Evaluative and Explanatory Reasoning

Evaluative and Explanatory Reasoning

Stuart S. Nagel

Q
QUORUM BOOKS
Westport, Connecticut • London

Library of Congress Cataloging-in-Publication Data

Nagel, Stuart S., 1934–
Evaluative and explanatory reasoning / Stuart S. Nagel.
p. cm.
Includes bibliographical references and index.
ISBN 0-89930-445-1 (alk. paper)
1. Policy sciences—Methodology. 2. Policy sciences—Decision making. 3. Law—Methodology. 4. Judicial process. 5. Reasoning. I. Title.
H61.N264 1992
320'.6—dc20 91-32381

British Library Cataloguing in Publication Data is available.

Library of Congress Catalog Card Number: 91-32381
ISBN: 0-89930-445-1

First published in 1992

Quorum Books, 88 Post Road West, Westport, CT 06881
An imprint of Greenwood Publishing Group, Inc.

Printed in the United States of America

∞

The paper used in this book complies with the Permanent Paper Standard issued by the National Information Standards Organization (Z39.48-1984).

10 9 8 7 6 5 4 3 2 1

Contents

Illustrations

Introduction

The essence of evaluative reasoning can be expressed in the form of a simple syllogism with a normative premise, an empirical premise, and a prescriptive conclusion. The normative premise takes the form, "*Y* is good." The empirical premise takes the form, "*X* causes *Y*." The prescriptive conclusion says, "Therefore adopt *X*." A definition of *evaluative reasoning* might therefore be reasoning that relates to drawing prescriptive conclusions about what a society, an individual, or other entity should do in light of the entity's goals and its perceptions of the relations between various alternatives and those goals.

The essence of explanatory reasoning can also be expressed in the form of a simple syllogism. The initial premise indicates what decision has been reached. One or more subsequent premises or items of information may indicate something about the goals or perceptions of the decision-maker. The conclusion offers an explanation of why the decision-maker reached the decision in light of those premises. Since the subsequent premises can relate to either goals or perceptions, one can classify explanatory syllogisms in terms of whether they draw conclusions about the decision-maker's goals or perceptions, or both.

In order to be more concrete with explanatory reasoning, one can start with an initial premise of the form, "*X* has been adopted," followed by "The decision-maker likes *Y* as a goal." The logical conclusion to be deduced is that "The decision-maker probably perceives that *X* will cause *Y*." The other form starts with "*X* has been adopted," followed by "The decision-maker perceives that *X* causes *Y*." It is then logical to deduce that "The decision-maker probably likes *Y*."

Those three syllogisms fit many situations. In reality, however, one normally works with many goals, like Y_1, Y_2, Y_3, and so on. Likewise, one normally works with many alternatives like X_1, X_2, X_3, X_4, and so on. If there are three goals and four alternatives, then there are 12 relations to be concerned with. If each of those 12 relations can be positive or negative, there would actually be 24 relations. There would be 60 relations if each of those relations can be scored, for example, if a 5 for the alternative is highly conducive to achieving the Y goal; a 4 is mildly conducive; a 3 is neither conducive nor adverse; a 2 is mildly adverse; and a 1 is highly adverse.

The situations become more challenging and more realistic when one takes into consideration the obstacles to systematic reasoning which this book seeks to overcome. For example:

1. Each of the Y goals may be measured differently, some being measured in dollars, some in crime occurrence units, and some in due process or justice units.

2. Information may be missing, or there may be a range of possibilities in any of the basic 12 relations in the hypothetical example. Information may also be missing on the relative importance of the goals to each other.

3. The problem may involve not merely choosing among X_1, X_2, and so on. If it is an allocation problem, one must decide how many units of some scarce resource should be allocated to X_1, X_2, and so on. When one must choose between X_1 and X_2, there are only four possibilities: (a) choosing X_1 and rejecting X_2; (b) rejecting X_1 and choosing X_2; (c) choosing both; or (d) rejecting both. In an allocation problem, there may be a very large or even an infinite number of ways of allocating a million dollars to X_1, X_2, and X_3.

4. The problem may involve realistic constraints so that one cannot simply choose the X that has the highest total score. The constraints may specify minimums and maximums on each X and each Y, these minimums and maximums being expressed in terms of absolute amounts or ratios. There may also be legal, political, economic, psychological, mathematical, and other constraints, some of which conflict with each other.

5. In spite of the multiplicity of goals, dimensions, missing information, weights, allocation possibilities, and constraints, there is a need for simplicity in drawing and presenting conclusions.

A key purpose of this book is to discuss evaluative and explanatory reasoning in the context of overcoming such obstacles to systematic reasoning.

The book devotes nine chapters to evaluative reasoning and six chapters to explanatory reasoning as they are applied to a policy studies orientation or a social science orientation in which the goal is to arrive at useful prescriptions for society, social groups, or individuals. Natural science tends to place more emphasis on theoretical explanations for why the sun rises, why earthquakes occur, why apples fall, and so on, although engineering aspects of natural science are also practically oriented.

An important related point, however, is that good evaluative reasoning is partly dependent on good explanatory reasoning, and vice versa. Good evaluative and good explanatory reasoning satisfy the following criteria:

1. The conclusions do logically follow from the premises in accordance with the rules of deductive reasoning, which ultimately rely on basic intelligence.

2. The empirical premises or relations do fit observed reality as determined by multiple observers.

3. The normative premises or goals do fit the desires of the people whose goals one is seeking to achieve, whether those people are the U.S. Supreme Court, the Illinois legislature, one's family, oneself, or some other person or group of persons.

4. The alternatives are those that are most likely to be capable of achieving the goals or that are most frequently mentioned in major viewpoints.

5. If the prescriptive or evaluative conclusion is implemented, it will actually achieve the goals better than any of the other alternatives that have been considered or that could have been considered.

6. If the explanatory conclusion is used for predictive purposes, it must accurately predict future decisions or occurrences.

Good prescriptive or evaluative reasoning requires good causal analysis because the empirical premises in a prescriptive syllogism are causal premises. When one says, "*X* causes *Y*," one should have an explicit or implicit understanding of what causation means and how to determine whether it exists. Likewise, good explanatory reasoning should take into consideration the goals of the person or group whose decisions one is trying to explain. One acquires substantially greater predictive power from knowing how specific people evaluate goals and alternatives than from knowing the kinds of easily measured but less useful demographic characteristics that social science sometimes overemphasizes.

Both kinds of reasoning can be considered high-leverage knowledge because they are so broadly applicable to all fields of knowledge. Some fields may be more concerned with explanation than with evaluation, such as chemistry as opposed to chemical engineering. All basic fields of knowledge, regardless of whether they are natural sciences, social sciences, or humanities, are concerned with explaining why things happen. Likewise, all applied fields, regardless of whether they are engineering, social work, or art performance, are concerned with prescribing what one ought to do in order to achieve certain effects.

The kind of evaluative reasoning emphasized in this book is not meant to evaluate alternative engineering projects or oil paintings. The emphasis is on making public policy, individual decision-making, allocating scarce resources, advocating and influencing decisions, mediating disputes, being a representative, assigning people to tasks, optimum sequencing, and reaching decisions that allow all sides to exceed their initial best expectations. Those kinds of evaluations are discussed in the first nine chapters. They are the main kinds of evaluation used in social policy, social science, public administration, business administration, and related fields.

Likewise, the kind of explanatory reasoning emphasized in this book does not explain natural science phenomena or what causes favorable reactions to different art forms. The emphasis is on explaining public policy-making, explaining individual decision-making, generalizing from cases, generalizing from facts, relational reasoning, and explaining why we do not always reach decisions that allow all sides to exceed their initial best expectations. Those kinds of explanation are discussed in the next six chapters. They are also the main kinds of explanation in social policy, social science, public administration, and business administration.

This book represents both a culmination and a beginning. It is the culmination of years of developing the ideas that are presented here in such more specifically focused books on evaluative and explanatory reasoning as *Law, Policy, and Optimizing Analysis* (Quorum Books, 1986) and *Causation, Prediction, and Legal Analysis* (Quorum Books, 1986). Those two books focus on legal process applications. Other previous methodology books, which focus on public policy applications, are *Evaluation Analysis with Microcomputers* (JAI Press, 1989) and *Policy Evaluation: Making Optimum Decisions* (Praeger, 1982). The scope of this book is broader than legal, policy, or other applications.

This book is also a beginning in the sense that the last chapter in each section points toward a new kind of evaluative and explanatory reasoning, which emphasizes not just evaluating a pair of alternatives to see which is the better one, or evaluating a set of alternatives to see which is the best one. Instead, it emphasizes trying to find an alternative that is better than the previous best that has been offered on each side of an evaluative dispute. That is, the outcome of this kind of reasoning should be better than that associated with compromises and trade-offs. There, the alternative chosen tends to provide a little of each of the conflicting alternatives, so that the disputants go away feeling they came out better than their worst expectations, although not better than their best expectations.

In the realm of causal explanation, this kind of super-optimum reasoning can be contrasted with the idea of answering the question: "Why not the best?" That question is frequently thought of as being naively optimistic. That kind of question, however, was frequently raised by such people as Robert Kennedy, John F. Kennedy, and Jimmy Carter. The even higher (but actually more feasible) question is "Why not better than the best?" That phrase is used in the sense of finding an alternative that is simultaneously better than the previous conservative best using conservative values and better than the previous liberal best using liberal values. What makes it more feasible is that its goal is not the best in some absolute sense, but in the relative sense of being better than what each disputant previously thought could be achieved.

Rather than being entirely new, every innovative idea or invention involves synthesizing previous ideas or inventions. Therefore innovators must understand the basics of their field before they can create something new in it: Einstein had to be well grounded in traditional physics in order to formulate the theory of relativity and Picasso had to learn how to paint realistically before he could paint in a more abstract style. Likewise, those who want to develop a new form of super-optimum evaluation or a new form of super-optimum explanation should have a good understanding of what is involved in basic evaluative and explanatory reasoning. The purpose of this book is to provide those basics and also to lay the groundwork for the formulation of even better methods of reasoning.

PART I

Evaluative or Prescriptive Reasoning

1

Choosing among Public Policies

The essence of decision-aiding software is that it is designed to process a set of (1) goals to be achieved, (2) alternatives for achieving them, and (3) relations between goals and alternatives, in order to choose the best alternative, combination, or resource allocation in light of the current goals, alternatives, and relations.

The main benefit of decision-aiding software is that it accurately and quickly handles five key methodological problems in decision-making:

1. The multiple dimensions of multiple goals. This is the apples-and-oranges program.
2. Much missing information.
3. A multiplicity of alternatives, so that it is impossible to determine the effects of each one.
4. Multiple and possibly conflicting constraints.
5. The need for simplicity in drawing and presenting conclusions in spite of the multiplicity of the elements involved.[1]

ADDING APPLES AND ORANGES

Decision-making problems often involve multiple goals that must be measured on a variety of different dimensions, such as miles, hours, dollars, 1–5 attitude scales, and yes–no dichotomies.

Some of the ways in which multiple dimensions are handled are

1. To multiply the apples by 2 if each apple is twice as desirable as each orange, and then to express everything in orange units.

2. To ask whether the gain in apples from choosing one alternative is worth more or less than the gain in oranges from choosing a second alternative.
3. To convert the apple units into percentages by dividing the raw scores on the apple goal by the sum of the apples, and to convert the orange units into percentages by dividing the raw scores on the oranges goal by the sum of the oranges.

These methods become clearer in the concrete example of choosing between two affirmative action programs for a medical school. One program produces a lot of minority students but treats few patients. The other program produces few minority students but treats a lot of patients. The example is shown in Table 1-1.[2]

MISSING INFORMATION

We often do not know the relation scores of each alternative for each goal, and we often do not know the relative weights of the goals.

The key way in which missing information is handled is to allow the user to quickly and accurately determine the effects of inserting various values for the missing information. More specific techniques include

1. What-if analysis, in which the computer shows what would happen if we make changes in the goals, alternatives, and/or relations.
2. Threshold analysis, in which the computer shows for each relation score and goal weight the value which would cause a tie between the second-place alternative and the first-place alternative.
3. Convergence analysis, in which the computer shows for each goal weight at what magnitude the goal tends to dominate the other goals so that nothing is to be gained by increasing the weight further.
4. Best–worst analysis, in which the computer shows the conclusion reached by using the values that most favor a given alternative, and then the values that least favor a given alternative. The two conclusions are then averaged.

These methods become clearer in the concrete example of deciding between nuclear energy and solar energy in light of their long-term value and cost, as shown in Table 1-2.[3]

ALLOCATING RESOURCES

Decision-aiding software can help in the allocating of resources, as contrasted to the generally easier problem of just finding a best alternative or combination.

A good way of allocating resources is to convert into percentages the raw merit scores of the objects to which the resources are to be allocated. One

Table 1-1
Four Methods for Dealing with Multidimensional Trade-Offs

POLICY	RAW SCORE INCREMENTS: Students Trained (S)	RAW SCORE INCREMENTS: Patients Treated (P)	PART/WHOLE PERCENTAGING: Students Trained	PART/WHOLE PERCENTAGING: Patients Treated	PART/WHOLE PERCENTAGING: Unweighted Sum	PART/WHOLE PERCENTAGING: Weighted Sum W=2
Policy A (X_1)	30	10	60%	36%	96%	132%
Policy B (X_2)	20	18	40%	64%	104%	168%
Total (Whole)	50	28	100%	100%	200%	300%
Difference (Increment)	+ 10S >>	− 8P?				
Threshold			$W60 + 36 = W40 + 64 \therefore W^* = 1.40$			

POLICY	PAIRED-COMPARISON MONETIZING: Students Trained $SY = (S)^{.92}$	PAIRED-COMPARISON MONETIZING: Patients Trained $SY = (P)^{.90}$	PAIRED-COMPARISON MONETIZING: SUM	WEIGHTED RAW SCORES: Students (Expressed in Terms of Patients) W = 2	WEIGHTED RAW SCORES: Patients	WEIGHTED RAW SCORES: Sum
Policy A (X_1)	$22.85	$ 7.94	$30.79	60	10	70
Policy B (X_2)	$15.74	$13.48	$29.22	40	18	58
Total	$38.59	$21.42	$60.01	100	28	128
Threshold				$W30 + 10 = W20 + 18 \therefore W^* = .80$		

NOTES:

1. Incremental analysis has the advantage of simplicity, especially where there are only a few policies and goals. It is also applicable to variables that are nonquantitative. It involves a minimum of transforming of the raw data. It reduces the value judgement to determining whether the incremental gain of one policy is preferred over the incremental gain of a second policy.

2. Percentaging analysis has the advantage of being applicable where there are many policies and goals. It reduces the value judgement to determining the relative weight of the goals.

3. Paired-comparison monetizing tends to consider all the values of the relevant decision-makers, although their values are not disaggregated into separate components. Working with monetized variables may also be more comfortable for many people. Paired-comparison monetizing reduces the value judgements to determining at what point a set of non-monetary benefits is equal to a quantity of dollars.

4. Weighted raw scores have the advantage of being relatively easy to apply where the goals have tangible units like students or patients, rather than intangible units like scores on a 1-9 attitude scale, where part/whole percentaging tends to be easier to handle.

Table 1-2
Threshold Values, Insensitivity Ranges, and Change Scores

POLICIES \ GOALS	Long-Term Value (Y_1)	Low Cost (Y_2)	WEIGHTED SUM
Nuclear (X_a)	a_1 +1 4 (3 to ∞)	a_2 -1 3 (2 to ∞)	7
Solar (X_b)	b_1 -1 5 (-∞ to 6)	b_2 -1 1 (-∞ to 2)	6
Weights	W_1 -1 1 (-∞ to 2)	W_2 -2 1 (.5 to ∞)	

NOTES:

1. The symbol in the upper-left-hand corner of each cell shows
   (1) The identifying symbol of each relation, with the letter indicating the goal.
   (2) The identifying symbol of each weight, with the subscript indicating the goal to which the weight refers.

2. The number in the middle of each cell shows
   (1) The value of the relation on a 1-to-5 scale.
   (2) The value of the weight with the least important goal having a weight of 1.

3. The number in the upper-right-hand corner of each cell shows by how much the gap changes between the two alternatives being compared if the input increases by one unit.

4. The number in parentheses in each cell is the threshold value for each input. At that value, there will be a tie in the weighted sum of the two alternatives being compared.

5. The range in parentheses in each cell is the insensitivity range. That range shows how far down and up each input can go without affecting which alternative is the winner.

can then apply the percentages to the grand total available to be allocated. A good way to convert the raw scores into percentages is to divide them by their total within the same goal in order to get part/whole percentages. Those percentages can then be summed across the goals, with the use of a weighted sum where the goals have different weights.

Table 1-3A shows how the P/G% software can be used in an allocation problem in which the bottom line consists of allocation percentages. The alternative methods shown are trials and plea bargains. Additional alternatives may be added, such as diversions or dismissals. The goals shown are to reduce delay and to increase respect for the legal system. Additional goals may be added, such as reducing expense and increasing the probability of innocent defendants being acquitted.

The raw data show that in our hypothetical court system, the average trial takes 120 days, and the average plea bargain takes 30 days from arrest to disposition. The data also show that the trial alternative receives a respect score of 6 on a 0–10 scale in a rough survey of attorneys, and pleas receive a score of only 2. It would not be meaningful to add 120 days to a respect score of 6 to get an overall score for trials because (1) delay is measured in

Table 1-3
Allocating Cases to Methods of Resolving: The Basic Data

A. THE RAW DATA

	Delay (Days)	Respect (0-10 Scale)
Trials	120	6
Pleas	30	2
	150	8

B. THE TRANSFORMED RAW DATA

	Speed (1/Days)	Respect (-5 to +5)
Trials	1/120 or .00833	+1
Pleas	1/30 or .03333	-3
	5/120 or .04166	-2

NOTES:

1. The raw data are hypothetical, but realistic. The object is to decide on the optimum allocation of cases to trials versus pleas in light of the facts that
   (1) "Trials" receives a score of 120 days on delay and "pleas" 30 days.
   (2) "Trials" receives a score of 6 on respect and "pleas" a score of 2.

2. Transferring the raw data involves
   (1) Calculating the reciprocals for the raw scores of the negative goal of delay.
   (2) Recalculating the raw scores on respect by using a scale which shows absolute zero. If N equals absolute zero, then subtract N from each of the original raw scores. For example, on a 0-10 scale, the number 5 (or below) might be absolute zero.

days and respect is measured on a 0–10 scale, so that a common measure must be devised to make these scores comparable; (2) delay is a negative goal, so that a high score is undesirable; and (3) a score of 2 for respect may be a negative score, so that each additional plea bargain decreases respect for the system.

To deal with those problems, we do the following:

1. We convert the delay scores into part/whole percentages by dividing each score by the sum of the delay column, but after inverting for the negative goal.
2. We do the inversion by working with the reciprocals of the delay scores. That means working with 1/120 and 1/30 rather than 120 and 30. In this way, we preserve the fact that trials are four times as bad as pleas on the goal of delay, while we make the pleas score higher than the trials score. We are then working with speed rather than delay as a goal. Speed should be given a weight of +1 if delay has previously been given a weight of −1.
3. We also convert the respect scores into part/whole percentages by dividing each score by the sum of the respect column, but after adjusting for the fact that pleas may have a negative score.
4. That means determining the value of a true zero on the 0–10 scale and subtracting that value from the 0–10 scores. Thus, if a 5 is the separation point between positive scores and negative scores, then a 6 is the equivalent of a +1, and a 2 is the equivalent of a −3. These transformed numbers are shown in Table 1-3B.

Table 1-4A converts the transformed data into part/whole percentages. Pleas is given 0% on respect because one would not want to allocate anything more than the minimum possible if pleas has a negative score and if more respect were the only criterion. We can now add across the percentages and obtain an aggregate percentage of 120% for trials and 80% for pleas. We then divide by 2 to bring the sum of those percentages down to 100% because we cannot allocate more than 100%.

Table 1-4B makes conversions based on the fact that respect is considered twice as important as speed: the percentages in the respect column are multiplied by 2. The new aggregate percentages are 220% and 80%. We then divide by 3, or the sum of the weights, to obtain the allocation percentages of 73% and 27%. Not all allocation problems involve multiple dimensions, negative goals, or negative scores. If, however, one can follow the allocation analyses in Table 1-3 and Table 1-4, one can deal with simpler allocation problems.[4]

ADJUSTING FOR CONSTRAINTS

Decision-aiding software can help in dealing with constraints that require setting minimums or maximums on the alternatives or the goals or other conditions that must be met, regardless of how high the scores of an alternative are.

Table 1-4
Allocating Cases to Methods of Resolving: Percentaging and Weighting

A. THE PART/WHOLE PERCENTAGES

	Speed P/W%	Respect P/W%	Aggregate P/W%	Allocation%
Trials	20%	100%	120%	60%
Pleas	80%	0%	80%	40%
	100%	100%	200%	100%

B. THE WEIGHTED P/W%'S

	Speed w=1	Respect w=2	Aggregate P/W%	Allocation%
Trials	20%	200%	220%	73%
Pleas	80%	0%	80%	27%
			300%	100%

NOTES:

1. Calculating the correct part/whole percentages involves
   (1) Calculating the part/whole percentages on the inverted negative goal.
   (2) Giving zero percent to any alternative that has a negative raw score and then calculating the part/whole percentages for the other alternatives.

2. Calculating the allocation percentages involves
   (1) Multiplying the part/whole percentages in each column by the relative weight of the goal to which the column pertains.
   (2) Summing the weighted part/whole percentages across each alternative.
   (3) Dividing those aggregate percentages by the sum of the weights. The results are the allocation percentages for each alternative or budget category.

The following are the main ways in which constraints are handled:

1. The constraints can be met *before* one allocates scarce resources or determines the relation scores. The result tends to be to give an alternative more than it is entitled to if it deserves only the minimum. That result cannot occur if adjustments are made *after* allocating, so as to bring alternatives up to their minimums.

2. The best way of resolving conflicting constraints is to expand the total benefits available or to reduce the total costs to be imposed so that all the constraints can be satisfied simultaneously. If that course is not possible, one can resolve conflicting constraints by developing compromises that satisfy each constraint in proportion to its importance. Other less desirable alternatives involve partially satisfying all constraints equally or fully satisfying certain constraints in the order of their priority.

Adjusting for constraints is illustrated with the problem of allocating a budget to police and the courts in light of crime reduction and fair procedure. The constraints specify giving minimum amounts to the police and the courts, but those minimums may add up to more than the total available.

A good way to adjust the allocations to satisfy the equity constraints in two, three, and four budget categories is as follows (see Table 1-5):

1. With two budget categories, suppose category A is below its minimum and category B is above its minimum. After allocating in proportion to their aggregate scores, give category A its minimum. Give the rest of the total budget to category B.
2. With three budget categories, suppose that A is below its minimum and that B and C are above their minimums. Give A its minimum. Divide the rest of the total budget between B and C in proportion to their aggregate scores.
3. With four or more budget categories, one can reason by analogy with the three-category situation. No matter how many budget categories are below their minimums in the initial optimizing, give them their minimums and then remove them from further allocating. The remainder of the total budget is then divided proportionately among the other budget categories.[5]

SIMPLICITY OF ANALYSIS

Decision-aiding software that is based on multicriteria decision-making (MCDM) can greatly simplify the analysis of a variety of decision-aiding problems that have traditionally used more complicated and often less valid methods, such as arrow diagrams, payoff matrices, decision trees, optimum level curves, indifference curves, functional curves, and multiobjective programming. The essence of MCDM software is that it works with a table, a matrix, or a spreadsheet with alternatives in the rows, evaluative criteria in the columns, relation scores in the cells, and a summation column at the right showing the overall score or allocation percentage for each alternative.

A good illustration of the simplicity of MCDM and P/G% software is the decision whether to take away an abused child or leave it with its family. Table 1-6A shows an analysis of the problem with a traditional payoff matrix, and Table 1-6B shows an analysis of the problem with a P/G% spreadsheet table. Both approaches show the alternatives in the rows. The payoff matrix shows contingent events and their probabilities in the columns, whereas the P/G% approach shows goals and their relative weights in the columns. The payoff matrix shows relative payoffs in the cells, whereas

Table 1-5
Raw Scores

ALLOCATION CRITERIA / BUDGET CATEGORIES	RAW SCORES		TRANSFORMED SCORES			ALLOCATION RESULTS				
	Crime Reduction (1)	Fair Procedure (2)	Aggregate Scores (3)	Allocation Percentages		Optimum Allocations		Minimums (6)	Adjusted Allocations	
				2-way (4a)	3-way (4b)	2-way (5a)	3-way (5b)		2-way (7a)	3-way (7B)
POLICE	2.00	1.00	3.00	43%	39%	$214	$195	$240	$240 (Min.)	$240 (Min.)
COURTS	1.00	3.00	4.00 ---- 7.00	57%	51%	$286	$255	$ 80	$260 (100% of $260)	$218 (84% of $260)
CORRECTION	.50	.25	.75	N/A	10%	N/A	$ 50	$ 40	N/A	$ 42 (16% of $260)
TOTALS	---	---	----- 7.75	----- 100%	----- 100%	----- $500	----- $500	----- $360	----- $500	----- $500

NOTES:

1. In Table 1-5 optimizing is done first and then adjustments are made to satisfy the constraints if they have not been satisfied already. In other words, if we optimally allocate without considering the minimums, we obtain what is shown in column 5a (for two budget categories) and column 5b (for three budget categories). If we then consider the minimums, we obtain what is shown in column 7a and 7b.
2. There is $500 available to be allocated this year. There was $450 available to be allocated last year. N/A = Not Applicable
3. The minimum in column 6 are equal to 80% of last year's budget. Last year, the police received $300. The courts received $100, and corrections received $50.
4. The numbers in column 1 and 2 are based on a rough survey of a small sample of people who are knowledgeable about the criminal justice system.
5. The formulas for the numbers in the other columns are:

   (3) = (1) + (2) (4a) = (3)/7.00 (4b) = (3)/7.75 (5a) = (4a) ($500)
   (5b) = (4b) ($500) (6) = 80% of last year's allocation (7a) = (5a) +/-$26 (7b) = (5b) +/-X, where X is clarified in the text.
6. The best way of making the adjusted allocation is to give any budget category its minimum (from column 6). If its optimum (from column 5a or 5b) falls below its minimum, divide the remainder among the other budget.

Table 1-6

Comparing a Payoff Matrix with Policy/Goal Percentaging on Decision-Making under Conditions of Risk (e.g., Deciding Whether to Take Away or Leave an Abused Child)

A. THE PAYOFF MATRIX

SEVERE SUBSEQUENT ABUSE

	Would Not Occur	Would Occur	Benefits	Costs
TAKE AWAY	a -50	b +100	(P) (100)	(1-P)(50)
LEAVE	c +50	d -100		

B. THE P/G% APPROACH

	Avoid Abuse (w=2)	Preserve Family Love (w=1)	Save Taxpayer Cost (w=1)	Weighted Sum
TAKE AWAY	4	2	2	12
LEAVE	2	4	4	12

NOTES:

1. The cell entries are arrived at by asking the decision-makers the following question
   (1) Of the four possible occurrences, which ones are desirable (marked plus), and which ones are undesirable (marked minus)?
   (2) Of the undesirable occurrences, which one is the most undesirable (marked -100)?
   (3) How much more undesirable is the more undesirable occurrence than the less undesirable occurrence (marked -50 to show cell d is twice as bad as cell a)?

2. With that information, one can determine the threshold probability as follows
   (1) At the threshold, the discounted benefits equal the discounted costs (i.e., 100P = 50 - 50P).
   (2) The solution for P in that equation is $P^* = d/(a+d)$ or $P^* = 100/(50 + 100) = .33$

3. The scoring of each alternative on each criterion is on a 1-5 scale where 5 = highly conducive to the goal, 4 = mildly conducive, 3 = neither conducive nor adverse, 2 = mildly adverse to the goal, and 1 = highly adverse. Decimal scores can be given between these numbers where appropriate.

4. Avoiding abuse is considered to be twice as important as preserving whatever family love might exist or saving taxpayer cost.

5. By considering multiple criteria rather than emphasizing the probability of severe subsequent abuse, the decision is a much closer decision, and more dependent on the specific facts or scores on the first two criteria than on a general threshold probability.

6. If the criteria are given equal weight and a threshold analysis is performed, then leaving the child wins 10 points to 8 points. The threshold or tie-causing values of the weights are then 2, 0, and 0. The threshold values of the relation scores are then 6, 4, 4, 0, 2, and 2, reading across the matrix.

in its cells, the P/G% approach shows relation scores on a 1–5 scale, assigned to the alternatives and the goals. The payoff matrix shows benefits minus costs on the right side with each element discounted by the probability of its occurring, whereas the P/G% approach shows the weighted summation scores for each alternative at the right side.

Both approaches are applied to the same empirical situation in Table 1-6. The payoff matrix tends to lead to a decision to take the child away because the probability of severe abuse is likely to be greater than the threshold probability. The P/G% approach leads to a closer decision because it emphasizes the multiple criteria of avoiding abuse, preserving family love, and saving the taxpayer cost. One could argue that those three criteria are taken into consideration in the relative payoffs in the cells of the payoff matrix. However, when all three criteria are lumped together, their separate existences and sensitivity values are overwhelmed by the criterion of avoiding abuse. The payoff matrix may thus lead to results that are less valid in terms of the decision-maker's goals than the P/G% approach.

The following are the advantages of the P/G% approach over a payoff matrix:

1. The P/G% can explicitly consider any number of criteria, such as the three shown in Table 1-6.
2. The P/G% can explicitly consider any number of alternatives, such as taking the child away to an institution, taking the child away to a foster home, taking the child away to a relative's home, leaving the child and counseling the family, or leaving the child without counseling the family.
3. Because it allows a consideration of multiple criteria and multiple alternatives, the P/G% approach conforms more with reality, rather than being a simplistic abstraction.
4. The P/G% is also simpler, with its 1–5 scales, weighted criteria, computerized threshold analysis, and logical way of analyzing a problem in terms of alternatives, criteria, and relations.[6]

SOME CONCLUSIONS

As mentioned at the beginning of this chapter, the main benefits of the decision-aiding software are its accuracy and speed in handling the five key methodological problems in evaluation analysis. To fully appreciate the relevance of the software, it is necessary actually to use it. We can, however, briefly describe how the software applies to each problem.

On the matter of *multiple dimensions* and multiple goals:

1. In comparing any two alternatives, one can show for each goal the incremental gain of the better alternative over the other alternative. This can be more easily done by putting the goals in the rows and the two alternatives in the columns,

since the software subtracts across the rows. One can then pick the alternative that has the more desired set of increments.

2. One can specify the importance of each goal relative to the least important goal. Those weights can consider both the importance and the nature of the measurement units where raw scores are used.
3. The software is capable of working with the relations either as raw scores or as part/whole percentages by exercising an option on the data management menu.

On the matter of *missing information:*

1. The software can do what-if analysis by allowing the user to change any of the inputs and to see quickly how those changes affect the conclusion.
2. The main menu gives the user an option to do a threshold analysis or a convergence analysis to determine the critical values for relation scores or goal weights, above which one alternative would be better and below which another alternative would be better.
3. In specifying the criteria, one can divide each criterion into a best version and a worst version, such as the best possible cost of each alternative and the worst possible cost. The computer can then show the overall best score, the overall worst score, and the midpoint for each alternative.
4. The software can also draw indifference curves or threshold curves showing the combination of scores on two or more variables which would lead to a tie between any two alternatives.

On the matter of *allocating resources:*

1. The user can specify the grand total available for allocation. The program will multiply that grand total by the allocation percentages for each alternative or budget category.
2. One calculates the allocation percentages by obtaining an overall score for each alternative and then dividing each overall score by the sum of the scores in order to obtain part/whole allocation percentages.
3. The program can transform the raw scores by determining their reciprocals where negative goals are involved, or by subtracting the value of absolute zero from each raw score where negative scores are involved. Those transformations may, however, be easier to do with a calculator. The results can then be entered into the data matrix.

On the matter of *adjusting for constraints:*

1. The user can enter minimum constraints for each alternative, and the program can guarantee that they will be met in whatever allocation is calculated. A better approach, though, would be to optimize ignoring the constraints, and then to make adjustments for any alternative or criterion that violates its minimum or maximum.

2. The ease of doing what-if analyses facilitates resolving conflicting constraints and conflicting decision-makers by enabling both sides or a mediator to try different alternatives, criteria, weights, constraints, relations, and other inputs until a mutually satisfying solution is found.

On the matter of *simplicity:*

1. The essence of the software is that it puts alternatives in the rows of a spreadsheet matrix, criteria and weights in the columns, relations in the cells, and overall scores for the alternatives in the right-hand column.
2. That system conforms with a great deal of systematic decision-making, as indicated by the popularity of spreadsheet software, payoff matrices, decision trees, and other formats that can be reduced to a decision matrix.

This kind of evaluation analysis could be done with pencil and paper or even in one's mind. The analysis is, however, facilitated substantially by the availability of the software and microcomputers. The software encourages thinking more explicitly about evaluation problems without confining the user to quantitatively measured variables. It facilitates creativity by allowing changes to be so easily made. We may be at the advent of new ways of thinking about program evaluation, policy analysis, and decision-making, to the benefit of the decision-makers and those who are affected by their decisions.[7]

NOTES

1. For further details on optimizing analysis in terms of goals, policies, relations, and conclusions, see S. Nagel, *Public Policy: Goals, Means, and Methods* (New York: St. Martin's, 1984), and Edward Quade, *Analysis for Public Decisions* (Amsterdam: North-Holland, 1982). The first book uses numerous legal examples. Other books that take an optimizing perspective on law include Richard Posner, *Economic Analysis of Law* (Boston: Little, Brown, 1977), and Gordon Tullock, *The Logic of Law* (New York: Basic Books, 1971).

2. On dealing with nonmonetary benefits and costs, see Mark Thompson, *Benefit-Cost Analysis for Program Evaluation* (Beverly Hills, Calif.: Sage, 1980), and Edward Gramlich, *Benefit-Cost Analysis of Government Programs* (Englewood Cliffs, N.J.: Prentice-Hall, 1981), although they may overemphasize monetizing nonmonetary variables, rather than working with them in their original form or a form close to the originals. Also see S. Nagel, "Nonmonetary Variables in Benefit-Cost Evaluation," 7 *Evaluation Review* 37–64 (1983), and S. Nagel, "Economic Transformations of Nonmonetary Benefits in Program Evaluation," in James Catterall (ed.), *Economic Evaluation of Public Programs* (San Francisco: Jossey-Bass, 1985).

3. On dealing with missing information without having to gather additional information, see Mark Thompson, *Decision Analysis for Program Evaluation* (Cam-

bridge, Mass.: Ballinger, 1982), and Clifford Harris, *The Break-Even Handbook* (Englewood Cliffs, N.J.: Prentice-Hall, 1978). Also see S. Nagel, "Dealing with Unknown Variables in Policy/Program Evaluation," 6 *Evaluation and Program Planning* 7–18 (1983), and S. Nagel, "New Varieties of Sensitivity Analysis," 9 *Evaluation Review* 772–779 (1985).

4. On diverse methods for dealing with the multiplicity of alternatives in allocation problems, see Philip Kotler, *Marketing Decision Making: A Model Building Approach* (New York: Holt, 1971) (calculus and statistical analysis); Claude McMillan, *Mathematical Programming: An Introduction to the Design and Application of Optimal Decision Machines* (New York: Wiley, 1970) (reiterative guessing and operations research); and S. Nagel, *Policy Evaluation: Making Optimum Decisions* (New York: Praeger, 1982) (variations on part/whole percentaging in Chapters 10–13). Also see S. Nagel, "Optimally Allocating Federal Money to Cities," 5 *Public Budgeting and Finance* 39–50 (1985).

5. On dealing with constraints in public policy analysis in general, see S. Nagel, *Public Policy: Goals, Means, and Methods* (New York: St. Martin's, 1984), especially the chapters on equity, effectiveness, human rights, discretion, economic structure, government structure, political feasibility, and ethical constraints. On quantitative constraints in allocation problems, see "Allocation Logic" in S. Nagel, *Policy Evaluation: Making Optimum Decisions* (New York: Praeger, 1982), where the problem of allocating to police, courts, and corrections is also discussed.

6. On the matter of simplicity in drawing and presenting conclusions in evaluation analyses, see S. Nagel, "Comparing Multi-Criteria Decision Making and P/G% with Traditional Optimizing," in Yoshikazu Sawaragi (ed.), *Multiple-Criteria Decision Making* (Berlin: Springer-Verlag, 1987), and "Simplifying Basic Methods" in S. Nagel, *Public Policy: Goals, Means, and Methods* (New York: St. Martin's, 1984). On the subject of removing abused children from their homes, see "Neglect," in George Cooper et al., *Law and Poverty: Cases and Materials* (St. Paul: West, 1973).

7. On policy/goal percentaging and the P/G% software, see Benjamin Radcliff, "Multi-Criteria Decision Making: A Survey of Software," 4 *Social Science Microcomputer Review* 38–55 (1986); S. Nagel, "P/G% Analysis: An Evaluation-Aiding Program," 9 *Evaluation Review* 209–214 (1985); and S. Nagel, "A Microcomputer Program for Dealing with Evaluation Problems," 9 *Evaluation and Program Planning* 159–168 (1987). On the applicability of the P/G% to all five analytical problems, see S. Nagel, *Evaluation Analysis with Microcomputers* (Beverly Hills, Calif.: Sage, 1987).

2

Individual Decision-Making

The first wave of microcomputer software consisted mainly of word-processing programs. A microcomputer can handle word-processing well by displaying typing on the TV screen. The typing can then be changed on the screen until the typist is satisfied with the contents and format. The typing can then be printed on letterhead, manuscript paper, or other stock.

The second wave of serious and popular microcomputer software consisted of programs for file management. Their main purpose is to enable the user to call up data, notes, files, recipes, court cases, or other forms of information that have been stored by key words, numbers, or other concepts.

The third wave of software consists of spreadsheet and bookkeeping programs. They provide tables of rows and columns into which one can enter information, especially with accounts or other economic items in the rows and time periods in the columns. The key feature of spreadsheets is that one can change any cell and quickly see how that change affects the row total, the column total, the grand total, or any subtotal.

The fourth wave of microcomputer software for home and business use consists of programs designed to aid the user in processing a set of (1) goals to be achieved; (2) alternatives for achieving the goals; and (3) relations between goals and alternatives in order to choose the alternative or combination that maximizes the desirable results and eliminates the undesirable. These programs are referred to as *decision support systems*, although sometimes that phrase refers to data sets and file management. These programs are better referred to as *decision-aiding systems* or *multiple-criteria decision-making*.

The purpose of this chapter is to discuss an especially important decision-aiding system for personal decision-making. It is called *policy/goal percentaging analysis* (abbreviated P/G%) because it relates alternative policies or decisions to goals, and it converts to simple percentages goals that are stated in different measurement terms, like years, miles, dollars, and apples.

THE EXAMPLE OF GETTING MARRIED

The best way to understand the program is to start with a simple example in which the goals are all measured in the same terms, and then to move on to an example in which the goals are measured in different terms. The first example involves the question of whether to get married or to stay single. The basic information is summarized in Table 2-1.

The Input Data and the Initial Results

This is a real-life example. It was developed at O'Hare Airport when I was on my way to demonstrate the P/G% program in Switzerland. My mother met me at the airport. I volunteered to demonstrate how the program could help her in making decisions. She was especially concerned about whether she should get married or stay single (she had been a widow for more than a year).

The basic alternatives were to get married or to stay single, as Table 2-1 indicates. The basic goals or criteria were companionship and privacy. On a 0–10 scale, getting married scored a 7 on companionship, but only a 3 on privacy in the eyes of my mother, who was thinking in terms of a specific prospective husband. On the other hand, staying single scored only a 4 on companionship, but an 8 on privacy.

If one gives equal weight to companionship and privacy, then the sum of 7 plus 3 for getting married adds to 10. The sum of 4 plus 8 for staying single adds to 12. Thus, staying single outscores getting married in the initial analysis. Up to this point, the computer is helpful in organizing one's ideas in terms of alternatives, goals, and relations. It is also helpful in scoring the relations so as to provide consistency within each goal, and so as to enable one to see quickly the summation score for each alternative.

Sensitivity of the Initial Results to Input Changes

The initial analysis, however, is only the beginning of what it would take to bring the second-place alternative up to the desirability level of the first-place alternative. Answering that important question involves first noting that there is a two-point gap between the overall score for staying single and the overall score for getting married.

If the user asks for a threshold or breakeven analysis, the computer will

Table 2-1
Deciding Whether to Get Married

Goals / Alternatives	Companionship	Privacy	Sum of Raw Scores
Get Married	7 (9)	3 (5)	10
Stay Single	4 (2)	8 (6)	12
Weights	1.00 (1.67)	1.00 (.60)	

NOTES:

1. The numbers not in parentheses are raw scores on a 0-10 scale for companionship and a 0-10 scale for privacy.
2. The initial weights are 1.00 for both goals.
3. The numbers in parentheses are the threshold values which will cause getting married to be of equal satisfaction to staying single. They each involve adding or subtracting 2 from the raw scores since 2 is the threshold difference when summing the raw scores for both alternatives.
4. Since it may be difficult to improve on the companionship and privacy of getting married by 2 points, and it may be difficult to recalculate companionship and privacy on staying single by 2 points, the program reduces to whether the weight of companionship is more than the weight of privacy or is the same.
5. Getting married in this context could refer to a specific person or just to the abstract idea.

indicate to what number each relation and weight would have to change in order to generate a tie between the second- and first-place alternatives. For example, there would be a tie if getting married moved up from a 7 to a 9 for companionship, or from a 3 to a 5 for privacy. Likewise, there would be a tie if staying single were considered worth only a 2 for companionship rather than a 4, or worth only a 6 for privacy rather than an 8.

Changing the relation scores may be difficult, however, since they do have some degree of objectivity, at least in the eyes of the person making the decision. It may be easier to change the weights of the goals from equal weights to different weights. The threshold analysis of the microcomputer says that if companionship is given a weight of 1.67 when privacy has a weight of 1, there will be a tie. It also says that if privacy is given a weight of .60 when companionship has a weight of 1, there will be a tie. The reason is that if privacy had a weight of .60, getting married would receive a weighted score of 7 plus 1.8 (which is .60 times 3), for a total of 8.8. Staying single would then receive a weighted score of 4 plus 4.8 (which is .60 times 8), for the same total of 8.8. One could also show that getting married and staying single would both be tied at 14.67 if companionship had a weight of 1.67 (or 1.66666 . . . to be exact), and privacy had a weight of 1.

The New Results

A better way to interpret the threshold weights is to say they mean that if companionship is only as valuable as privacy, one should stay single. On the other hand, if companionship is worth at least twice as much as privacy (rounded to the nearest whole number), then one is better off getting married in view of the goals to be achieved, the alternatives available, and the relations between the alternatives and the goals.

Incidentally, my mother decided that she did value companionship more highly than privacy. As a result, she decided to marry a man she had met in Florida shortly before the O'Hare Airport analysis in the summer of 1984. They were married that December.

THE EXAMPLE OF BUYING A HOUSE

The second example involves the question of whether to stay in one's present house or to buy a new house. This, too, is a real-life example. It was developed when my secretary asked if she could use the P/G% program to aid in her house-buying decision.

The Input Data

In this example, the basic alternatives are the present house versus a specific new house. We could change the problem to involve a comparison among a number of houses, just as the marriage problem could involve comparing a number of prospective spouses. The basic goals are cost and space, although one could include many more goals. The Champaign-Urbana *News Gazette* lists 21 goals in the table which it provides for comparing houses in its weekly real estate supplement. The computer can easily handle multiple goals, but the methodology is more easily understood with two goals.

According to Table 2-2, the present house costs $400 a month for expenses and mortgage payments. The new house would cost $500 a month. The present house, however, only has 1,400 square feet, whereas the new house has 1,600 square feet. In the marriage example, we could meaningfully add 7 to 3 because both numbers came from the same 0–10 measurement scale. We cannot, however, add $400 to 1,400 square feet and arrive at a meaningful sum. The sum would tend to give too much weight to the space goal because it is expressed in larger numbers, not because it is more important.

Table 2-2
Deciding Whether to Buy a New House

GOALS / ALTERNATIVES	Cost (dollars 100's) (W = -1)		Space (100 sq. feet) (W = 2)		Sum of Unweighted P/W%'s	Sum of Weighted P/W%'s
	Raw Score	Part/Whole Percent	Raw Score	Part/Whole Percent		
Present House	4	-44%	14	47%	+3%	49%
New House	5	-56%	16	53%	-3%	51%
Total	9	100%	30	100%	0%	100%

NOTES:

1. This problem reduces to the question of whether house size is more or less than twice as important as monthly cost. If more, than buy the new house. If less, than retain the present house.

2. Another way of viewing this problem is to note that the present house has the advantage of costing $100 less per month. The new house has the advantage of providing 200 extra square feet per month. Thus, from a raw score perspective, the problem reduced to the question of whether $100 a month or 200 square feet is more desired. If $100, then choose the present house since it saves the money. If 200 square feet, then choose the new house since it provides the most space.

Handling the Different Dimensions and Weights

One way of handling goals that are measured on different dimensions is to convert the measurement into dimensionless part/whole percentages. That operation simply involves adding the raw scores of $400 and $500 to get $900 and then dividing $400 (the part) by $900 (the whole) to obtain 44% (the part/whole percentage). The result of applying the same operation to the second alternative is a P/W% of 56%. For the second goal (space) 1,400 square feet is added to 1,600 square feet to yield 3,000 square feet. The part/whole percentages are 14/30, or 47%, and 16/30, or 53%.

Since cost is a negative goal, it should receive a negative weight, and space should receive a positive weight. If the two goals are treated equally, the weights are −1 and +1. For the present house, the sum of the unweighted or equally weighted part/whole percentages would be −44% plus 47%, or +3%. For the new house, the sum of the unweighted percentages would be −56% plus 53%, or −3%. Thus, when the goals receive equal weight, the present house wins.

However, if space is given a weight of 2 and cost stays at a weight of −1, the sum of the weighted part/whole percentages for the present house becomes −44% plus 94% (2 times 47%) for a total of slightly less than 50% when the numbers are carried out to more places. The weighted P/W% for the new house becomes −56% plus 106% (2 times 53%), for a total of slightly more than 50% when the numbers are carried out to more places.

Making a Decision

One can conclude from this example that the decision-maker who gives equal importance to cost and space should stay in the present house, given the alternatives available and the relations between the alternatives and the goals. On the other hand, the decision-maker who considers the space goal (as measured in units of 100 square feet) at least twice as important as the cost goal (as measured in units of $100 per month) should buy the new house. Incidentally, my secretary decided she did not consider the space units twice as important as the cost units, at least for now, so she stayed in her present house.

FURTHER APPLICATIONS AND COMPARISONS

Applications

The program can perform a variety of useful decision-making analyses, such as:

1. Choosing, ranking, or allocating to alternatives categories.
2. Working with goals that have a common measurement unit or that are multidimensional.
3. Doing what-if variations on goals, alternatives, and relations.
4. Doing a threshold or convergence analysis to indicate the scores for the goals, alternatives, or relations that will make a difference in the winning alternative or how resources are allocated.
5. Adjusting results for minimums, maximums, and other constraints.
6. Comparing optimum choices with actual choices in order to reduce the gap between the actual and the optimum.

The P/G% approach differs from other decision-aiding approaches by virtue of being able to deal meaningfully with all of the following decision-making situations:

1. Multidimensional goals.
2. Choosing the one best alternative.
3. Choosing the best combination of alternatives.
4. Making choices that involve risks and probabilities.
5. Making choices where doing too much or too little is undesirable.
6. Allocating scarce resources, even where there are millions of alternative ways of allocating a given budget to a set of budget categories.
7. Situations with multiple missing information.
8. Situations involving public policy, law, business, medicine, or personal decision-making.
9. Situations where all the goals are measured on the same dimension.
10. Situations involving prediction as well as prescription.
11. Minimums or maximums on the alternatives, goals, or other constraints.

Along with the program, there are a variety of demonstration datafiles. They include applications from the fields of law, public policy, health care, and personal decision-making. They also include applications that involve predicting decisions as well as prescribing decisions. One can easily create new applications by inserting a set of tentative alternatives, goals, and relations for various problems.

Comparisons

The approach also differs from other approaches by virtue of having the following characteristics:

1. P/G% can easily go from alternatives, goals, and relations to drawing a conclusion.
2. It has been translated into a highly user-friendly microcomputer program.
3. It is based on mathematical justifications that relate to classical calculus optimization, especially if one views the part/whole percentages as proxies for nonlinear regression coefficients.
4. It comes with many illustrative applications and years of relevant experience.
5. It is analogous to mathematical programming procedures such as linear, nonlinear, integer, goal, and multiobjective programming, but without the complexity and unrealistic assumptions.
6. The program can systematically compare optimum choices or allocations with actual choices or allocations in order to bring the optimum closer to the actual, and vice versa.

The program has the potential for outperforming spreadsheet programs like Lotus 1-2-3. Lotus does "what-if" analysis, in which one asks what would be the effect of a cell change on a row total, a column total, or a grand total. Such an analysis is highly cumbersome if one has 100 cells (as one does with a 10 × 10 matrix), and each cell is reasonably capable of taking five different values. P/G% analysis instantly tells the user the threshold values for all 100 cells. For example, if the cell in row 4, column 6, has a threshold value of 89, any number greater than 89 will result in alternative 5's being the winner, and any number less than 89 will result in alternative 7's being the winner. Thus one does not have to experiment with what would happen with a score of 95, 117, 43, or 11.

Conclusions

For further information concerning this decision-aiding tool, write Stuart Nagel, 361 Lincoln Hall, University of Illinois, Urbana, Illinois 61801, or telephone (217) 359-8541. A copy of the program, the present manual, and the periodic updates can be obtained for experimental purposes for only $40 to cover the cost of two floppy disks, photocopying, postage, and handling.

Microcomputers are revolutionizing information access and processing. Decision-aiding systems are revolutionizing ideas concerning what microcomputers can do. The P/G% software is, in turn, revolutionizing decision-aiding systems with its unique methods of percentaging, threshold analysis, allocation, and other features. It is an important part of the fourth wave of serious, popular microcomputer software.

3

Allocating Scarce Resources

This chapter deals with allocating money, budgets, and other scarce resources to places and activities. The first part of the chapter deals with allocating to places, and the second part with allocating to activities. Within each part, there is a discussion of allocating by marginal rates of return and by part/whole percentages. The main illustrative example involves allocating anticrime dollars to either places or activities, although one could reason by analogy to allocation in other areas.

The third part of the chapter deals with missing information in allocation problems. It is often difficult to answer questions that relate to how much weight to give a criterion, or to how high to score a relation between an alternative and a criterion. One object of the analysis here is to convert such questions into questions that merely ask whether a weight or relation score is above or below a convergence or critical level. The fourth part of the chapter deals with distinguishing allocating from choosing and clarifying the implications in terms of developing a feasible and meaningful microcomputer algorithm for allocating scarce resources.

The fifth part covers the somewhat tricky problem of how to deal with negative goals where having a low score is desirable. It also covers the problem of how to deal with negative scores for positive goals, where a high temperature, for example, may be desirable, but it is possible to have scores below zero. The sixth part covers how not to handle negative goals in an allocation problem. There are many wrong ways, but only one right way that satisfies the criterion of inverting the scores while preserving their ratios.

ALLOCATING TO PLACES

Allocating by Marginal Rates of Return

In this context, marginal rates of return are the increase in benefits that occurs as a result of a one-unit increase in expenditures. Table 3-1 provides an illustrative example. It involves a reallocation of the $41 million which the Law Enforcement Assistance Administration (LEAA) allocated to 10 large cities in 1974. The object is to reallocate that money to see how much additional crime reduction could have been obtained by allocating the money in proportion to the marginal rates of return for each city, as contrasted to the more subjective methods used by the LEAA.

The Actual Expenditures

Perhaps the best way to analyze Table 3-1 is to explain each column separately. The first column shows the minimum number of dollars that LEAA had to use in deciding how many anticrime dollars would be allocated to each city. Each minimum indicates how much each city had spent in 1973. It could be anticipated that each city would spend approximately the same in 1974 relative to the other cities. Those minimums were not equity minimums in the sense of what each city should have had in order to stay below a maximum crime level, or what each city should have had in view of its population or wealth. The reason for being concerned with how much each city was already spending is that LEAA dollars have less effect on a city that is already spending a lot, because of the principle of diminishing returns. As more dollars are spent on a city, crime is likely to go down but at a decreasing rate, so that the marginal rate of return decreases.

The second column shows how much anticrime money had actually been spent in each city in 1973. That column represents the minimum dollars (i.e., the dollars spent by each city) plus the LEAA dollars. Thus, by subtracting the minimum from the actual amount, one can determine how much the LEAA spent in each city. For Boston, the minimum or self-expenditure was $54 million, and the LEAA expenditure was $13 million, for a total actual expenditure of $67 million, or 67 monetary units.

The Optimum Expenditures

The third or optimum column is especially important. It shows how much money should have been spent on each city to do two related things. The first was to produce as little crime as possible, as measured by the sum of the predicted crime scores across the 10 cities. The second was to spend all $41 million which the LEAA had available, taking into account the idea that the more the LEAA spent, the less crime there would be, and also taking into account the diminishing marginal returns. One would not want to spend all $41 million on the one city that had the best marginal rate of return because the

Table 3-1
Allocating Anti-Crime Dollars to Cities by Marginal Rates of Return

City	Minimum $ (M) #1	Actual $ (X) #2	Optimum $ (X*) #3	$ Difference (Act.-Opt.) #4	Predicted Crime from Actual $ (Y) #5	Predicted Crime from Optimum $ (Y*) #6	Crime Diff. (Act.-Opt.) #7
1. Boston	54	67	57.96	9	24	27	-3
2. Cincinatti	19	21	22.41	-1	35	34	1
3. Dallas	26	32	28.37	4	58	59	-1
4. Houston	29	34	29.41	5	71	71	0
5. Kansas City	26	26	32.03	-6	14	8	6
6. Milwaukee	35	37	35.00	2	23	23	0
7. New Orleans	22	27	22.00	5	40	37	4
8. Pittsburgh	18	21	22.11	-1	23	23	0
9. San Fransisco	59	62	76.59	-15	21	4	17
10. Seattle	20	22	22.97	-1	31	30	1
TOTAL	308	349	349.00	0	340	315	25

All dollars are in millions for 1973. All crimes are in thousands for 1974.

Minimum $ = Non-LEAA dollars. Actual $ = Non-LEAA + LEAA dollars. Optimum $ or X^* = Minimum $ + $41(b/\Sigma b)$.

1974 Predicted Crime from Actual 1973 $ $= a + b_1(\log X_{73}) + b_2(Y_{73})$.

1974 Predicted Crime from Optimum 1973 $ $= a + b_1(\log X^*_{73}) + b_2(Y_{73})$.

phenomenon of diminishing returns would cause much of that money be wasted whenever the negatively sloping crime reduction curve became too flat. The best or optimum allocation would have been to spend the total $41 million in such a way that each allocation would be at the same slope or marginal rate of return for each city. With that set of 10 points, there would be nothing to gain by switching some dollars from one city to another, since the cities would then all be at the same marginal rate of return, even though some of the cities might have curves that were generally steeper than those of other cities.

A key question is: How does one determine the marginal rate of return for each city. A meaningful approach is to put information into a statistical calculator for a set of time periods for each city, concerning its crime quantity (Y) and its total anticrime expenditures (X). Doing so under a linear regression assumption would result in providing the numerical parameters for an equation of the form $Y = a + bX$. To consider the nonlinear diminishing returns, one can put into the calculator the logarithms of the expenditure scores. The result will be the numerical parameters for an equation of the form $Y = a + b(\log X)$. To take into account the reciprocal causation of crime and anticrime expenditures, as well as the other variables that influence both crime and expenditures, one can statistically control for those influences by also putting into the calculator the expenditure and crime scores for each year or time period prior to the year ($t - 1$) for which we are trying to predict or explain crime quantity. Doing so will result in an equation of the form $Y_t = a + b_1(\log X_{t-1}) + b_2 Y_{t-1}$. That kind of analysis, which deals with reciprocal and spurious causation, is referred to as *cross-lagged panel analysis.*[1]

With one equation like that for each city, one can establish, through the use of calculus and simultaneous equations, that the optimum allocation of a grand total of dollars (G) to each city is a quantity of dollars (X^*) equal to $G(b/\Sigma b)$. That expression simply says to allocate to each city in accordance with the ratio between its semilog regression coefficient and the sum of all the negative coefficients across the cities.[2] The cities with positive coefficients just get the minimum amount because the positive coefficient implies that extra money will bring more crime, even though additional statistical analysis might show that the positive coefficient is spurious. The figures in the third or optimum column were determined by means of that approach. For example, Boston had a semilog regression coefficient of −44. The sum of the negative coefficients was 453. Boston therefore had about 10% of the total, and it was thus efficiently entitled to 10% of the $41 million to be allocated. The optimum LEAA allocation was $3.96 million. That amount was added to the $54 million which Boston spent itself to yield the total optimum of $57.96 million. The optimum amounts in column 3 for the other cities were similarly calculated.

Actual versus Optimum

Column 4 of Table 3-1 shows the difference between the actual allocation for each city in 1973 and the optimum allocation, as just described. The differences are generally small, with two exceptions. One exception is Boston, which seems to have received \$9 million more than it should. The explanation may be that Senator Edward Kennedy was chairing the Senate Judiciary Committee in 1973, and the LEAA may have especially wanted to provide anticrime dollars to his state and its main city. Part of the explanation may also be that there were a number of research programs in the Boston area which had received substantial funds from the LEAA, including programs at Harvard, MIT, and Abt Associates. Those expenditures might eventually have been relevant to national crime reduction, but not necessarily to Boston crime reduction in the following year, although LEAA research money was small in amount relative to LEAA action money. The other city which shows a big difference between actual and optimum is San Francisco. It seems to have received \$15 million less than it should. The explanation may be that Jerry Brown, who was then governor of California, had denounced LEAA money as a terrible waste, and he may have been rewarded by receiving substantially less of it than he otherwise would have received.

Column 5 shows the predicted crime from the actual expenditures in column 2. The bottom of Table 3-1 on the left side shows the equation for calculating predicted 1974 crime from actual 1973 dollars. That equation has the form previously mentioned of $Y_t = a + b_1(\log X_{t-1}) + b_2 Y_{t-1}$. To determine predicted 1974 crime, one inserts \$67 in place of X_{t-1}, and -44 in place of b_1. The 1973 Boston crime quantity is substituted for Y_{t-1}. The statistical regression analysis previously discussed provides a numerical value for a and b_2. By inserting those numbers in the Boston equation, one gets a predicted-crime score for 1974 of 24,000 crimes.

Column 6 shows the predicted crime from the optimum expenditures in column 3. The bottom of Table 3-1 on the right side shows the equation for calculating predicted 1974 crime from optimum 1973 dollars. To apply that equation requires inserting the \$57.96 in place of X^*_{t-1}. All the other numbers remain the same. After making that insertion, taking the logarithms, and performing the multiplication and addition, one finds that the predicted 1974 crime rate for Boston from the optimum 1973 dollars is 27,000 crimes. The other amounts in column 6 are similarly calculated.

Column 7 involves subtracting column 6 from column 5 in order to show how much of a predicted improvement in crime quantity one gets from the optimum allocation, rather than the actual allocation to each city. For every city, the optimum allocation results in lower predicted crime than the actual allocation with the exception of the results for Boston. For Boston, the number of crimes with the optimum dollars is 3,000 more than the number with the actual dollars. The explanation is that the actual dollars received by Boston were substantially more than the optimum that Boston deserved in light of Boston's relatively low marginal rate of return (MRR) or logarithmic regression coefficient. One might also note that San Francisco would have had 17,000 less crimes with the optimum dollars than with the actual dollars. The explanation is that the actual dollars received by San Francisco were substantially fewer than San Francisco deserved in light of its relatively high MRR or logarithmic coefficient.

An especially important number to note is the bottom-line number of 25 in the lower-right-hand corner of Table 3-1. That number indicates that with the optimum allocation, there would have been 25,000 fewer predicted crimes than with the actual allocation. One might question why the difference is not bigger, since 25 on a base of 340 is only a 7% difference. One could answer by saying that the 25,000 extra crime victims might greatly welcome that 7% difference. One might also recognize that no matter how optimally the LEAA allocates its anticrime money, the LEAA cannot have very much effect on crime occurrence for two reasons. First, it does not have much money to allocate. In our context, it had only $41 million, compared to the $308 million which the 10 cities had. Thus the LEAA had only 12% of the total $349 million being allocated. Second, the regression coefficients between anticrime dollars and crime reduction are rather low, and the LEAA has little control over those marginal rates of return. The MRRs for expenditures on police, criminal courts, and prisons, for example, are close to zero when one relates crime occurrence to expenditures for those three activities. In other words, if the LEAA had much more money and could somehow use the money to influence job opportunities or other more potent crime-deterring factors, then optimally allocating anticrime dollars to cities could make a much bigger difference than allocating anticrime dollars to cities in accordance with more traditional political and other criteria.[3]

Allocating by Part/Whole Percentages

Relevant Attributes

As a substantially different approach to allocating money to cities, one might determine the attributes or characteristics of those cities which should get more federal money than others to fight crime. The attributes are likely to be of two kinds. Some relate to the need for money, and some relate to the ability to use it efficiently. Need or equity attributes might be population size, crime occurrence, and wealth of the city. These attributes are similar to those used allocating income in accordance with need, in which each family receives an income in accordance with the number of people in the family, disease occurrence, and other variables that require expenditures, as well as how much wealth or other income the family already has.

An ability attribute in the anticrime context might be the quality of the police recruitment system measured on a 1–10 scale. This would be analogous to allocating income on the basis of ability or potential contribution, whereby those with more education or intelligence are allocated higher incomes, in anticipation that they will put the money to better use or that such a system will stimulate others to get more education. Ability may also be applied ability, not just potential ability. In the anticrime context, such an ability might be the scoring of cities by knowledgeable people on how well they have been actually fighting crime. This would be analogous to allocating income to people in terms of how much they have actually been contributing to the betterment of society or the economy as measured by marketplace factors or by a national planning commission.

The need attributes are generally determined through (1) the legislative process; (2) the judicial process, where constitutional equal protection issues may be involved; and/or (3) the administrative process, where administrative agencies have been delegated the authority to make such decisions. Need attributes and their weights can also be determined by surveying relevant people, deducing from other related allocation procedures, or making assumptions and then determining how the allocations are influenced by alternative assumptions. Ability attributes and their weights can be determined by the same methods. One can also use a relational analysis, whereby proposed ability attributes are correlated with such goals as crime occurrence per capita to show how much empirical regression weight they have in such relations.

Scoring the Cities on the Attributes and Obtaining Total Scores

Once an appropriate set of allocation attributes or criteria has been determined, one might then ask what can be done with that information. Suppose we want to allocate to two cities only on the basis of their population. City A has 40 people, and City B has 10 people, as is shown in Table 3-2. If we have $200 to allocate, we would logically give 40/50, or 80% to City A, and 10/50, or 20% to City B. Because we recognize the phenomenon of diminishing returns or diminishing utility, we would not give everything to City A. This means that City A may have more need or ability in general than City B, but the 200th dollar given to City A is likely to produce less need satisfaction or goal achievement than the 1st dollar given to City B. We thus allocate proportionately, as if we were allocating in accordance with nonlinear elasticity coefficients, rather than in accordance with linear slopes. This simple kind of analysis can be extended easily to more than two cities. We simply allocate to each city in accordance with the ratio of its population to the total population of all the cities, or in accordance with

Table 3-2
Allocating Anti-Crime Dollars to Cities by Part/Whole Percentages

City	People (Wt = 1)	P/W%	Crime (Wt = 2)	P/W%	Wealth (Wt = 1)	P/W%	Unweighted Sum (3 criteria)	Weighted Sum	Allocation Percentages
A	40	80%	90	60%	$500	-83%	57%	117%	58.5%
B	10	20%	60	40%	$100	-17%	43%	83%	41.5%
Whole	50	100%	150	100%	$600	-100%	100%	200%	100%
City	Police Efficiency (Wt = 3)	P/W%	Judicial Efficiency (Wt = 2)	P/W%	Corrections Efficiency (Wt = 1)	P/W%	Unweighted Sum (6 criteria)	Weighted Sum	Allocation Percentages
A	6	75%	5	50%	3	33%	215%	475%	59.4%
B	2	25%	5	50%	6	67%	185%	325%	40.6%
Whole	8	100%	10	100%	9	100%	400%	800%	100%

Symbols

* = Optimum amount to give to a city.

G = Grand total available to allocate (e.g., $200)

S = Raw attribute score or part.

N = Attribute score expressed as a part/whole percentage (P/W%) of the sum of the scores.

W = Relative weights (Wt) of each attribute.

Formulas

One Attribute: $X^* = (G)(P)$, where $P = S/\Sigma S$

Two or more attributes unweighted: $X^* = (G)(\Sigma P/N)$

Two or more attributes weighted: $X^* = (G)(\Sigma WP/W)$

the ratio of its attribute score to the sum of the attribute scores of all the cities.

Suppose we want to work with two attributes, such as population and crime. Suppose further that City A has 90 crimes, and City B has 60 crimes. If we are allocating only in accordance with crime, City A would receive 90/150, or 60%, of the $200 and City B would receive 60/150, or 40%, of the $200. However, since we are allocating in accordance with two attributes, each of which has equal weight, the logical thing to do is to compromise between the $160 that City A would receive in accordance with the population allocation and the $120 that it would get in accordance with the crime allocation. Thus, in terms of these two attributes, City A should receive $140, and City B should get $60. We can easily extend this simple kind of analysis to more than two attributes by determining how much each city would be allocated if we use the proportional allocation for each attribute separately. We then arrive at an average allocation for each city by averaging across those differing attribute allocations. Preferably each attribute should be scored so that a high score indicates a desirable characteristic.

Suppose we want to allocate to each place in proportion to the people, crime, and wealth, all three criteria being weighted equally. In golf, the lower the score the better; the player with the lowest score wins. Analogously, wealth has the golflike characteristic that the less of it a city has, the more money the federal government should allocate to the city. A logical way to do so would be to give City A a composite score equal to 80% + 60% − 83%, which equals 57%. We would likewise give City B a composite score equal to 20% + 40% − 17%, which equals 43%. That tells us that City A should get 57% of the $200, and City B should get 43% of the $200. If we are allocating to a golflike criterion like wealth, and it is the only criterion, we can allocate in proportion to the complements of the part/whole percentages. If, however, it is one of a set of criteria, then we calculate a composite score for each place or other object of the allocations. The composite score is the algebraic sum of the positive percentages and the negative percentages. Then we allocate in proportion to those algebraic sums.

To further clarify the distinction between equity or needs criteria and efficiency criteria, the second part of Table 3-2 provides hypothetical data for each place on the efficiency of their police, judicial, and corrections systems. We could obtain such data by asking knowledgeable police chiefs, state supreme court justices, prison wardens, or other such people to rank-order each place on a 1–*N* scale, or to rate each place on a 0–100 scale, just as college department heads have often been asked to rank or rate each other's departments. The most knowledgeable people might be those who are officers or staff members of cross-city associations like the International Association of Police Chiefs, the American Judicature Society, or the American Probation and Parole Association. Those scores can be treated arithmetically like the equity scores of population, crime, and wealth. If we allocate only in accordance with efficiency scores, we may get more crime reduction for our $200 than if we allocate in accordance with the equity scores. We may, however, be violating our sense of fairness that no place should receive less than a certain minimum allocation in view of its population, crime problems, and lack of wealth.

Weighting the Attributes

Suppose that our initial two attributes of population and crime are not equally important. More specifically, suppose that a survey of legislators, the public, or some other relevant group determines that crime is twice as important in allocating as population is. In this situation, we simply figure that City A would receive 80% of the $200 budget if population were the only criterion, and 60% of the budget, times 2, if crime were the only criterion, with a weight of 2. That means that we sum 80%, 60%, and 60%, divide by 3, and obtain 67%. If the two attributes were weighted equally, City A would get 70%. Since crime is given a weight of 2, City A gets only 67%, and City B gets 33% rather than just 30%. In more general terms, we allocate to each city by summing the weighted percentage scores and dividing by the sum of the weights. The weights should consider not only the relative importance of each attribute, but also the measurement units used and the other attributes that are present. Thus an income attribute measured in $1 units would get a smaller weight than one measured in $1,000 units. Likewise, crime would get a greater weight if population were not also included as an attribute, since crime occurrence and population size are closely related.

On the matter of weighting the equity and efficiency attributes, a compromise might be to weight the three equity allocations equally along with the three efficiency allocations. We can also use a differential weighting, as described above in the discussion of weighted composite allocation. An alternative to allocating according to equity and efficiency criteria simultaneously is to allocate according to those criteria sequentially. Doing that involves making a decision about what is roughly the minimum which each place, group, or person needs in order to be at a minimum level of decency with regard to health, education, freedom from crime, or other societal benefits. If it is determined that City A needs a minimum of $4 beyond what it can afford and City B needs a minimum of $8 beyond what it can afford, then the sequential method would allocate that $12 to those two places and then allocate the remaining $188 in accordance with the efficiency criteria. The simultaneous method may be easier, since it does not require determining a minimum constraint level for each city, but it is less accurate in guaranteeing that each city will be at or above a minimum level.[4]

In light of all the above considerations, we can summarize the part/whole percentaging approach by saying it defines the optimum allocation to each city as being the minimum per city plus a proportion of the new grand total to be allocated across the cities. The minimum per city is what the city spends on itself plus a federal amount necessary to bring the city up to a minimum level. The new grand total is the original total minus the sum of amounts needed to bring the cities up to those minimum levels. The proportion that each city gets is then equal to the ratio between the sum of its weighted part/whole percentages divided by the sum of the weights.

Some Conclusions on Allocating to Places

How does a part/whole percentaging approach compare with an approach that allocates in proportion to the marginal rates of return? The marginal analysis approach seeks to relate benefits to alternative allocations. It then arrives at an optimum allocation in light of (1) the regression coefficients of each place or activity and (2) certain minimum equity constraints. The minimum constraints are like need attributes, and determining them involves the same problems. Marginal analysis produces more effective or goal-achieving allocations when we are confident that the regression coefficients are capturing the true causal relationships between benefits and alternative allocations. That confidence is often difficult to achieve, since there are problems of reciprocal causation and spurious causation that are difficult to control for. Under such circumstances, a part/whole percentaging approach may be more meaningful, especially if the attributes, the weights, and the scoring can be agreed upon by those whose opinions are considered relevant.

Both approaches involve considerable subjectivity. The MRR approach is highly subjective when used to decide what dependent variable should be optimized. One could argue that crime reduction should be only one goal in allocating anticrime dollars. At least one other goal should be procedural fairness. The MRR approach tends to avoid such goals, which are difficult to measure. The percentaging approach is more comfortable with multiple goals and with goals that can be measured by knowledgeable insiders. The relative weights of the goals and the relation scores in the percentaging approach are subjective, but they may be more meaningful than having only one criterion in the MRR approach and having regression scores that cannot be trusted to be in the right direction, let alone to be the right magnitude. The best way to deal with the subjectivities of both approaches is to make sure they are resolved in accordance with the values and the perceptions of whatever persons have the responsibility for making the allocation decisions. One can also observe that there is often room for substantial variation in the allocation inputs without their substantially affecting the allocation outputs.

The best test of these two basic approaches to optimum or effective allocation is to try them both, and to see how they compare on goal achievement. The most meaningful way to do that would be to arrange for a random sample of about 30 cities to be allocated anticrime dollars in accordance with their marginal rates of return, and to arrange for another random sample of about 30 cities to be allocated the same quantity of anticrime dollars in accordance with their part/whole percentages. If the cities are randomly chosen, then in the period before these allocations, the total crime for each group should be about the same, which might be 10,000 crimes at time $t - 1$. The year after the allocations at time $t + 1$, the total crime for the P/W% cities might be 8,000, and the total crime for the MRR cities might be 9,000. The difference or change score for the P/W% cities would thus be −2,000, and the change score for the MRR cities would be −1,000. These figures would show, in this substantive context, that allocating with part/whole percentages is more effective or optimum than allocating in accordance with marginal rates of return.

Such an experiment might be objected to on various grounds such as:

1. *Expensiveness.* The experimental allocations, however, would be no more expensive than the nonexperimental allocations. The grand total to be allocated would not be changed.
2. *Methodological complications.* The methodology here is simple and effective. There is a large number of cities, unlike states, to choose among randomly. Any substantial differences between the two sets of cities cannot be readily attributed to other factors, which the randomization would tend to equalize.
3. *Ethical complications.* This is not the equivalent of putting human beings at risk. Both sets of cities are being given substantial anticrime funds in accordance with different, but rational, formulas. If we knew that one set of the cities was going to be subjected to much more crime than the second set of cities, we would have an ethical problem.
4. *Unnecessary experimentation.* This objection implies that if we could conduct such an experiment, we would already know enough so the experiment would be unnecessary. On the contrary, our reason for conducting such an experiment would be because we do not know whether allocating by marginal rates of return is more or less effective than allocating by part/whole percentages or multiattributes.

There is a need for more such research on allocating federal money to cities. Most of the present research relates to (1) descriptions of how much money various cities receive and what they do with it; (2) descriptions of the political process for deciding how to allocate or how a proposal becomes a law; and (3) recommendations for allocations in specific substantive fields, rather than general principles of optimum allocation.[5] Doing research on the effects of alternative allocation systems could pay off in terms of developing ideas for improving allocation procedures and thereby improving the benefit/cost ratio of the allocation dollars spent in many areas that involve allocating federal money to cities, such as crime, housing, transportation, education, health, welfare, urban development, and other areas that are relevant to the quality of urban life.

ALLOCATING TO ACTIVITIES

Allocating by Marginal Rates of Return

Instead of allocating the anticrime budget to 10 cities, we can think of allocating in terms of the three activities: police, judges, and corrections. This approach would involve working with the same data for 10 cities over a number of points in time. However, instead of generating 10 equations, with 1 for each city relating crime to anticrime expenditures, we would generate one equation relating crime to the three anticrime activities. The data matrix would thus show for the total set of cities for each year (1) the crime occurrence score; (2) the expenditures on the police; (3) the expenditures on judges; and (4) the expenditures on corrections.

To obtain the marginal rate of return for an anticrime dollar expended on the police, we compute the regression parameters for the equation $Y_t = a(P_{t-1})^{b1}(J_{t-1})^{b2}(C_{t-1})^{b3}(Y_{t-1})^{b4}$. In that regression equation, Y represents crime; P represents dollars spent on the police; J represents dollars spent on judicial activities; and C represents dollars for corrections. The parameters are based on 50 units of analysis consisting of five years for each of the 10 cities. All the variables are logged to take nonlinear diminishing returns into consideration and are also lagged to consider the delayed effect of anticrime dollars on crime. Crime for the previous year is again held constant so that we can indirectly get at variables other than anticrime dollars which influence crime. Performing that simple regression analysis on the data yields the equation $Y_t = 1.86(P_{t-1})^{-.07}(J_{t-1})^{-.001}(C_{t-1})^{-.001}(Y_{t-1})^{.89}$.

We can prove algebraically that the optimum allocation to each activity (in light of the above equation and elementary calculus) can be determined by the formula $X_i^* = G(b_i/\Sigma b)$, where X_i^* equals the optimum incremental allocation to activity i, and b equals the elasticity coefficient of activity i. There is no need to consider the scale coefficient a, since all the activities share the same scale coefficient. Similarly, they share the same Y_{t-1}, although its presence influences the values of b_1, b_2, and b_3, particularly by generally making them negative rather than positive. This X_i^* formula is applied only to activities which have negative elasticity coefficients. An activity with a positive coefficient should receive only the minimum allocation, which is equal to an estimate of what the cities spent on that activity independent of the LEAA. This estimate assumes that the LEAA spent its \$41 million on police, judicial, and corrections in the same proportions as the cities did.

Allocating by Part/Whole Percentages

The illustrative example involves a budget of $500 and two budget categories. One is money for the police, and the other is money for the courts. There are two allocation criteria. One is crime reduction, and the other is fair procedure. The scoring of the alternatives on the criteria is relative scoring, which means noting the budget category that does better and roughly how much better. Those basic concepts about the budget categories and the allocation criteria are shown in Table 3-3A.

Scoring the Alternatives

To score the alternatives on crime reduction, one asks which budget category is less effective in crime reduction. Nearly everyone would say that the courts are less effective than the police in reducing crime:

1. The courts, however, do reduce crime by the sentencing of convicted criminals, which does have some deterrent effect on the general public, although it may not have much deterrent effect on the specific defendant.
2. Proof that the police are somewhat effective in reducing crime are studies that show highway speeding is reduced by the presence of more visible police cars. The Kansas experiment which found virtually no change in the crime rate of a neighborhood in which the police were temporarily removed is not inconsistent, since would-be criminals were not notified that the police were being removed.
3. After giving the less effective category a score of 1, one asks how much more effective the next category is. People might disagree about how much more effective a 10% increase in police expenditures might be than a 10% increase in court expenditures, but they might generally say twice as effective. Therefore, we give the police a score of 2 on crime reduction.

To score the alternatives on fair procedure, we ask which budget category is less effective. Nearly everyone would say the police are less effective than the courts in the separation of the innocent from the guilty, which is the essence of fair procedure:

1. The police, however, do some separation of the innocent from the guilty when they decide who should be given warnings and who should be arrested.
2. Proof that the courts are somewhat effective in separating the innocent from the guilty is the fact that there are so few cases of convicted people who are subsequently found to have been innocent. There are many cases of people who have not been found guilty who subsequently do commit crimes, although that does not necessarily indicate that they were previously guilty. The concept of fair procedure, however, places more weight on freeing the innocent than on convicting the guilty.
3. After giving the less effective category a score of 1, one asks how much more effective a 10% expenditure increase would be for the courts than a 10% expenditure increase for the police. Most people would probably say that there is a bigger

Table 3-3
Using Policy/Goal Percentaging to Allocate Resources to Budget Categories

A. THE ALTERNATIVE BUDGET CATEGORIES AND THE ALLOCATION CRITERIA

Alternative	Criterion	Meas.Unit	Weight
1 POLICE	1 CRIME REDUCTION	RELATIVE X	1.00
2 COURTS	2 FAIR PROCEDURE	RELATIVE X	2.00

B. THE RELATIVE SCORING OF THE ALTERNATIVES ON THE CRITERIA

ALTERNATIVE/CRITERIA SCORING

	CRIME RE	FAIR PRO
POLICE	2.00	1.00
COURTS	1.00	3.00

C. ALLOCATION PERCENTAGES IN LIGHT OF EACH CRITERION

PART/WHOLE %

	CRIME RE	FAIR PRO
POLICE	66.67	25.00
COURTS	33.33	75.00

D. WEIGHTED ALLOCATION PERCENTAGES (With One Criterion Considered Twice as Important)

WEIGHTED PART/WHOLE %

	CRIME RE	FAIR PRO
POLICE	66.67	50.00
COURTS	33.33	150.00

E. AVERAGING THE WEIGHTED ALLOCATION PERCENTAGES

Alternative	Combined W P/W	%
1 POLICE	116.67	38.89
2 COURTS	183.33	61.11

F. APPLYING THE AVERAGE PERCENTAGES TO THE TOTAL RESOURCES

Total Resources = 500.00

Alternative	Allocation
1 POLICE	194.44
2 COURTS	305.56

gap regarding the effectiveness of the courts on fair procedure than there is regarding the effectiveness of the police on crime reduction. The courts are supposed to be a more substantial part of the crime reduction system than the police are in the guilt determination system. Therefore we tentatively give the courts a score of 3 on fair procedure.

In technical terms, the 2-1 on crime reduction, and the 1-3 on fair procedure are substitutes or proxies for nonlinear elasticity coefficients or regression equation exponents. The relative scores of police and courts on crime reduction and fair procedure are shown in Table 3-3B. Also, technically speaking, we should not talk in terms of how much more effective the police are than the courts in crime reduction. Rather, we should talk in terms of how much more effective an extra $1 or $100 to the police would be in reducing crime than an extra $1 or $100 to the courts would be. Likewise, it is the general effect on fair procedure of incremental dollars to the police and courts that we are interested in, not incremental quantities of police or judges. We can obtain these relative scores by averaging the general opinions of knowledgeable insiders, subject to the kind of sensitivity analysis that will be discussed later.

Weighting the Goals

The criteria of crime reduction and fair procedure need to be weighted in terms of their relative importance. To do the weighting, we ask which of these two criteria is less important for the purposes for which the money is being allocated. More people associated with the legal system would say that crime reduction is less important than fair procedure. They would implicitly agree with William Blackstone, in direction although not necessarily in magnitude, that it is 10 times better to acquit the innocent than it is to convict the guilty, or that it is 10 times worse to convict the innocent than it is to acquit the guilty.

After giving the less important criterion a weight of 1, we ask how much more important or desirable the next criterion is. In this context, 10 to 1 would be too high, since we are talking not about convicting or acquitting a specific defendant, but about crime reduction and fair procedure, which are only analogous concepts. For the sake of simplicity and illustrative purposes, we can tentatively say that fair procedure is about twice as important as crime reduction to whoever has the responsibility for allocating the $500 budget that needs to be allocated. The far right of Table 3-3A shows those relative weights.

Doing the Allocating with Separate Allocation Percentages

Table 3-3C shows that if the $500 were to be allocated to the police and the courts only on the basis of crime reduction, and the police do twice as well as the courts on that criterion, it would be logical to allocate 2/3 or 67% of the budget to the police and 1/3 or 33% to the courts. The reason we do not allocate all of the budget to the police is diminishing returns, whereby additional funds allocated to a budget category produce increased returns, but at a diminishing rate. That means that each additional dollar allocated to the police may produce an additional crime reduction, but each reduction gets smaller as the easy crime is reduced and the crime that is more difficult to deal with remains. The first dollar allocated to the courts will not produce as much reduction as the first dollar allocated to the police. The 499th dollar, however, will do more good if allocated as the 1st dollar to the courts than as the 499th dollar to the police.

If we do not allocate all to the police in crime reduction, then how much do we allocate? We can prove by classical calculus optimization that the budget will produce a maximum crime reduction if it is allocated to the police and the courts in proportion to those relative scores or proxies for elasticity coefficients.

Table 3-3C also shows that if the $500 were to be allocated to the police and the courts only on the basis of fair procedure, and the courts do three times as well as the police on that criterion, it would be logical to allocate 1/4 or 25% of the budget to the police and 3/4 or 75% to the courts. This is true for the same reasons that we would not allocate all of the $500 to the police if we were considering only crime reduction. For effectiveness, efficiency, and equity, we would generally make only a proportionate allocation, assuming for the moment that there are no political, legal, or other requirements of certain minimum or maximum allocations to the police or to the courts. If there were, adjustments would have to be made for those requirements after we first allocate optimally without considering them.

Doing the Allocating with Weighted Allocation Percentages

Table 3-3D is the same as Table 3-3C except that the allocation percentages associated with fair procedure have been doubled because we tentatively consider fair procedure twice as important as crime reduction. Thus, the 25% and 75% allocation percentages to the police and the courts become, under the criterion of fair procedure, 50% and 150%.

Table 3-3E adds the allocation percentages across the row that pertains to the police budget category: 67% plus 50% equals 117%. Table 3-3E also adds the allocation percentages across the row that pertains to the courts budget category: 33% plus 150% equals 183%. Those are the combined or aggregate allocation percentages. They cannot be used directly for allocation since we cannot allocate more than 100%. They need to be divided by the sum of the weights, which is 1 plus 2, or 3. If we divide 117% by 3, we get 39%. If we divide 183% by 3, we get 61%. Those two percentages represent the weighted average of the allocation percentages. That is, they average the separate allocation percentages from Table 3-3C, taking into consideration the relative importance of each set of percentages.

Table 3-3F applies the 39% and the 61% to the $500 in total resources to be allocated by multiplying $500 by .39 and .61. The results are $194 to the police and $306 to the courts, based on the use of only crime reduction and fair procedure as the allocation criteria, with weights and relative scores like those shown in Tables 3-3A and 3-3B. If we add another goal, like providing employment, we would probably increase the allocation to the police. If we had a constraint that said neither the police nor the courts could receive less than 70% of what they received last year nor more than 150%, then the police probably would receive a larger proportion of the $500.

Postoptimizing Analysis in Systematic Allocation

Table 3-4 shows some forms of analysis that can occur after one has arrived at the initial allocations shown in Table 3-3F. Table 3-4A compares the past allocation amounts for police and courts of $300 and $100 with the recommended amounts of $194 and $306. One would expect the recommended amounts to be about 125% higher than the past amounts since the past total resources were only $400, and the present total resources are $500. The differences or residuals between the actual and the recommended are, however, too big to be explained by an increase in the total resources, in which case the police would receive $375 and the courts would receive $125.

The following are explanations for why the police may be overallocated and the courts may be underallocated:

1. The people doing the allocating may consider crime reduction as important as or maybe even more important than fair procedure.
2. The people doing the allocating may perceive that fair procedure can be bought more cheaply than it can be. They may thus provide only a small allocation to the public defender's office within the courts, thinking that the public defender can adequately represent all potentially innocent defendants on such a small budget.
3. There may be other goals operating in the minds of the decision-makers that we have not included, such as the employment goal mentioned; the police are viewed in some cities as providing important employment opportunities, whereas the courts are not.

Table 3-4B shows what it would take to bring the police allocation up to the level of the court allocation if the two allocation criteria had equal weights. The table shows the threshold value for each relation score and each weight. At that value, there would be a tied allocation of 50% apiece between the two budget categories. Thus, the six threshold figures would be as follows:

1. If the police were to score 3 to 1 rather than 2 to 1 on crime reduction.
2. If the courts were to score .67 to 2 on crime reduction, rather than 1 to 2.
3. If the police were to score 1.5 to 3 rather than 1 to 3 on fair procedure.

Table 3-4
Post-Optimizing Analysis in Policy/Goal Percentaging Allocation

A. COMPARING THE PAST ALLOCATION AMOUNTS WITH THE RECOMMENDED AMOUNTS

Total Resources = 500.00

Alternative	Actual	Allocation	Residual
1 POLICE	300.00	194.44	105.56
2 COURTS	100.00	305.56	-205.56

B. BRINGING THE POLICE ALLOCATION UP TO THE COURT ALLOCATION
(With the Criteria Having Equal Weight)

THRESHOLD ANALYSIS

	POLICE	COURTS	Weight
CRIME REDUCTION	3.00	0.67	1.500
FAIR PROCEDURE	1.50	2.00	0.667

C. BRINGING THE POLICE ALLOCATION UP TO THE COURT ALLOCATION
(With Fair Procedure Having Twice the Weight of Crime Reduction)

THRESHOLD ANALYSIS

	POLICE	COURTS	Weight
CRIME REDUCTION	??	0.00	3.000
FAIR PROCEDURE	2.14	1.40	0.667

D. THE WEIGHT AT WHICH EACH CRITERION REACHES A MAXIMUM INFLUENCE

CONVERGENCE ANALYSIS

	Weight
CRIME REDUCTION	8.00
FAIR PROCEDURE	8.00

Stopping difference set at:
5.0 percentage points.

4. If the courts were to score 2 to 1 on fair procedure, rather than 3 to 1.
5. If the weight of crime reduction to fair procedure were to go up to 1.5 to 1, instead of 1 to 1.
6. If the weight of fair procedure to crime reduction were to go down to .67 to 1, instead of 1 to 1.

One can substitute any of those changes in Table 3-3A or 3-3B and then apply the procedures of Table 3-3C through 3-3F. The result will be $250 to the police, and $250 to the courts.

Table 3-4C shows the threshold values per the more realistic situation in which some criteria are more important than others. The threshold values become less obvious than when the criteria have equal weight. Nevertheless, all the threshold values are still tie-causing values. For example, if the courts were to score zero on crime reduction, the police would get 100% of the budget on the crime reduction criterion. Adding 100% to 50% instead of 67% to 50% in Table 3-3B would now give a combined score of 150%. That would exactly equal adding 0% to 150% in the courts row. The pair of question marks shows that no matter how high the police score is on crime reduction, there will not be an equal allocation if the courts give three times the effectiveness on fair procedure, and if fair procedure is twice as important as crime reduction.

If we were to allocate only on the basis of crime reduction, the allocation percentages would be 67% and 33% as is shown in Table 3-3C. That is the equivalent of giving crime reduction a weight of infinity so that it totally overwhelms fair procedure. Table 3-4D shows that with a weight of only 8 for crime reduction, the allocation percentages will be within five percentage points of 67% and 33%. With a weight higher than 8 for crime reduction, there is very little incremental gain toward the maximum figures of 67% and 33%, in view of diminishing returns. Likewise, with a weight of only 8 for fair procedure, the allocation percentages will be within five percentage points of the 25% and 75% shown in Table 3-3C. Thus there is no need to argue whether fair procedure should receive a weight of 8 to 1 or 10 to 1 compared to crime reduction, since anything above 8 to 1 produces approximately the same allocation and is roughly the equivalent of a weight of infinity.

A special form of allocating is allocating people to activities. It is not like allocating money to activities because money is a homogeneous resource: one dollar is like any other dollar. One person is, however, not like any other person. People differ in how well they do and enjoy doing different activities. We may need to take those ability and interest scores into consideration in allocating people to activities or tasks. Allocating people also involves special constraints. In allocating money, the main constraints are the total budget and the minimums or maximums to be given to each activity. In allocating people, we may need to recognize that each person must be given a minimum and a maximum amount of work to do. We must also consider how much of each task there is available to do. There may also be constraints specifying that no persons may perform certain tasks without a minimum level of qualification. The best way to handle allocating people to tasks is probably through a linear programming routine, although P/G% can provide insights, starting points, and feasible solutions, if not optimum solutions.[6]

MISSING INFORMATION IN ALLOCATION PROBLEMS

Choosing and Allocating Compared

Three major ways of dealing with missing information in choosing problems (as contrasted to allocation problems) are threshold analysis, best-worst analysis, and graphics analysis. Threshold analysis has only limited applicability in an allocation problem. It applies when one wants to know what it would take in terms of input changes to cause a certain budget category to receive the same allocation as another budget category. Threshold analysis also applies where one wants to know what it would take to cause a budget category to receive an allocation equal to a specific percentage of the resources, such as 80%. One might create a hypothetical budget category that does get 80% of the resources to compare with the budget category in which one is interested.

Best–worst analysis can apply to either an allocation problem or a choosing problem. In either situation, one shows the controversial input items at their best and at their worst and then calculates the overall best choosing scores or allocation scores, the overall worst, and the midpoint between the overall best and the overall worst. One normally goes with the midpoints in either choosing among the alternatives or allocating resources to the alternatives. One may go with the overall best where the midpoint approach does not cross a minimum constraint of the benefits received. Likewise, one may go with the worst case in choosing or allocating, where the midpoint approach exceeds a maximum constraint on costs. The worst case involves choosing the best alternative given the worst that could happen.

The graphics approach is an extension of threshold analysis to cover two or more unknowns. It has the same defect of emphasizing either–or thinking as threshold analysis does when applied to an allocation problem. Thus there is a region above the threshold curve that might be called *Favor Alternative 1* and a region below the threshold curve that might be called *Favor Alternative 2*. That makes sense in a choosing problem where only one alternative can be the winner overall or in a paired comparison. It does not make so much sense in an allocation problem where each alternative receives a percentage of scarce resources.

In an allocation problem, what we mainly want to know regarding missing information is whether the input item could be big enough or small enough so that all the allocation percentages are within 5%, or some other percentage, of the maximum that they could be. If the allocation percentage is within 5% (i.e., five percentage points) of the maximum, there is no need to argue that the input item should be changed further, since the incremental results are probably not worth the incremental arguing. That is where the concept of convergence analysis comes in as a form of sensitivity analysis especially applicable to allocation problems.

Convergence Analysis in General

To explain convergence analysis, it is helpful to define some basic concepts such as the following:

1. *Convergence weight or score.* This is the value of a weight or a relation score which generates allocation percentages that are exactly five percentage points from the maximum allocation percentage possible. We normally only talk about convergence weights since the weights are generally more subject to argument than the relation scores are.

2. *Allocation percentage.* This is the percentage showing the portion of some scarce resources or some other whole that should be allocated to each alternative or budget category in order to maximize total goal achievement. The scarce resources could be money, time, people, cases, or virtually anything. The alternatives or categories could be places, activities, people, or anything that is capable of receiving whatever is being allocated. The allocation percentages add up to 100%. The sum of the absolute allocations add up to the grand total of whatever is available to be allocated.

3. *Maximum allocation percentage.* This is the allocation percentage that would occur with a weight of infinity or a score of infinity for a weight or relation score in which one is interested. The maximum allocation is normally not 100%, given the occurrence of diminishing returns when one keeps adding to a budget category. The maximum allocation percentage is normally the allocation percentage that would occur if the criterion under consideration were the only criterion. With one criterion, the allocation percentages would be the same as the part/whole percentages.

4. *Convergence range.* This is the range around a maximum allocation percentage. It is usually from five percentage points below the maximum allocation percentage up to five percentage points above the maximum allocation.

5. *Perceived weight or score.* This is the weight or score that is put into the data matrix. It can be contrasted to the convergence value, which is a near-maximum-causing value. This is also in contrast to a threshold weight or score, which is a tie-causing value.

6. *Convergence equation.* This is the analytical equation which enables one to find a convergence weight or score analogous to the threshold equation discussed in threshold analysis. The right side of the convergence equation is the maximum allocation percentage plus or minus five percentage points, or .05 where everything is expressed as decimals. The left side of the convergence equation is the formula for calculating an allocation percentage for the alternative or budget category involved.

7. *Convergence analysis.* This is an analysis that determines the convergence weights or scores in a multiple-criterion allocation problem.

8. *Allocation problem.* This is a problem where we have alternatives, criteria, weights for the criteria, and relations between alternatives and criteria. The object is to determine the allocation percentages for each alternative. The allocation percentages add to 100%.

Convergence Weights

To obtain a better understanding of convergence analysis, it is helpful to be aware of the equation for calculating convergence weights. The equation is as follows:

$$(W\% + \Sigma\%O) / (W + \Sigma WO) = \text{Max}\% \pm .05$$

The left side of the equation shows the formula for the actual allocation percentage. The right side of the equation shows the formula for the maximum allocation percentage plus or minus 5%. The left side is a weighted average percentage. The numerator is equal to the sum of the allocation percentages for all the criteria with a given alternative. The denominator is equal to the sum of the weights for all the criteria. The key variable is *W*, which is the weight of the criterion under consideration. The object is to determine how far up *W* would have to go to generate an allocation percentage within five percentage points of the maximum allocation percentage if that criterion were the only criterion.

Reading the left side of the equation from left to right, using words rather than symbols, we have, "The actual allocation to an alternative is equal to the part/whole percentage of the alternative on the criterion in question multiplied by the weight of the criterion, with that percentage added to the sum of the other part/whole percentages of the alternative on the criterion, with that sum then divided by the weight of the criterion, plus the sum of the other weights when they are all set equal to 1.00." Reading the right side of the equation, we have, "The maximum allocation percentage is equal to the part/whole percentage of the alternative on the criterion in question, and we should add or subtract .05." The symbol *O* stands for "other." The symbol % stands for part/whole percentage. The symbol Σ stands for "sum of."

This equation is much easier to follow if actual numbers are used, such as those given in Table 3-3. For example, suppose one wants to know by the above equation the convergence weight of fair procedure. One could determine that value by inserting numbers in place of the symbols in the above equation. Doing so would generate the following equation with W as the one unknown:

$$(.75W + .33) / (W + 1) = .75 \pm .05$$

The left side of the equation shows that the actual allocation percentage is .75 + .33, or 1.08 divided by 2, or .54 if all the criteria have weights of 1.00. The right side of the equation shows that we want to know how much *W* has to be raised above 1.00 to yield an allocation percentage of .70. The .70 is five percentage points away from the maximum allocation percentage of .75, which would occur if the criterion in question were the only criterion or if it had a weight of infinity.

Simplifying the above equation, we get $.75W + .33$ on the left side and $.70W + .70$ on the right side by multiplying both sides by $W + 1$. By transposing terms, we get $.75W - .70W$ on the left side and $.70 - .33$ on the right side. That further simplifies to $.05W$ equals .37, so that *W* equals .37 divided by .05, which is a convergence weight of 7.4.

If one now inserts a weight of 7.4 for fair procedure and a weight of 1.00

for crime reduction, then exactly 70% of the resources will be allocated to the courts and 30% to trials, give or take a slight rounding error since 1/3 is not exactly .33. The computer shows a convergence weight of 8.0 because it normally rounds off to the nearest whole number. One can, however, specify smaller increments than whole numbers such as increments of .10, rather than 1.00. The computer will then show a convergence weight of 7.4. The Lotus spreadsheet version of P/G% which is now being developed uses the above equation to arrive directly at the convergence weight, rather than using a reiterative guessing process.

Convergence Scores

To obtain a better understanding of convergence analysis, it is helpful to be aware of the equation for calculating convergence scores. The equation is as follows:

$$[WR/R + \Sigma RO) + \Sigma W\%O] / \Sigma W = [(\Sigma W\%O + W / \Sigma W] \pm .05.$$

The left side of the equation is the formula for the actual percentage allocated to the alternative in question. The right side of the equation is the maximum percentage allocated to the alternative plus or minus five percentage points if the relation score were infinity or close to it. The left side has two parts. The numerator is equal to the sum of the allocation percentages for all criteria. The key variable is R, which is the raw score of the relation under consideration. The object is to determine how far up R has to go to generate an allocation percentage within five percentage points of the maximum allocation percentage.

Reading the left side of the equation from left to right, using words rather than symbols, we have, "The actual allocation to an alternative is equal to the raw score of the cell in question divided by the column total and multiplied by the weight of the column, plus the sum of the other part/whole percentages divided by the sum of the weights." Reading the right side of the equation, we have, "The maximum allocation is equal to the sum of the other weighted part/whole percentages, plus the weight of the criterion of the raw score under consideration, divided by the sum of the weights." We add or subtract .05 to or from that figure. The symbols and parts of this convergence score equation are thus similar to those of the convergence weight equation, except here the emphasis is on solving for R, rather than W. The symbol R stands for relation score, and the symbol W stands for weight.

This equation is much easier to follow if actual numbers are used, such as those given in Table 3-3. For example, suppose one wants to know by the above equation the convergence score of the courts on fair procedure. One can determine that value by inserting numbers in place of the symbols in the above equation. Doing so would generate the following equation with R as the one unknown:

$$[2R/(R + 1) + .33] / 3 = (.33 + 2.00) / 3 \pm .05.$$

Simplifying the equation above means dividing by 3 as indicated in the equation and thus obtaining $[2R/(3R + 3) + .11] = .78 - .05$. That equation further simplifies to $2R/(3R + 3) = .73 - .11$, which then becomes $2R/(3R + 3) = .62$. That equation is equal to $2R = .62(3R + 3)$, which in turn equals $2R = 1.86R + 1.86$, and $2R - 1.86R = 1.86$, or $.14R = 1.86$. That means $R = 1.86/.14$, or 13.00.

We can test whether 13 is the convergence value of the cell that shows the relation score between courts and fair procedure. To do so, we insert a 13 in place of the 3 in the data matrix and observe the results. The results are 73% to the courts, which is exactly five percentage points less than the 78% maximum. We could have determined the convergence value of that cell plus or minus 10 percentage points through the same equation, but using .10 rather than .05. The new answer is then 1.71/.29, or 5.90. This tells us that there is no use arguing whether the courts are more than six times as effective as the police on fair procedure or separating the innocent from the guilty. The reason is that any figure higher than 5.90 times as effective is likely to result in about the same high bottom-line allocation to the alternative in question, assuming one is willing to tolerate as much as a 10% deviation from the maximum allocation.

DISTINGUISHING ALLOCATING FROM CHOOSING

The most common type of decision-making other than allocation decisions occurs in optimum choice decisions, where one processes a set of alternatives, criteria, and relations in order to pick the best alternative or combination of alternatives. Allocating, on the other hand, involves a set of persons, places, activities, or other objects to which resources are being distributed in light of various criteria and the relations between the objects and criteria.

The bottom line in a choosing problem takes the form of "Choose alternative 16" (where only one alternative can be chosen) or "Choose alternatives 16, 4, and 9" (where more than one alternative can be chosen). The bottom line in allocating takes the form of "Give 40% of the scarce resources to category 1, 25% to category 2, and 35% to category 3." In a choosing problem, each alternative must be completely adopted or completely rejected. In an allocating problem, each category can receive anywhere from 0% to 100% of the scarce resources being allocated, and the sum of the percentages adds up to 100%.

Those definitions of choosing and allocating lead to six important distinctions between the two kinds of decision-making. Those distinctions relate to (1) budget categories for allocating versus alternatives for choosing; (2) allocation percentages versus ranking percentages; (3) the need for an absolute zero point on the scales of each goal only when allocating; (4) the irrelevance of the concept of dominance in allocating; (5) the need for special handling of negative goals in allocating; and (6) the irrelevance of the concept of breakeven values as contrasted to the concept of convergence value.

Budget Categories versus Alternatives

The first distinction is that the alternatives in allocating are not really alternatives, but budget categories. For example, if we are allocating $1,000 to two budget categories like police and courts, then we would have 1,001 alternative ways of allocating the $1,000 only involving integer amounts. We could allocate $1,000 to the police and $0 to the courts. Another alternative is $999 to the police and $1 to the courts, and so on down to $0 to the police and $1,000 to the courts. If we had $1 million to allocate, we would have 1,000,001 alternatives. If we have three budget categories, the number of alternatives becomes quite huge. With more budget categories and more dollars to allocate, the number of alternatives becomes astronomical. A large quantity of alternatives is quite time-consuming to analyze even with computers, and distinctions concerning how each alternative scores on the criteria become meaningless. We therefore work with budget categories instead of alternatives when making allocating decisions.

Allocation Percentages versus Yes–No Answers

Allocating also differs from choosing with regard to what one does with the bottom-line percentages. In a choosing situation, the bottom-line percentages are used mainly to rank-order the alternatives in order to pick the best one or the best five or *N* alternatives. The percentages could also be divided by cost figures to yield a form of benefit/cost ratios. They in turn could be used to indicate the order in which the alternatives should be chosen until one's budget runs out. In allocating, the bottom-line percentages need to be divided by the sum of the weights in order to add up to 100%, since we cannot allocate more than 100% of what we have. We then multiply those allocation percentages against the grand total of dollars that we have available in order to determine how much goes to each budget category.

Absolute Zero Point versus Relative Scoring

A third important distinction between choosing and allocating relates to the meaning of the scales on which the relations are measured between the alternatives or budget categories and the criteria. For example, a common scale is a 1–5 scale when no better measurement is available. The 5 means highly conducive to the criterion; 4 means mildly conducive; 3 means neither conducive nor adverse; 2 means mildly adverse; and 1 means highly adverse. That scale needs no absolute zero point in a choosing problem, regardless of whether one works with raw scores in the absence of multidimensionality, or with part/whole percentages where multidimensionality is present. That is so because the important thing in a choosing problem is getting the alternatives in the proper order, or at least determining which alternative is in first place. It is generally not so important to determine how far each alternative is above each other alternative, or above or below an absolute zero on one or more criteria. In allocating on the other hand, if one budget category receives a 5 on a 1–5 scale, and another budget category receives a 1, then the first category will receive 5/6 or 83% of the budget, and the other category will receive 1/6 or 17% of the budget. That may not make sense if a 1 on the 1-5 scale means that additional money given to the second category will result in a worsening on the criterion. If the part/whole percentages were elasticity coefficients, we would not give more than the minimum required to a budget category that has a negative coefficient with a positive goal. Likewise, relation scores below an absolute zero should therefore be converted into zeros.

Resources to Dominated Alternatives

A fourth important distinction relates to the concept of dominance and diminishing returns. In a choosing problem, if one alternative dominates the other alternatives on all the criteria, then that one alternative is obviously the best alternative regardless of multidimensionality and diminishing marginal returns. For example, if the police were to receive a higher score than the courts on both crime reduction and fair procedure, then the police category would clearly be the better category in a choice between the categories. That would be so if the police were to receive a score of 2 on crime reduction and a 3 on fair procedure, and the courts were to receive scores of 1 and 1. Even though the police receive a higher score on both criteria, we do not give the police the complete $500 allocation available. If we did so, we would then be allocating dollars to the police when diminishing returns would provide a very low marginal rate of return. At some point, we are better off switching some dollars to the courts. If the police category dominates, it would be better to give all $500 to the police than all $500 to the courts. However, we would still be better off giving about 5/7 or 71% of the $500 to the police and 2/7 or 29% to the courts. The first $100 given to the police may be more productive than the first $100 given to the courts, but the last $100 between $400 and $500 given to the police may be less productive than the first $100 given to the courts. One can show that if those crime reduction and fair procedure scores can be treated as proxies for elasticity coefficients, then one should allocate the budget to the categories in proportion to those scores, and not give all the budget to the category with the best combined raw scores, even if it is best on all the criteria.

Handling Negative Goals

Allocating also differs from choosing with regard to the handling of negative goals. Those are goals in which it is desirable to have a low score, as in golfing. As a general matter, negative goals are to be avoided in either allocating or choosing since it is easier to work with positive numbers than with negative numbers, both conceptually and arithmetically. Thus, in using 1-5 scales, it is preferable to have 5 mean highly desirable, 4 mildly desirable, 3 neutral, 2 mildly undesirable, and 1 highly undesirable, or variations in that general direction, even if the criterion is a cost. Sometimes, however, a negative goal cannot be avoided, such as delay measured in time units, crime measured in quantity of crimes, or cost measured in dollars. If multidimensionality is present, the weighted part/whole percentages for the negative goals may be subtracted from those for the positive goals. That causes no problems in a choosing situation, since one chooses the alternative that has the highest aggregate score regardless of the sign when one has to make a choice. Thus an alternative with a −40 score is better than an alternative with a −60 score. In allocating, however, one cannot meaningfully give one alternative −40% of the scarce resources and another alternative −60%. Both should possibly get nothing, since those negative percentages may imply that giving those alternatives anything more than the required minimum will do more harm than good.

If, however, one must allocate to those two categories, it would be logical to give 60% to the first alternative and 40% to the second. In doing so, one is in effect saying that alternative 1 received a 40 on a negative goal (like favoring the prosecution) and alternative 2 received a 60. If the goal were conceptually and semantically reversed (to be like favoring the defense), then alternative 1 would logically receive a 60 and alternative 2 a 40. Those new raw scores translate into 60% and 40% allocations. Making those semantic reversals properly depends on the specific subject matter, but they tend to be more of a problem in allocation situations than in choosing situations. A general rule to follow when dealing with negative goals is (1) to calculate the reciprocals of the raw scores; (2) to determine the part/whole percentages for those reciprocals, and (3) to allocate in proportion to those part/whole percentages. Thus, in the example, the 40 would be converted to 1/40 and the 60 to 1/60. The sum of those two fractions is 3/120 plus 2/120, or 5/120. Expressing those fractions or reciprocals as part/whole percentages yields 60% and 40%. One might ask why not just take the complements. The answer is that taking the complements will not work with more than two budget categories because the sum of the complements will add up to more than 100%, and the ratios will not be preserved.

Convergence versus Breakeven Values

When choosing among alternatives, alternative 3 may be the winner or alternatives 6 and 7. A key sensitivity analysis question might then be what changes need to occur in the weights or relation scores in order to bring alternative 5 up to the same total score as 3, 6, and 7. Those new values are referred to as breakeven, tie-causing, or threshold values. This is not such a meaningful concept in allocation analysis. The reason is that no budget category is considered the winner in the way that an alternative wins in a choosing problem. In an allocation problem, all the alternatives are likely to win by receiving some of the resources, as long as they have a positive total relation with the criteria. More meaningful in an allocation problem is the concept of convergence value. As previously mentioned, it refers to the value of a weight or a relation score which generates allocation percentages that are exactly 5 or 10 percentage points from the maximum allocation percentage possible.

WORKING WITH NEGATIVE GOALS OR NEGATIVE SCORES

In the literature on policy/goal percentaging, a classic example is allocating criminal cases to trials and plea bargains. Trials average 120 days from arrest to disposition, and pleas average 30 days. Trials average a respect score of 6 on a 0–10 scale and pleas average a respect score of 2. Thus trials do better on respect but pleas do better on delay.

Delay is measured in days, and respect is measured on a 0–10 scale. The way the multidimensionality problem is handled is to convert the scores on both goal variables into part/whole percentages. Thus the 120 days and the 30 days become 80% and 20%. Likewise, the respect scores of 6 and 2 become 75% and 25%. We then multiply the 80% and the 20% by −1, since delay is a negative goal, like a cost. Likewise, we multiply the 75% and the 25% by 2, since respect is considered twice as important as delay.

That gives us scores of −80% and 150% for trials on the two criteria. Those scores add to 70%. We also have scores of −20% and +50% for pleas on the two criteria. Those scores add to 30%. The number 70% is obviously greater than the number 30%. We could therefore declare trials to be the better alternative. Doing so would be correct if this were simply a problem of choosing the better alternative.

Negative Goals

Doing so, however, is not correct is this is considered a problem of how to allocate 100% of the criminal cases between these two methods of resolving cases. The incorrectness can be seen more clearly if we deal with just one goal at a time. If, for example, the only goal were to pick the alternative that does best on delay, then pleas is clearly the winner. Suppose, though, that the goal is to allocate 100% of the cases between trials and pleas in light of how those alternatives do on delay. It is then meaningful to convert the 120 days and the 30 days into percentages. Doing so initially generates 80% and 20%. We would not, however, want to allocate 80% of the cases to trials, since trials receives a higher score on delay and delay is considered an undesirable occurrence. The situation is not helped by multiplying by −1 since we cannot allocate a −80% to trials and a −20% to pleas.

What can and should we do in allocating to trials and pleas in light of how they do on the negative goal of delay? The idea of multiplying by −1 to deal with negative goals is fine in a choosing problem. A score of −20% is higher than a score of −80%. The most logical thing to do in an allocation problem is to work with the complements of 80% and 20%. Thus we should allocate 20% to trials (or 100% − 80%) and 80% to pleas (or 100% − 20%).

Taking the simple complements may work with two alternatives, but not with three or more alternatives. Suppose we add the alternative of diversion out of the system as a third method of case disposition. It averages 20 days. The three delay figures of 120, 30, and 20 days can be converted into part/whole percentages of 70%, 18%, and 12%. If we obtain the complements of those three numbers, then we are talking about percentages of 30%, 82%, and 88%. Those complements, however, cannot be used as allocation percentages because they add up to 200%.

What we need to do when working with a negative goal is to determine the reciprocal of each raw score on the goal and work with those reciprocals (rather than with the original raw scores) in arriving at the part/whole percentages. Thus, in Table 3-5B, the 120 days for the average trial is converted to 1/120, and the 30 days for the average plea bargain is converted to 1/30. Those fractions can be expressed as decimals, but they may be easier to work with as fractions because decimals in this context may require many places to avoid rounding errors. After determining the reciprocals, we add them together to obtain the total or whole for the column or goal. In this instance, the total is 1/120 plus 1/30, which is 5/120 since 1/30 equals 4/120. Table 3-6A shows that 1/120 is 20% of 5/120, and 4/120 is 80% of 5/120.

Thus, the general rule for dealing with negative goals in an allocation problem is to:

1. Convert the raw scores on a negative goal into their reciprocals, expressed as either fractions or decimals.
2. Add the reciprocals on the goal to obtain the total.
3. Divide each reciprocal by the total to obtain the part/whole percentage for each raw score.
4. Work with those part/whole percentages in determining the overall allocation for each alternative or budget category.

Table 3-5
Allocating Rather than Choosing with Negative Goals and Negative Scores: The Raw and Transformed Data

A. THE RAW DATA

	Delay (Days)	Respect (0-10 Scale)
Trials	120	6
Pleas	30	2
	150	8

B. THE TRANSFORMED RAW DATA

	Speed (1/Days)	Respect (-5 to +5)
Trials	1/120 or .00833	+1
Pleas	1/30 or .03333	-3
	5/120 or .04166	-2

NOTES:

1. The raw data are hypothetical, but realistic. The object is to decide on the optimum allocation of cases to trials versus pleas in light of the facts that
   (1) "Trials" receives a score of 120 days on delay and "pleas" 30 days.
   (2) "Trials" receives a score of 6 on respect and "pleas" a score of 2.

2. Transferring the raw data involves
   (1) Calculating the reciprocals for the raw scores of the negative goal of delay.
   (2) Recalculating the raw scores on respect by using a scale which shows absolute zero. If N equals absolute zero, then subtract N from each of the original raw scores. For example, on a 0-10 scale, the number 5 (or below) might be absolute zero.

The reason this method of dealing with negative goals makes sense is that it is the only method which satisfies all the following criteria:

1. The part/whole percentages on a negative goal should always add up to 100% (just as on a positive goal), since one cannot allocate more than 100% of what is available.
2. All the part/whole percentages on a negative goal should be positive (just as on a positive goal), since one cannot allocate less than 0% to a budget category.

Table 3-6
Allocating Rather than Choosing with Negative Goals and Negative Scores: The Unweighted and Weighted Part/Whole Percentages

A. THE PART/WHOLE PERCENTAGES

	Speed P/W%	Respect P/W%	Aggregate P/W%	Allocation%
Trials	20%	100%	120%	60%
Pleas	80%	0%	80%	40%
	100%	100%	200%	100%

B. THE WEIGHTED P/W%'S

	Speed w = 1	Respect w = 2	Aggregate P/W%	Allocation%
Trials	20%	200%	220%	73%
Pleas	80%	0%	80%	27%
			300%	100%

NOTES:

1. Calculating the correct part/whole percentages involves
   (1) Calculating the part/whole percentages on the inverted negative goal.
   (2) Giving zero percent to any alternative that has a negative raw score and then calculating the part/whole percentages for the other alternatives.

2. Calculating the allocation percentages involves
   (1) Multiplying the part/whole percentages in each column by the relative weight of the goal to which the column pertains.
   (2) Summing the weighted part/whole percentages across each alternative.
   (3) Dividing those aggregate percentages by the sum of the weights. The results are the allocation percentages for each alternative or budget category.

3. The proper rank order on a negative goal (just as on a positive goal) should involve (a) the highest part/whole percentage going to the best budget category; (b) the lowest part/whole percentage going to the worst budget category; and (c) an appropriate rank order for the middle budget categories.
4. The same ratios should exist among the part/whole percentages as existed among the raw scores. Thus, if one budget category is four or *X* times as bad as a second

budget category (such as the relations between trials and pleas on delay), then the second budget category ought to have a part/whole percentage that is four or X times as big as the part/whole percentage from the first budget category.

5. The method for dealing with negative goals should transform raw scores that are tied into part/whole percentages that are tied. Thus, if two raw scores are tied, their reciprocals will also be tied.
6. The method should provide that if a raw score is zero, then its part/whole percentage will also be zero.

Negative Scores

We should now look at what the allocation results would be if respect were the only criterion. Trials receives a score of 6 on respect, and pleas receives a score of 2. The part/whole percentages are thus 6/8 or 75% for trials and 2/8 or 25% for pleas. Once again, that is fine if we are just trying to decide which alternative is better: 75% is higher than 25%. If, however, we are allocating scarce resources to two alternatives, and one alternative receives a score as low as a 2 on a 0–10 scale, we should ask whether that alternative should be allocated anything.

If the 0–10 scale were a −5 to 0 to +5, pleas would receive a score of −2 and trials would receive a score of +1, because we have shifted the scale by five notches and a +2 thus becomes a −3, and a +6 becomes a +1. If the −2 is considered a proxy for an elasticity coefficient in the equation $Y = (X_1)^{+1}(X_2)^{-2}$, then we would want to give all our scarce resources to X_1 and none to X_2, assuming we want to maximize Y, which we do when Y is respect. A negative elasticity coefficient means that every additional unit given to X_2 causes respect to go down rather than up. Therefore, we must ask whether a +2 on a 0–10 scale is the equivalent of a negative score. If it is (as it does seem to be in this context), then we should give 100% of the cases to trials and 0% to pleas when we are allocating only in accordance with the respect criterion.

Putting the Two Together

If trials should get 20% of the cases on the basis of the delay criterion and 100% on the basis of the respect criterion, its aggregate score or combined part/whole percentage is 120%. If pleas should get 80% on the basis of delay and 0% on the basis of respect, its aggregate score is 80%. Those two aggregate scores add to 200%. They need to be divided by 2 to be converted into allocation percentages that add up to 100%. The bottom line is thus 60% to trials and 40% to pleas.

If, however, respect is twice as important as delay reduction, then the 100% and the 0% on respect should be doubled, giving 200% and 0%. That means the weighted aggregate score for trials becomes 220%, and the score for pleas becomes 80%. Dividing those aggregate scores by the sum of the weights, which is 3, gives a new bottom line of 73% and 27%.

One might note that those figures are close to the 70% and 30% arrived at when we use the subtraction method rather than the complements method to consider delay and when we give trials and pleas part/whole percentages of 75% and 25% on respect. That outcome is purely coincidental, since properly considering negative goals and negative scores in allocation analysis as contrasted to a choosing situation should produce a different, but more correct, set of allocations.

How P/G% Handles Negative Goals and Scores in Allocating

One might ask how the current version of the P/G% program handles negative goals in allocation situations. The best approach is probably through the following steps:

1. Insert the raw scores into the P/G% data matrix regardless of whether the goals are positive goals or negative goals.
2. For the negative goals, determine the reciprocals with a hand calculator by hitting the reciprocal button when the display shows the raw score. Type those reciprocals into the data matrix in place of the original raw scores. Do so to as many places as are shown on the calculator. The computer display will round each reciprocal to a number with two decimal places even though it retains the full number in its memory. The P/G% program can then work with those reciprocals as if they were the raw scores. Those negative goals, however, should be given positive weights because, in effect, working with the reciprocals converts delay into speed, or whatever term one wants to use for the opposite of delay. The word *speed* can be substituted for *delay* in listing the criteria to provide further clarification.
3. In a future version of P/G% for allocating situations, one will be able to indicate which goals are negative goals. The computer will then automatically work with the reciprocals of the raw scores and with positive weights for the goals, without one's having to use a calculator or to reenter any data.

Likewise one might ask how the current version of the P/G% program handles negative scores in an allocation situation. The best way is probably through the following steps:

1. Give a zero score to any alternative that has the equivalent of a negative score on a positive goal, so that the alternative would be allocated nothing if that goal were the only criteria.
2. The remaining alternatives should be given new raw scores in light of the transformed scale. For example, suppose the working scale is 1–5 but the true scale is −1 to 0 to +2. Suppose further that there are two nonzero alternatives with working scores of 4 and 5. Each of those scores should be converted into +1 and +2, so that 3 is subtracted from each original score because 3 is really zero.

3. Then proceed to work with the newly converted raw scores. Thus, in the example, one alternative would receive 1/3 or 33% of the scarce resources, and the other alternative would receive 2/3 or 67%, rather than 4/9 and 5/9.
4. Negative goals and positive goals with negative scores can be given multiplier weights to indicate negative importance in an allocating situation the same as in a choosing situation.
5. A further version of P/G% could automatically handle negative scores in allocating situations. The user would be required to inform the computer of what number on the working scale corresponds to a zero on the true scale, which includes negative scores. By *true scale* is meant one that provides for an absolute zero, as contrasted to a relative scale, in which all the scores have proper rank order or interval relations but do not indicate where the dividing point is between positive and negative scores.

ALTERNATIVE APPROACHES TO HANDLING NEGATIVE GOALS

The previous sections of this chapter indicated that the best way to handle negative goals is by working with the reciprocals of the raw scores so as to achieve the relevant criteria mentioned. The purpose of this section is to show that all the other suggested alternatives fail to achieve those criteria, or else they produce results identical to working with the reciprocals.

Table 3-7 summarizes the suggested methods for inverting negative goals. The example used involves three budget categories, since methods that make sense with two budget categories may fail to do so with three budget categories. This is true of working with complements of the part/whole percentages, as previously mentioned. The example uses only one allocation criterion (delay reduction), since a second criterion might obliterate the nonsense that is obvious with one criterion.

Eleven Unsatisfactory Approaches

Column 1 gives the *raw scores* on the delay negative goal for the three allocation categories of trials, pleas, and diversion as ways of disposing of criminal cases. The raw scores cannot be used as allocation percentages mainly because they are not percentages. Column 2 converts those raw scores to *part/whole percentages*. The part/whole percentages cannot be used as allocation percentages because the worst category would get the highest allocation.

Column 3 *multiples by −1* the part/whole percentages. The effect is to give trials the lowest transformed score and diversion the highest. Those transformed scores would be meaningful if we were interested just in rank-ordering the alternatives of diversion, pleas, and trials. They are, however, meaningless as allocation percentages since one cannot allocate −70% or any negative percentage to a budget category.

Column 4 works with the *complements* of the part/whole percentages.

Table 3-7
Methods for Inverting Negative Goals in Policy Evaluation

Criteria / Alternative	(1) Raw Scores for Delay	(2) P/W%	(3) -P/W%	(4) 1-P/W%	(5) 1-P/W% / N-1	(6) 2/N-P/W%	(7) Flipped P/W%
A. Trials	120 days	70%	-70%	30%	15%	-3%	12%
B. Pleas	30	18%	-18%	82%	41%	49%	18%
C. Diversion	20	12%	-12%	88%	44%	55%	70%
Totals	170	100%	-100%	200%	100%	100%	100%

Criteria / Alternative	(8) Highest Raw Score	(9) 1-5 Scales Defined Numbers	(10) 1-5 Scale Interpolation	(11) Rankings	(12) Reciprocal Raw Scores
A. Trials	0 = 0%	1 = 10%	1.0 = 10%	1 = 17%	.0083 = 9%
B. Pleas	90 = 47%	4 = 40%	4.6 = 43%	2 = 33%	.0333 = 36%
C. Diversion	10 = 53%	5 = 50%	5.0 = 47%	3 = 50%	.0500 = 55%
Totals	190 = 100%	10 = 100%	10.6 = 100%	6 = 100%	.0916 = 100%

NOTES:

1. Some equivalent methods are
   (1) Reciprocal P/W% or 1/P/W% is the equivalent of 1/RS, highest/RS, and whole/part.
   (2) Flipped P/W% is the same as flipped RS.

2, Working with the reciprocals for the raw scores is the only inverting method that satisfies all the criteria of providing (1) positive percentages that add to 100%, (2) the proper rank order so that the best raw score gets the highest part/whole percentage, (3) the same ratios among the part/whole percentages as existed among the raw scores, and (4) a meaningful way of dealing with ties and zero scores.

The sum of the complements, however, adds up to more than 100%, or 1.00 expressed as a decimal number. One cannot allocate more than 100%. One can show that the sum of the complements always adds to $N - 1$. Thus, if there are three alternatives, the sum is 2. If there are N alternatives, the sum is $N - 1$.

This logically leads to column 5, which involves *dividing each complement* by $N - 1$ in order to bring the sum down to 1.00, or 100%. The result, however, is to obliterate the differences between the alternatives or the budget categories. The original part/whole percentages indicated that raw score A and percentage A are six times as large or as bad as raw score C and percentage C in columns 1 and 2. In column 5, however, that difference has been reduced to three times as large. One can prove that as the number of categories goes up, the differences between the complements divided by $N - 1$ goes down to nothing. Thus, with 20 alternatives, the complements divided by $N - 1$ are about 5% for every alternative regardless of the original raw scores or percentages. That is about as bad a method as one could possibly have with regard to preserving the original ratios.

As an alternative to dividing the complements by $N - 1$ to bring the sum down to 1, one might consider *subtracting from each complement*. The something to be subtracted is X in the equation $(N - 1) - X = 1$. The $N - 1$ on the left is the sum that is too large. The 1 on the right is the desired sum. The X in the middle is the difference. If we solve for X, we obtain $(N - 2)/N$. We are thus saying that if we subtract $(N - 2)/N$ from each complement or $1 - P/W\%$, the sum of the adjusted complements will be 1.00. The expression $(1 - P/W\%) - (N - 2)/N$ algebraically simplifies to $2/N - P/W\%$, which is shown at the top of column 6. That approach does succeed in forcing the sum of the adjusted complements to add to 1.00. The price of doing so, however, is not only to distort the original ratios, but also often to cause negative percentages. The method of column 6 thus has the disadvantages of both columns 5 and 3, although not of column 4.

Another approach to inverting the raw scores on negative goals might be simply to *physically flip* them over. That means considering alternative C as taking 120 days and alternative A as taking 20 days. One obtains the same result by flipping the part/whole percentages of column 2, as is shown in column 7. At first glance, that method looks fine. The percentages are just as positive and add to 100% in column 7, as they do in column 2. Likewise, the new rank order makes sense, and the 6-to-1 ratio has been preserved between alternatives A and C. The method, however, is incapable of preserving the ratios between any of the alternatives other than the ones at the extremes. Thus, the ratio between A and B was originally 4 to 1, but now it is 1½ to 1. The ratio between B and C was originally 1½ to 1, but now it is 4 to 1, give or take a little for the rounding involved in calculating percentages. The distortion is magnified if there are ties. Suppose, for example, both pleas and trials involve 120 days. Then, after the flipping, pleas and trials would have very different percentages, but pleas and diversion would have the same percentages. The flipping method thus also causes alternatives with very different raw scores to wind up with the same percentages.

As another approach, one might suggest *subtracting each raw score from a high number,* analogous to subtracting each part/whole percentage from 100%. The logical high number would be the highest raw score, as is shown in column 8. The result is a sum equal to 100%, no negative percentages, and the proper rank order. However, the ratios are meaningless. This approach also adds a new defect: if any of a raw score happens to be zero, no transformed raw score can be meaningfully calculated since any number divided by zero gives infinity. Thus, any alternative that has a raw score of zero would always be allocated all of the resources or would have to divide them equally with other alternatives that also have zero raw scores, regardless of the other raw scores.

Subtracting each raw score from the highest raw score does preserve the distances which existed in the original raw scores. For example, there is a 90-day distance between the 120 days of alternative A and the 30 days of alternative B. There is likewise a 90-day distance between the 0 of alternative A and the 90 of alternative B in the transformed scores, although desirably in the opposite direction. Preserving ratios, however, is the relevant matter in an allocation problem, not preserving distances. If one alternative is four times as bad as another alternative, it should get only 1/4 as much of the resources, as with trials and pleas. Multiplying by −1 preserves both the distances and the ratios when one is inverting but provides unacceptable negative allocation percentages.

A *1-5 scale* is an approach that often works well for scoring alternatives on a subjective goal where numerical information is not available. One type of 1–5 scale defines each number from 1 to 5 in terms of words appropriate to the subject matter with or without equal intervals. In this context, the words might be 1 = more than 100 days; 2 = 80 to 99 days; 3 = 60 to 79 days; 4 = 40 to 59 days; and 5 = less than 40 days. The raw scores thus translate into 1, 4, and 5, as is shown in column 9. Such a method obviously distorts the ratios and therefore loses valuable information. It also adds the new defect of being highly subjective in the words or criteria chosen to be associated with each of the five scores, whereas all the other methods at least have objectivity in their application.

To provide objectivity to 1–5 scales, one can use the method of *interpolation*, which involves arbitrarily, although objectively, a score of 1.0 to the worst category and a score of 5.0 to the best category. The 1–5 scores of all the other budget categories are then determined though interpolation. Thus, if there are 100 days between 120 and 20, and 4 points between 1 and 5, the 90 days between 120 and 30 should be proportionate to the difference between 1 and the score that goes with 30 days. That translates into solving for

X in the equation $100/4 = 90/X$. The value of X is 3.6, and the score corresponding to 30 days is thus 1.0 plus 3.6, or 4.6. The method has objectivity, but it both distorts the ratios and adds the highly arbitrary element that the worst score always gets a 1 and the best score always gets a 5. This method has no way of distinguishing whether the worst and best raw scores are close together or far apart.

Another method that is sometimes used for scoring alternatives is to score them in terms of their *rank order,* as is shown in column 11. Rank ordering tends to lose information even more than a 1–5 scale does, since the top and bottom ranks may in reality be very close or very far, as in the 1–5 interpolation method. Worse, however, the scores of the intermediate alternatives are not proportionate to the original raw scores, as they are in the 1–5 interpolation method. Ranking does have the advantage over the 1–5 interpolation method of being simpler, since interpolating is a big chore when there are many alternative budget categories.

Some negative goals can be *phrased as positive goals.* For example, one can measure the negative goal of pollution on a 0–100 scale, and one can also measure the positive goal of cleanliness on a 0–100 scale. Instead of talking about percentage of illiteracy, unemployment, or infants that do not survive to one year, one can talk about percentage of literacy, employment, or infants who do survive to one year. Some negative goals, however, cannot be rephrased as positive goals. For example, the category crimes per capita does not have a positive counterpart like noncrimes per capita, or percentage in compliance with the law when there are opportunities not to comply. Likewise, a delay of 120 days cannot be reworded into a positive measure of speed. One could subtract 120 days from some number that represents an arbitrary maximum or optimum, but doing so yields the same distortion of the ratios as subtracting the raw score from the highest score in column 8.

All the methods shown in columns 1 through 11 have some major defect such as wrong rank order (1 and 2), negative percentages (3 and 6), not adding up to 100% (4), not being able to deal with zero scores (8), not being able to deal with ties (7), losing information (9, 10, and 11), being highly arbitrary (10), being complicated to calculate (10), and especially distorting the original ratios (4 through 11).

The Optimum Approach

In spite of those complications, column 12 shows the one method that does satisfy all the criteria. This method involves working with the reciprocals of the raw scores, as previously described. Doing so can be shown to be algebraically the equivalent of working with (1) the reciprocals of the part/whole percentages; (2) the highest score divided by each raw score; or (3) the total divided by each raw score, which is the whole/part percentage.

All four methods are algebraically equivalent since they produce the same bottom-line allocation percentages, which in this situation are 9%, 36%, and 55%.

A proof that working with the reciprocals makes good sense is to reason as follows:

1. What we want to do is solve for X in the equation $X + 4X + 6X = 1.00$, where X is the allocation percentage for the worst budget category, which in this situation is trials.
2. That equation also tells us that the allocation percentage for the best budget category should be six times whatever the worst category gets. The 6 equals the ratio between the worst raw score and the best raw score.
3. That equation also tells us that the coefficient for every middle category should be equal to the ratio of the raw score of each middle category to the worst raw score.
4. Solving for X in this equation yields .0909 or 9%.
5. Thus the worst category should receive only 9%. The middle category should receive four times 9%, or 36%. The best category should receive six times 9%, or 55%, give or take a little for rounding.
6. By reducing the above analysis and the method of working with reciprocals to algebraic symbols like A for 120, B for 30, and C for 20 days, one can prove algebraically that working with reciprocals gives exactly the same result as the above reasoned-equation approach.

None of the methods shown in Table 3-7 (including working with reciprocals) explicitly accounts for the possibility that a delay of 120 days is more than four times as bad as a delay of 30 days, or more than six times as bad as a delay of 20 days. Such a consideration requires making a transformation for nonlinearity on the raw scores separate from the transformations designed to consider the negative nature of the goal. Here we have increasing costs in the sense that 120 days of delay may cost 10 times the damage done by 20 days of delay. We thus want to convert the 120 and the 20 into two numbers, so that the first number will be 10 times as large as the second number, not just 6 times as large.

A simple way to make such a conversion is to raise each raw score to a power designed to reflect the degree of increasing returns. For example, if there were only two raw scores, we would want to know the value of X in the equation $120^x/20^x = 10$. Solving for X through the use of logarithms yields a value of 1.28. Substituting 1.28 for the exponent gives the numbers 460 and 60, which do have a 10 to 1 ratio, give or take a little for rounding. If there is a series of raw scores and a corresponding set of relative disutility scores, then it would be appropriate to develop a translation formula by fitting a power function to those data of the form $Y = aX^b$. In this equation, Y is the transformed score, X is the original raw score, b is the exponent, and a indicates the value of Y when X is 1. The numerical value of b

and a can be determined by inputting the logarithms of the X and Y scores into a hand calculator that can do regression analysis. Such an equation is especially helpful when we want to determine the disutility score that corresponds to a given raw score.

If working with the reciprocals makes so much sense in an allocation problem, then why do we multiply by −1 in a choosing problem? The answer is that in a choosing problem we are concerned with which alternative is in first place and by how much. For example, suppose that alternative A has $100 in benefits and $60 in costs for a net profit of $40, and suppose that alternative B has $120 in benefits and $70 in costs for a net profit of $50. Alternative B is then the better investment because it has a $10 higher net profit. The sensitivity analysis question is what changes it would take to make up that $10 gap. The changes include decreasing by $10 the $120 in benefits of B or the $60 in cost of A, or increasing by $10 the $100 in benefits of A or the $70 in costs of B. Here we logically multiply the costs by −1 and then add to determine the overall score on each alternative. Here we are concerned with the distance between those overall scores, not the ratio. It would make no sense to add the reciprocal of $60 to $100 and the reciprocal of $70 to $120.

In an allocating problem, on the other hand, we are concerned with percentages in the bottom line. For example, suppose we wanted to allocate $1,000 to the above two projects, recognizing that we do not want to give the whole $1,000 to the best project in view of diminishing returns. If the $40 profit and the $50 profit can be considered proxies for elasticity coefficients, then we give 4/9 to the first project and 5/9 to the second project. Even then, we would not work with reciprocals of the cost figures.

The only time we work with the reciprocals of a negative goal is in an allocation problem in which multidimensionality is present. This is not true of the above B–C problem, since both goals are measured in dollars. Multidimensionality, however, is present in the problem of allocating cases to trials versus pleas. There, one goal is respect measured on a 0–10 scale, which translates into a −5 to +5 scale. The other goal is the negative goal of delay measured in days. In those multidimensional circumstances, the raw scores are converted into part/whole percentages. It is then quite meaningful to work with the reciprocals of the delay raw scores before converting them into part/whole percentages, for all the reasons previously mentioned.[7]

SOME CONCLUSIONS

From this analysis, we can conclude that we can rationally and feasibly allocate to budget categories by answering the following series of questions:

1. What are the budget categories to which we want to allocate, and what are the goals that we are seeking to achieve?

2. On the first goal, which budget category has the lowest marginal rate of return for an extra dollar or monetary unit? Give it a score of 1 on the first goal.
3. On the first goal, how do the other budget categories compare with that lowest MRR budget category? Is the second budget category twice as effective in putting one monetary unit to use in achieving the goal or three times as effective. If three times as effective, give it a score of 3, and do likewise with the other budget categories.
4. Do likewise with the second goal and however many goals there are.
5. Looking across the goals rather than down the budget categories on a single goal, answer the question of which goal is the least important to whoever the decision-makers are. Give that goal a weight of 1.
6. How do the other goals compare with that base goal? If another goal is four times as important, give it a score of 4. An alternative approach would be to give all the goals a weight of 1, and then to have the computer program indicate for each goal what its convergence weight or critical weight is. Above that weight, little is to be gained, because of diminishing returns.
7. Convert the raw scores on the first goal into part/whole percentages. Allocate in proportion to those part/whole percentages, or simply use those part/whole percentages as allocation percentages. Do likewise with the second goal, and so on through all the goals.
8. Give each budget category a weighted average allocation by averaging across the separate allocations, taking the weights of the goals into consideration.

There are variations and other aspects of these basic procedures, such as variations to take into consideration (1) missing information; (2) minimums or maximums for the budget categories; (3) minimums or maximums for the goals; (4) conflicting constraints, such as minimums that add up to more than the total budget; and (5) situations where one is seeking to minimize costs while meeting a minimum satisfaction level, as contrasted to seeking to maximize benefits while meeting a maximum budget constraint. The overall conclusion might be that it is possible to allocate a budget or other scarce resources both rationally and feasibly. Normally, to achieve rationality, one has to sacrifice feasibility or simplicity, and vice versa. That does not have to be so. With the above procedures and their variations, one can develop and apply a system of rational and feasible budget allocation.

From the examples of (1) allocating anticrime dollars to cities, (2) allocating a personnel budget to police and courts, and (3) allocating cases to trials and pleas, one can conclude a budget can be allocated meaningfully by the following principles:

1. One should have a reasonably clear notion of the goals one is seeking to achieve and their relative importance.
2. One should know what the categories are to which the budget is to be allocated, regardless of whether those categories are places, activities, or other objects.

3. Indicating how each budget category scores on each goal. Sufficient and valid information can often be obtained by asking knowledgeable insiders to score the relations on 1–5 scales, 0–10 scales, or scales of relative degrees of relationship.
4. If different scoring systems are used for different goals, weighted part/whole percentaging may be used to deal with the multidimensionality. If the same scoring systems are used on different goals, working with weighted raw scores should be sufficient.
5. By adding the weighted scores across each budget category, one can obtain meaningful aggregate scores by which the budget can be proportionately allocated.
6. When negative goals and multidimensionality are present, one works with the reciprocals of the raw scores in calculating part/whole percentages.
7. When a measurement scale provides for an absolute zero point (either explicitly or in translation), one converts all truly negative scores into zero part/whole percentages.
8. If there are minimum amounts that must be allocated to some budget categories, one (1) allocates first in an optimizing way ignoring those minimums; (2) observes which categories would receive less than their minimums; (3) gives those categories the minimum amounts; and (4) reallocates the remainder of the resources to the other budget categories.

These general principles can be applied to a variety of public management problems that involve allocating resources to different places or activities. The principles can also be applied to allocating a personnel budget to different members of a government agency in light of how well they have scored on various criteria. Applying the principles is also likely to result in obtaining insights into other relevant applications with regard to allocating money, time, people, or other scarce resources to places, activities, or other objects in order to maximize societal benefits and to minimize societal costs.[8]

NOTES

1. For further detail on cross-lagged panel analysis, see D. Heise, "Causal Inference from Panel Data," in Edgar Borgatta and G. Bornstedt (eds.), *Sociological Methodology* (San Francisco: Jossey-Bass, 1970); and D. Pelz and F. M. Andrews, "Detecting Causal Priorities in Panel Study Data," 29 *American Sociological Review* 836–848 (1964). Those are relatively accurate methods for relating a social indicator like crime to a public policy like anticrime expenditures while attempting to control for reciprocal and spurious causation. The time-lagging is designed to get at reciprocal causation, since crime at time t cannot cause anticrime expenditures at time $t - 1$, although crime has a strong influence on anticrime expenditures at time $t + 1$. The auto correlation of Y_{t-1} on the right side of the equation is designed to get at spurious causation since it indirectly holds constant all factors that influence crime except anticrime expenditures. The logging is designed to get at the diminish-

ing-returns relation between anticrime expenditures and crime. Those methods, however, may not be accurate enough where the magnitudes of the regression coefficients are going to be used as the basis for allocating expenditures to places or activities in order to maximize a desired social indicator like literacy or to minimize an undesired social indicator like crime.

2. If we had only two cities, we would want to solve for $\$X_1$ and $\$X_2$ in a pair of equations that say $\$X_1 + \$X_2 = G$, and $b_1/\$X_1 = b_2/\$X_2$. The G is the grand total available to be allocated. The b_1 is the semilog regression coefficient of the first city, and the b_2 is the semilog regression coefficient of the second city. If $Y_1 = a_1 + b_1(\log \$X_1)$, then the slope of Y_1 relative to $\$X_1$ is $b_1/\$X_1$, and likewise with the expression on the right side of the second equation. The first equation says that we want to spend all of the grand total available on the two cities. The second equation says that we want the slopes of the two cities to be equal to each other at the optimum allocation points so that nothing can be gained by switching some dollars from one city to the other. The solution for $\$X_1$ in that pair of equations is $G \times b_1/(b_1 + b_2)$. The solution for $\$X_2$ is $G \times b_2/(b_2 + b_2)$. Likewise, the solution for any X is G times its semilog regression coefficient divided by the sum of the regression coefficients for all the cities that have negative regression coefficients. See footnote 5 and the accompanying text in Chapter 13 on "Allocation Logic" in S. Nagel, *Policy Evaluation: Making Optimum Decisions* (New York: Praeger, 1982), for further details.

3. For further details on allocating by marginal rates of return, see "Service Distribution" in Werner Hirsch, *The Economics of State and Local Government* (New York: McGraw-Hill, 1970); "Multiple Territories," in Philip Kotler, *Marketing Decision Making: A Model Building Approach* (New York: Holt, 1971); and "Finding an Optimum Geographical Allocation for Anti-Crime Dollars and Other Governmental Expenditures," in S. Nagel and M. Neef, *Legal Policy Analysis: Finding an Optimum Level or Mix* (Lexington, Mass.: Lexington-Heath, 1977).

4. For further details on allocating by part/whole percentages, see Ward Edwards and Robert Newman, *Multi-Attribute Evaluation* (Beverly Hills, Calif.: Sage, 1982); Thomas Saaty, *The Analytic Hierarchy Process: Planning, Priority Setting, and Resource Allocation* (New York: McGraw-Hill, 1980); and "Multiple Goals and Policies" in S. Nagel, *Public Policy: Goals, Means, and Methods* (New York: St. Martin's, 1984).

5. For further details on allocating federal money to cities, see George Hale and Marian Palley, *The Politics of Federal Grants* (Washington, D.C.: Congressional Quarterly Press, 1981); Deil Wright, *Federal Grants-in-Aid: Perspectives and Alternatives* (Washington, D.C.: American Enterprise Institute for Public Policy Research, 1968); George Break, *Intergovernmental Fiscal Relations in the United States* (Washington, D.C.: Brookings Institution, 1966); Michael Reagan and John Sanzone, *The New Federalism* (New York: Oxford University Press, 1981); Richard Nathan and Charles Adams, *Revenue Sharing: The Second Round* (Washington, D.C.: Brookings Institution, 1969); General Accounting Office, *Perspectives on Intergovernmental Policy and Fiscal Relations* (Washington, D.C.: Government Printing Office, 1979); and House Committee on Banking, Finance, and Urban Affairs, *Small Cities: How Can the Federal and State Governments Respond to Their Diverse Needs?* (Washington, D.C.: Government Printing Office, 1978).

6. For further details on allocating people to tasks, see S. Nagel and M. Mills,

"Systematic Allocation of Lawyers to Case Types," 15 *Capital University Law Review* 223-242 (1986); and Warren Erikson and Owen Hall, *Computer Models in Management* (Reading, Mass.: Addison-Wesley, 1986).

7. On dealing with multiple alternatives and allocating, see Philip Kotler, *Marketing Decision Making: A Model Building Approach* (New York: Holt, 1971); Claude McMillan, *Mathematical Programming: An Introduction to the Design and Application of Optimal Decision Machines* (New York: Wiley, 1970); James Schockley, *The Brief Calculus: With Applications in the Social Sciences* (New York: Holt, 1971); and S. Nagel, "Optimally Allocating Federal Money to Cities," 5 *Public Budgeting and Finance* 39-50 (1985).

8. For further detail relevant to comparing allocative decision-making with choosing a best alternative or combination, see S. Nagel, *Policy Evaluation: Making Optimum Decisions* (New York: Praeger, 1982), 47-80, 230-254. The author thanks Gordon Pitz of the Department of Psychology at Southern Illinois University for emphasizing that allocative decision-making may be substantially different from choosing among alternatives.

4

Advocating for and Influencing Decisions

The purpose of this analysis is to describe how microcomputers can aid in the appellate and trial advocacy work of public defenders and legal services lawyers.

Computer-aided advocacy is using a computer (especially a personal computer) to aid in determining what to advocate on appeal or in trial in order to increase the probability of victory for one's client. The idea of computer-aided advocacy (CAA) is a law variation on computer-aided manufacturing (CAM) and computer-aided design (CAD), which are becoming increasingly important in the American economy.

Computer-aided advocacy is a substantially higher level of computer usage than litigation support, a system of information retrieval for handling litigation matters that involve many separate items. CAA should also be distinguished from document-drafting software, which incorporates decisions about what to advocate into a well-typed brief by drawing on a brief bank of related arguments.

The most appropriate software for computer-aided advocacy is probably software that enables one to process a set of (1) goals that the decision-makers have for reaching a decision; (2) the alternative positions they may take regarding the overall issue or subissues in the case; and (3) the relations between each position and each goal, showing how conducive or adverse each position is to each goal. An example of such software is policy/goal percentaging (abbreviated P/G%). It is called that because it was originally developed to relate public policies to societal goals, and it uses percentaging to handle goals measured in different ways.

THE *RODRIGUEZ* CASE: AID FOR LOW-INCOME SCHOOLS

The Inputs in a Spreadsheet Brief

Table 4-1 provides an example of a case brief using the P/G% software. The case is *San Antonio v. Rodriguez,* 411 U.S. Supreme Court 1 (1973). This landmark case in the field of legal services dealt with the extent to which a state is constitutionally required to help equalize expenditures per student across school districts within the state. This type of brief can be prepared after a case has actually been decided so that plans can be made for

Table 4-1
Appellate Advocacy in *San Antonio v. Rodriguez*

A. THE ALTERNATIVES AND THE CRITERIA

Alternative	Previous Outcome	Criterion	Meas.Unit	Weight
1 NO EQUALITY REQD.	YES	1 EDUCATED POP.	1-3 SCALE	1.00
2 = $ PER STUDENT	NO	2 - DISCONTENT		1.00
3 MIN.$ PER STUDENT	NO	3 - DOWNGRADING		1.00
4 HIGH $ PER STUDENT	NO	4 ADMIN.EASE		1.00
5 OTHER	?	5 CONSIST.W/CASES		1.00
		6 - EXPENSE		1.00

B. THE SCORES OF THE ALTERNATIVES ON THE CRITERIA

	EDUCATED	-DISCONT.	-DOWNGR.	ADMIN.EA.	CONSIST.	EXPENSE
NO EQUALITY REQ	1.00	1.00	3.00	3.00	2.00	3.00
= $ PER STUDENT	2.00	2.00	1.00	1.00	2.00	2.00
MIN.$ PER STUD.	2.00	2.00	2.00	1.00	2.00	1.50
HIGH $ PER STUD.	3.00	3.00	2.00	1.00	1.00	1.00

C. THE TOTAL SCORES OF THE ALTERNATIVES

Alternative	Combined Raw Scores	Previous Outcome
1 NO EQUALITY REQD.	13.00	YES
2 = $ PER STUDENT	10.00	NO
3 MIN.$ PER STUDENT	10.50	NO
4 HIGH $ PER STUDENT	11.00	NO

D. WHAT IT WOULD TAKE TO BRING THE SECOND-PLACE ALTERNATIVE UP TO FIRST PLACE

	NO EQUALITY	MIN.$ PER STUD.	Weight
EDUCATED POP.	-1.50	4.50	3.500
- DISCONTENT	-1.50	4.50	3.500
- DOWNGRADING	0.50	4.50	-1.500
ADMIN.EASE	0.50	3.50	-0.250
CONSIST.W/CASES	-0.50	4.50	??????
- EXPENSE	0.50	4.00	-0.667

future advocacy strategy. Such a brief can also be prepared while the case is still in process so that better decisions can be made about what ideas to emphasize.

Table 4-1A of the brief shows that the Supreme Court was faced with (or could be faced with) the four basic alternatives of (1) no equality required; (2) equal expenditure per student; (3) a minimum expenditure per student, but otherwise allowing inequality; or (4) a requirement of equality at a high level. The first part of the brief also shows that the court answered yes to the first alternative (or could answer yes), but no to the others.

The right side of Table 4-1A shows that there are six relevant criteria, including (1) having an educated population; (2) decreasing discontent due to educational disparities; (3) avoiding the downgrading of affluent schools; (4) administrative ease; (5) consistency with prior cases; and (6) avoiding heavy taxpayer expense. All six goals seem quite reasonable for the Supreme Court to have, although not to give equal importance.

Table 4-1B of the brief shows how each alternative scores on each criterion with a simple 1–3 scale, where 3 = conducive to the goal, 2 = neither conducive nor adverse, and 1 = adverse to the goal. Table 4-1C of the brief shows the combined raw scores for each alternative based on 1–3 scoring. The alternative with the highest combined raw score is "no equality required," which is the alternative that the Supreme Court adopted.

Converting a Loser into a Winner

Table 4-1D of the brief is the threshold analysis. It shows what it would take to bring the second-place alternative up to first place. There is a gap of 2.50 points between first and second place on the combined raw scores. That gap would be eliminated if the "no equality" alternative were to drop 2.50 points on any of the six criteria. That would be too big a drop on any one criterion since these criteria cannot go below 1.00. The gap would also be eliminated if the second-place alternative of having a minimum expenditure per student were to increase by 2.50 points on any of the six criteria. That would be too big an increase on any one criterion since these criteria cannot go above 3.00. The gap could also be eliminated if the Supreme Court were to place substantially more weight on having an educated population or on decreasing discontent due to educational inequalities. Those are two areas which the advocates of a minimum-dollars position should emphasize. The gap would be eliminated if the other criteria were given negative weights, which is unlikely. Changing the weight would not help with regard to consistency with prior cases, since both alternatives score the same on that criterion.

In computer-aided advocacy, the most helpful computer output is information like that shown in Table 4-1D with regard to what it would take to bring a second-place or other alternative up to first place. The most useful part of that threshold analysis is generally how the relative weights of the criteria or goals would have to change for the second-place alternative to become a winner. This is so because the relative importance of the criteria is more subjective and more subject to change through convincing advocacy than the relations between the alternatives and the criteria.

We might note that high dollars per student came in second in the initial analysis shown in Table 4-1C. High dollars per student, however, does not do so well when compared with no equality required because high dollars per student does so poorly on avoiding extra expense. In other words, the third-place alternative does better on the threshold or sensitivity analysis than the second-place alternative. The third-place alternative has the economic feasibility which the second-place alternative lacks. It also has the political feasibility which may be lacking in the alternative of equal dollars per student. That alternative would probably mean bringing down the influential school districts which spend high dollars per student. For a third-place alternative to do better than a second-place alternative in capturing first place is like a third-place baseball team that is physically fit doing better in capturing first place (at the end of the season) than a second-place team which has a number of injured players.

What incremental benefits does this kind of briefing have over more traditional briefing? The benefits include:

1. Thinking more explicitly about the alternatives that were or are available to the court, rather than working with just what the court defined as the issue or the adopt–reject decision.
2. Thinking more explicitly about the goals that might be achieved by whatever decision is reached.
3. Recognizing that consistency with prior cases as a goal is generally not enough to explain court decisions, especially decisions on new issues.
4. Seeing more clearly from an appellate advocacy perspective the position that the court might be most likely to be encouraged to adopt.

THE *DANDRIDGE* CASE: AID FOR LARGE BUT POOR FAMILIES

Background on the *Dandridge* Case

In addition to losing the *Rodriguez* case, the Legal Services Program also lost the landmark *Dandridge* case, 397 U.S. 471 (1970). These cases together represented a turning point in the decisions of the Supreme Court concerning poverty law cases. The court had previously decided a number of important cases in favor of the Legal Services Program, such as (1) *King v. Smith,* 392 U.S. 309 (1968), in which it was held that merely being found with a man in the house was not enough to deprive a family of welfare benefits; (2) *Shapiro v. Thompson,* 394 U.S. 618 (1969), in which it was held that one could establish residency for welfare and related purposes without having to live in a place for an extended period of time, such as a year; and (3) *Goldberg v. Kelly,* 397 U.S. 254 (1970), in which it was held that welfare recipients were entitled to at least minimum due process in a termination case, including the right to have notice, present witnesses, cross-examine accusers, and have a judge who was not the complaining welfare worker.

The turnaround in the Supreme Court's decisions in the 1970s is often attributed to changes in the court personnel, especially Chief Justice Burger's replacing Chief Justice Warren. That explanation, however, may be questionable since in 1972 Chief Justice Burger wrote the opinion in the *Argersinger* case, 407 U.S. 25 (1972), in which it was held that indigent defendants were entitled to court-appointed counsel in any criminal case, no matter how minor, as long as there was a possibility of serving as much as one day in jail. An alternative explanation is that the Legal Services Program brought the cases first, in the 1960s, that were easy to win (like *King, Shapiro,* and *Goldberg*), as contrasted to *Rodriguez* and *Dandridge*. Another at least partial explanation might be that the Legal Services Program became overly confident and a bit sloppy by late 1970 and lost the *Rodriguez* and *Dandridge* cases partly through bad appellate advocacy.

The *Rodriguez* case has already been discussed with regard to how advocating the alternative of a minimum expenditure per student might have been a winning position before the Supreme Court, as contrasted to advocating that students in poor schools should be brought up to the level of the most well-funded students in the state. The *Dandridge* case involved a related failure to present an acceptable alternative and a resulting total loss for the position of the Legal Services Program.

Inputs in the *Dandridge* Case

In abbreviated form, Table 4-2 shows the three alternative positions that could have been argued before the Supreme Court. The Legal Services Program argued that if the family allowance for three children is $300 a month, then for four children it should be $400 a month, and so on, with $100 added for each successive child. The State of Maryland argued that there should be a maximum grant of approximately $300 per family, regardless of how many children there are, even though the maximum is reached with only three children. The Legal Services Program (LSP) justified its position by claiming that Maryland's argument represented a blatant denial of equal protection because the third child in the family would get $100 and the fourth child would get nothing. The State of Maryland, however, justified its position by claiming that the allowance for three children averages $100 apiece and for four children averages $75 apiece, so that the fourth

Table 4-2
Appellate Advocacy in *Dandridge v. Maryland*

A. THE ALTERNATIVE POSITIONS AND THE CRITERIA FOR EVALUATING THEM

Alternative	Previous Outcome	Criterion	Meas.Unit	Weight
1 MAXIMUM GRANT	APPROVED	1 -TAXPAYER BURDEN	1-5 SCALE	1.00
2 PROPORTION.GRANT	REJECTED	2 MIN.FOOD ETC.		1.00
3 DIM.RETURNS GRANT	-PRESENT	3 CONSISTENCY CASES		1.00
		4 ECONOMIES/SCALE		1.00
		5 -ADMIN.BURDEN		1.00

B. THE 1-5 SCORING OF THE ALTERNATIVES ON THE CRITERIA

	-TAXPAYER	MIN.FOOD	CONSIST.	ECON/SCALE	-ADMIN.
MAXIMUM GRANT	5.00	1.00	4.00	1.00	3.00
PROPORTION.GRANT	1.00	5.00	2.00	1.00	3.00
DIM.RETURNS GRANT	3.00	3.00	3.00	5.00	2.00

C. THE OVERALL SCORES OF THE ALTERNATIVES

Alternative	Combined Raw Scores	Previous Outcome
1 MAXIMUM GRANT	14.00	APPROVED
2 PROPORTION.GRANT	12.00	REJECTED
3 DIM.RETURNS GRANT	16.00	-PRESENT

D. BRINGING THE MAXIMUM GRANT POSITION UP TO THE LEVEL OF THE DIMINISHING RETURNS POSITION

	MAXIMUM GRANT	DIM.RETURN	Weight
-TAXPAYER BURDEN	7.00	1.00	2.000
MIN.FOOD ETC.	3.00	1.00	0.000
CONSISTENCY CASES	6.00	1.00	3.000
ECONOMIES/SCALE	3.00	3.00	0.500
-ADMIN.BURDEN	5.00	0.00	3.000

child gets $75, rather than nothing. The State of Maryland further claimed that children are cheaper by the dozen, and that it makes sense for the amount of family allowance to go down with each successive child.

The position that was never argued is that the increment should go down with each successive child, given economies of scale, but not down to zero. The LSP position was that the increment should not go down at all. The Maryland position was that it should, in effect, go down to nothing, since a family of four children gets nothing more than a family of three. A logical alternative position would be that if a family of three children gets $300, then a family of four children should get, not $400, but about $350. That alternative recognizes that if three children average $100 apiece in a three-child family, then four children should average less than $100 apiece in a four-child family. The figure of $350 averages to $87.50 apiece, which is between the $100 asked for by the LSP and the $75 asked for by the State of Maryland.

The second part of Table 4-2A shows some of the criteria that were explicitly or implicitly mentioned by the Supreme Court in deciding between the two alternatives of the proportionate grant system advocated by the LSP and the maximum grant position advocated by Maryland. The criteria are (1) minimizing the taxpayer burden; (2) providing at least a minimum amount of food, shelter, and clothing to dependent children; (3) preserving consistency with past cases; (4) recognizing economies of scale; and (5) minimizing the burden on public administrators.

Table 4-2B shows how each of the three alternatives score on each of the five criteria on a 1–5 scale. On such a scale, a 5 means highly conducive to the goal or criterion, a 4 means mildly conducive, a 3 means neither conducive nor adverse, a 2 means mildly adverse, and a 1 means highly adverse. On the matter of minimizing taxpayer burden, the maximum grant position is clearly the best, and the proportionate grant is the worst. On providing minimum food, shelter, and clothing to dependent children, the situation is reversed, with the proportionate grant the best and the maximum grant the worst.

On consistency with prior cases, the differences are not as great among the three alternatives, but the maximum grant position is probably more consistent than the proportionate grant. The Supreme Court tends to regard the equal protection clause as being satisfied by minimal constitutional positions, rather than requiring optimum positions. On the matter of economies of scale, diminishing returns does well, whereas the other two alternatives ignore diminishing returns. On the matter of minimizing the administrative burden, both the maximum grant and the proportionate grant score equally well, at about neutral. Figuring the diminishing-returns amount may require more research and analysis, although not necessarily, if one simply splits the difference between the maximum grant and proportionate grant positions, as was done above.

Results of the *Dandridge* Case

Table 4-2C shows the overall scores for each alternative added across the rows of Table 4-2B. Table 4-2C shows that when it comes to a contest between a maximum grant and a proportionate grant, the maximum grant is likely to be the winner, which it was in the *Dandridge* case. More interesting, however, is that the alternative of a diminishing-returns grant (which was not presented in the *Dandridge* case) gets more points than either of the two alternatives which were presented.

Not only is the diminishing-returns grant the winner in a three-way contest, but it is also a big winner over the maximum grant position which the Supreme Court approved in the two-way contest. The size of the win of the diminishing-returns grant is not measured just by the number of points it receives over the maximum grant position. It is also measured by what would be required to bring the maximum grant position up to the level of the diminishing-returns position, as is shown in Table 4-2D. That table shows that for the maximum grant position to be the overall winner, one would have to do such things as giving no weight whatsoever to providing minimum food to dependent children, or giving no weight to economies of scale. Table 4-2D also shows one could make the maximum grant position a winner by giving it unreasonably high scores on the five criteria, such as a score of 7 on minimizing the taxpayer burden, when it has already received a score of 5 on a 1–5 scale. One could also give unreasonably low scores to diminishing returns on the five criteria to make the maximum grant the winner; that is, one could take the position that diminishing returns is highly adverse to providing dependent children with minimum food. One could also make the maximum grant position the winner by giving unreasonably high weights to minimizing the taxpayer burden, relative to providing minimum food needs and economies of scale.

Thus this analysis tends to show that the Legal Services Program could have turned the *Dandridge* case from a total failure into a substantial success if they had more carefully thought out the advocacy alternatives available and how those alternatives would be likely to score on the criteria that the Supreme Court might consider. Losing the *Dandridge* case not only meant establishing a bad precedent in calculating benefit levels for all public aid programs but also tended to demoralize appellate advocacy at the LSP. It may thus have had an unreasonably adverse effect on the willingness to bring future cases before the Supreme Court on the possibly mistaken theory that the Court was not receptive to reason.

THE *McCLESKEY* CASE: RACIALLY DISCRIMINATORY CAPITAL PUNISHMENT

The Alternatives, Criteria, and Relations

Table 4-3 shows an appellate advocacy analysis for the 1987 Supreme Court case of *McCleskey v. Georgia,* 107 S.Ct. 1756 (1987). Table 4-3A shows the alternative positions in the case. The position approved by the Supreme Court was to allow capital punishment even though a racially discriminatory pattern might be shown. The position of the American Civil Liberties Union (ACLU), the National Association for the Advancement of Colored People (NAACP), and other groups opposed to capital punishment

Table 4-3
Appellate Advocacy in *McCleskey v. Georgia*

A. THE ALTERNATIVE POSITIONS AND THE CRITERIA FOR EVALUATING THEM

Alternative	Previous Outcome	Criterion	Meas.Unit	Weight
1 ALLOW DISCRIM.CP	APPROVED	1 -HOMICIDE	1-5 SCALE	1.00
2 DISALLOW DISCRIM.	-PRESENT	2 SEPARATE INNOCENT		1.00
3 DISALLOW CP	REJECTED	3 -DELAY & COST		1.00
		4 RACIAL EQUALITY		1.00
		5 PUBLIC OPINION		1.00
		6 PREDICTABILITY		1.00
		7 -OVER PRECEDENT		1.00

B. THE 1-5 SCORING OF THE ALTERNATIVES ON THE CRITERIA

	-HOMICIDE	SEPARATE	-DELAY	EQUALITY	PUB.OP.	PREDICT.	-OVER
ALLOW DISCRIM.CP	3.50	2.00	2.00	1.00	2.00	2.00	2.50
DISALLOW DISCRIM.	3.00	3.00	3.00	5.00	4.00	4.00	4.00
DISALLOW CP	2.50	4.00	4.00	4.00	2.00	3.50	2.00

C. THE OVERALL SCORES OF EACH ALTERNATIVE

Alternative	Combined Raw Scores	Previous Outcome
1 ALLOW DISCRIM.CP	15.00	APPROVED
2 DISALLOW DISCRIM.CP	26.00	-PRESENT
3 DISALLOW CP	21.50	REJECTED

D. BRINGING THE ALLOWING OF DISCRIMINATORY CAPITAL PUNISHMENT UP TO THE LEVEL OF DISALLOWING ALL CAPITAL PUNISHMENT

	ALLOW DISC.	DISALLOW CP	Weight
-HOMICIDE	10.00	-4.00	7.500
SEPARATE INNOCENT	8.50	-2.50	-2.250
-DELAY & COST	8.50	-2.50	-2.250
RACIAL EQUALITY	7.50	-2.50	-1.167
PUBLIC OPINION	8.50	-4.50	??????
PREDICTABILITY	8.50	-3.50	-5.500
-OVER PRECEDENT	9.00	-4.50	14.000

E. BRINGING THE ALLOWING OF DISCRIMINATORY CAPITAL PUNISHMENT UP TO THE LEVEL OF DISALLOWING DISCRIMINATORY CAPITAL PUNISHMENT

	DISALLOW DISC.	ALLOW DISC.	Weight
-HOMICIDE	-8.00	14.50	23.000
SEPARATE INNOCENT	-8.00	13.00	-10.000
-DELAY & COST	-8.00	13.00	-10.000
RACIAL EQUALITY	-6.00	12.00	-1.750
PUBLIC OPINION	-7.00	13.00	-4.500
PREDICTABILITY	-7.00	13.00	-4.500
-OVER PRECEDENT	-7.00	13.50	-6.333

was that the presence of racial discrimination should be a justification for abolishing capital punishment. The middle position, which was not advocated, is to disallow capital punishment for those states where a discriminatory pattern is shown beyond a certain acceptable threshold.

The discriminatory threshold could be regarded as being exceeded in a state if the percentage of blacks convicted of capital crimes who are sentenced to die is more than 20 percentage points higher than the percentage of whites convicted of capital crimes who are sentenced to die. For example, if a state has sentenced 50% of convicted blacks to die and less than 30% of the convicted whites, that threshold would be violated. The percentage threshold could be any percentage difference that the Supreme Court considers too great. Perhaps 10 percentage points is too great, or 30 percentage points might be considered the threshold. The important idea is that there should be some critical difference between the percentage of blacks and the percentage of whites sentenced to die so that the Court says that difference is too large. Actually the key percentages to compare are not the percentages of blacks and whites sentenced to die but the percentage of defendants with white victims and the percentage of defendants with black victims. The *McCleskey* case found a substantially stronger discriminatory pattern in the race of the victims than in the race of the defendants.

If the Court were to take such a position, it would be up to any individual state found to have violated the threshold to decide how it will remedy that disparity. In the meantime, capital punishment would be suspended in that state. The remedy might be commuting the death sentences of some black defendants to life imprisonment to bring down the black percentage. In theory, the remedy might also be raising the white percentage. This could not be done with white defendants who have already been sentenced to life imprisonment, since resentencing would be a violation of the double jeopardy clause. However, the new standards could be applied to new white defendants. However, the result would be to equalize the disparity by having more capital punishment, not less, and that result would probably be undesirable to the groups attacking capital punishment and possibly also undesirable to the sentencing authorities in the states involved.

Table 4-3A also shows the criteria which the Court may have had in mind in deciding among the alternatives presented: (1) reducing homicides; (2) separating the innocent from the guilty; (3) reducing delay and court costs; (4) promoting racial equality; (5) satisfying public opinion; (6) encouraging predictability; and (7) avoiding overly broad precedents. To begin with, we operate under the assumption that those goals have approximately equal weight, although that assumption is subject to change when we see the threshold analysis, which shows the effects of different weights on the relative desirability of the competing alternatives.

Table 4-3B shows how each alternative is likely to score on each criterion. For example, allowing capital punishment even with discrimination may be thought of as helping to reduce homicides, although not greatly, whereas completely disallowing capital punishment would have the opposite effect. On the other hand, allowing capital punishment may interfere with separating the innocent from the guilty: innocent defendants are more likely to be convicted in capital crimes, where there is no victim to testify, and such a conviction would be irretrievable if implemented. Disallowing capital punishment would help to reduce delay and the expense of the lengthy appeal process, which capital punishment encourages. On the matter of equality, the conditional disallowance would promote more equality than total disallowance. It would also score relatively high on promoting predictability, especially predictability based on the law and facts, regardless of the race of the defendant or the victim. Limiting the decision to states with unduly discriminatory patterns would also be in conformity with not having an overly broad precedent. The scoring indicates that public opinion would probably be opposed both to allowing discriminatory capital punishment and to totally disallowing capital punishment, but it might favor the conditional disallowance alternative. Even if that criterion is wrongly perceived or scored, reasonable changes in the scoring would not affect the overall scores.

The Overall Scores and the Sensitivity Analysis

As for the overall scores, the conditional disallowance alternative seems to be a clear winner. One might ask why it did not win. The answer is largely that it was not presented. The overall scores also show that total disallowance scores higher than continuing capital punishment with racially discriminatory patterns. One might then ask why the low-scoring alternative came out the winner. The answer might be that the Court did not give equal weight to all the criteria.

Table 4-3D shows that the alternative of allowing discriminatory capital punishment will win over total disallowance if the Court gives extra weight to decreasing homicide and avoiding overly broad precedents. That may have been exactly what happened in the Justices' minds in the *McCleskey* case. They may have been thinking that the total-disallowance alternative would be unacceptable by virtue of the assumed adverse effect on decreasing homicide, and especially by virtue of the broadness of the precedent that would be established. If capital punishment were declared unconstitutional because it is administered in a racially discriminatory way, such a precedent would possibly be used to obtain a declaration of unconstitutionality regarding all sentencing and many other forms of governmental behavior.

Table 4-3E tends to reinforce the idea that if the conditional disallowance position had been advocated, it would have been a strong winner. Table 4-3E shows that in order to allow discriminatory capital punishment over the conditional disallowance, the Court would have to give an extremely high weight to decreasing homicide. Furthermore, the Court would have to give negative weight to such goals as separating the innocent from the guilty, reducing delay and cost, and the other goals. Those negative weights seem unlikely. Especially unlikely is the idea that the Court would perceive that disallowing discriminatory capital punishment would score such low negative scores on the criteria, or that allowing discriminatory capital punishment would score such high positive scores on other criteria. Those negative scores are below 1 on the 1–5 scale, and those positive scores are above 5 on the 1–5 scale.

GENERAL IDEAS AND CONCLUSIONS

Comparing the Cases

There are a number of ideas that cut across these three case studies. Let us first consider some important similarities and differences between the cases. In each of the three cases, three alternative positions are discussed. One position is a highly liberal position that the Supreme Court (at least at the time of these decisions) was unlikely to adopt, including (1) upgrading poor schools to the quality of the richest schools; (2) providing for welfare payments at a constant amount per child regardless of the number of children; and (3) totally abolishing capital punishment because it often involves racial discrimination. A second position is a highly conservative position, which the Supreme Court did adopt in all three cases, (1) ruling that the states have no obligation at all to upgrade poor schools; (2) ruling the states have no obligation to provide any additional money at all for an additional child beyond a certain low number of children; and (3) allowing capital punishment regardless how it might be associated with racial discrimination. The third position was left out of the advocacy in each case, although it could have been a winner: (1) advocating that poor schools be upgraded to at least the minimum level; (2) advocating that incremental children receive some incremental food, shelter, and other allowance, although permissibly at a diminishing rate of increase; and (3) advocating that capital punishment be suspended in those states where the racial disparity is beyond an acceptable threshold until it is brought down to that threshold.

In the *Rodriguez* case, the middle position might have been a winner if it had been advocated and if the Supreme Court had been convinced of the importance of having an educated population and reducing the discontent that comes from having less than the average educational opportunities for one's children. In the *Dandridge* case, the middle position might have been a winner even without a change in the Supreme Court's values since it does seem to be an objectively more tenable position than the conservative position, although the conservative position may be more tenable than the liberal position. In the *McCleskey* case, the middle position might have been a winner if it had been advocated since it also seems to be objectively more tenable than either the conservative or the liberal position.

Half a Loaf Is No Better than None

On a higher level of generality, we should address ourselves to the point that pursuing the middle position is rather unambitious. One might even be able to argue in some situations that the middling position is almost worthless where one is dealing with an *S*-shaped takeoff curve. In those circumstances, there is no real achievement until one gets above the takeoff point. For example, a lawyer working 1, 2, or 3 hours in developing an appellate brief may be just as much a loser as a lawyer working 4 or 5 hours because the case requires between 6 and 10 hours' work to be handled successfully. Thus anything at 5 hours or below is the equivalent of half a time-loaf and is equally worthless.

Possibly worse is that one may win the case by putting in a small amount of time but win a very low-level victory. Just winning, however, may cause a feeling of accomplishment that promotes a lower future standard of work than would have been motivated by a complete loss. In such a case, one can argue that half a loaf is worse than none.

Benefits of Incremental Optimizing

On the other side of this issue are a number of arguments that are much stronger, although the specific facts must be taken into consideration. One of the main arguments in favor of pursuing half a loaf is that if one does so in terms of successive halves, one very soon has the whole loaf. For example, if one achieves half of whatever the total achievement is in one day, then on a second day one can go to the 75% level by cutting the remaining 50% in half. On the third day, one could arrive at the 87.5% level by cutting the remaining 25% in half. On the fourth day, one can go over the 90% level, which should generally be enough for all but the most greedy. In other words, *just* settling for half a loaf may conceivably be worse than none. There is, however, no reason why, in appellate advocacy, one cannot pursue the middle position today and then come back tomorrow to court to pursue the 75% position, and then next week the 87.5% position. In fact, that is the way the constitutional revolution has worked in the U.S. Supreme Court process. The desegregation case of *Brown v. Board of Education* was not built in a day. Nor was the right to counsel for indigent parties established with a single case. It took a series of cases, starting with the right to counsel in capital cases, felony cases, appellate cases, police interrogation, and misdemeanor cases; the next step will probably be civil cases.

The incremental process may sound like slow going. In reality, it may work faster than going for the top all at once. There is nothing inherently slow about incrementalism. For example, the half-life of some newly found radioactive elements is less than a second. In effect, those elements chop themselves in half in successive choppings until they have reached the point where they cease to exist, before even one second has gone by. Incremental court cases do not work that fast, but it is quite possible that if the foundation had not been laid for *Brown v. Board of Education,* by way of chipping away the more blatant forms of education discrimination and segregation, we might still be trying to convince the Supreme Court to declare segregated schools unconstitutional.

Even if one could achieve the big win all at once, the incremental approach might be more desirable because it allows the opposition, the neutrals, and even the supporters to digest the gains in such a way as to facilitate implementation with a minimum of problems. The learning experience at each step enables the next step to be handled better. Civil liberties change has proceeded in the United States through a set of events that could not have been easily compressed. For example, the first modification of unrestrained capitalistic activity occurred in the Woodrow Wilson era. It established the Federal Trade Commission and the Pure Food and Drug Administration, which were early forms of middle-class consumer protection. The New Deal era of the 1930s saw the establishment of the rights of workers to form unions without being subject to dismissals. In the 1960s, the rights of blacks and women were established, more easily than could have been done without the precedents of workers' rights and consumers' rights.

A key point is that taking the incremental approach does not mean having low goals. One may seek to achieve very high goals through a series of steps, partly to avoid the risk of going for the top all at once and winding up with nothing, and partly to avoid the demoralization of such a total defeat, which may discourage one from trying again. The incremental approach is like climbing a ladder. Obviously it makes more sense to go up one rung at a time than it does to try to jump for the top rung.

Computer-Aided Advocacy and Multiple Alternatives

One question that might be asked is: Even if middle positions do make sense, what value does computer-aided advocacy have? Why could we not come to the conclusion that the middle position makes more sense than the extreme liberal position in *Rodriguez, Dandridge,* and *McCleskey,* without decision-aiding software? The answer is that anything a computer can do we can probably also do without a computer if we want to work long enough and hard enough at it. Why, though, should we handicap or deprive ourselves of what could be a useful tool for broadening our perspectives and for stimulating the behavior of the appellate court that we are going to argue in front of? Decision-aiding software that is based on a spreadsheet format and multicriteria decision-making, like the software described in this chapter, does encourage thinking in terms of both multiple criteria and multiple alternatives. Otherwise there is a tendency to think in terms of two alternatives—the plaintiff's position and the defendant's position, or the liberal position and the conservative position—rather than three or more alternatives. Likewise, there is a tendency to think in terms of one criterion in appellate advocacy, namely, consistency with prior decisions. That one criterion is not likely to enable one advocate to win over the other, since both positions are likely to be reasonably consistent with prior decisions. If one position is so obviously consistent or inconsistent, the Supreme Court probably would not even hear the case.

A related point is that the demonstration of the software looks impressive only because the cases have already been decided, and that all we are seeing is hindsight in action. The answer to that argument is that all the information used in Tables 4-1, 4-2, and 4-3 was available before the cases were decided. Although it is true that it is easier to analyze cases after they have been decided than before, one can still do a systematic, meaningful analysis before cases are decided. The more there is at stake, the more justification there is for finding and analyzing all of the possible alternative positions and all of the criteria that the Court may use in reaching a decision. Such an analysis should enable the appellate advocate to arrive at the best alternatives to argue, the best criteria to emphasize, and the best perceptions of the relations between the alternatives and the criteria to convince the Court.

In spite of all that has been said above about the importance of systematic appellate advocacy, it may be that appellate advocacy now has considerable limitations even in (and maybe especially in) the kinds of civil liberties cases that were used as examples. The big limitation is that the Supreme Court cannot do much more with regard to broadening the interpretation of the equal protection clause of the Constitution or other civil liberties. The most blatant forms of discrimination have been declared unconstitutional or statutorily illegal regarding race, gender, class, and geography, and regarding rights that relate to voting, criminal justice, education, employment, housing, and being a consumer. The new frontiers in these areas may be mainly in the realm of congressional and presidential action, concerning subsidies, tax breaks, and other incentives designed to better the opportunities of blacks, women, poor people, rural people, and others. Thus spreadsheet analysis should perhaps be expanded to include alternatives relating to congressional and presidential action, not just Supreme Court action.

The spreadsheet format emphasizes multiple alternatives (rather than dichotomies) and multiple criteria (rather than single objective functions or goals). That kind of perspective can be helpful in deciding not only what position to argue in a given Supreme Court case or whether to go to the courts or the legislature, but also in deciding among alternatives like (1) going through the federal courts versus the state courts; (2) deciding among alternative test cases; (3) deciding whether to appeal; (4) deciding whether to pursue a constitutional abuse that affects a lot of people in a small way, like pretrial detention, or one that affects a few people in a big way, like capital punishment; and (5) pursuing alternative forms of dispute resolution which are becoming increasingly popular, such as mediation, including computer-aided mediation. Thus the spreadsheet format of decision-aiding software has many possibilities for the appellate advocate beyond traditional appellate advocacy. It is hoped that this chapter will help bring out some of those possibilities for making appellate advocacy more effective, efficient, and equitable.[1]

NOTE

1. For further details on computer-aided legal decisions (CALD), see David Johnson and Paul Mode, *Improving Law Firm Productivity by Encouraging Lawyers' Use of Personal Computers* (New York: Harcourt Brace Jovanovich, 1985); John Burns and Jim Hodde, "Decision Analysis: Using Computers to Make Better Choices," 6 *Attorney's Computer Report* 1-4 (February 1988); S. Nagel, "Computer-Aided Law Decisions," 21 *Akron Law Review* 73-96 (1987); and S. Nagel, *Microcomputers as Decision Aids in Law Practice* (Westport, Conn.: Greenwood-Quorum, 1987). On computer-aided decision-making in general and decision-aiding software, see Patrick Humphreys and Ayleen Wisudha, *Methods and Tools for Structuring and Analyzing Decision Problems* (London: London School of Economics and Political Science, 1987); and Gautam Mitra (ed.), *Computer-Assisted Decision Making: Expert Systems, Decision Analysis, Mathematical Programming* (Amsterdam: North-Holland, 1986). On decision-making from the perspective of multiple criteria and multiple alternatives, see Ching-Lai Hwang and Kwangsun Yoon, *Multiple Attribute Decision Making: Methods and Applications* (Berlin: Springer-Verlag, 1981); and Milan Zeleny, *Multiple Criteria Decision Making* (New York: McGraw-Hill, 1982).

5

Mediating Disputes

Super-optimum dispute resolution involves both sides coming out ahead of their best expectations, not just ahead of their worst expectations. The latter is sometimes referred to as a *win–win solution*, or Pareto optimum, rather than a super-optimum solution. Such super-optimum or win-plus solutions are facilitated by microcomputers because microcomputers allow for easy trial-and-error experimenting, especially with multiple criteria, until the contending sides achieve a super-optimum solution.

An important part of administrative decision-making is the adjudicating of disputes. There is an increasing movement toward using alternative dispute resolution in administrative adjudication. The movement is partly designed to save time, but it is also designed to resolve disputes in more productive ways, especially where disputes involve employers and workers, sellers and consumers, landlords and tenants, and others who may need to cooperate with each other in the future.

This chapter uses criminal cases and civil cases as illustrative examples. Criminal cases are analogous to administrative regulation. Civil cases are analogous to the filing of claims in workers' compensation, veterans' benefits, and welfare cases.

CRIMINAL CASES

Suppose that in a criminal case, the prosecutor's optimum position is a five-year sentence; that is, the prosecutor considers five years the maximum realistic number of years that the defendant would be willing to go to prison. Five years may be less than the maximum which the statute allows. If five years is the prosecutor's optimum, then the prosecutor might be willing to settle for as little as two years. On the other hand, the defendant's optimum might be one year as the best possible settlement. Thus the defendant might be willing to settle for as much as three years in prison.

An optimizing solution would be one which allows the prosecutor to have a settlement of more than five years and that allows the defendant to have a settlement of less than one year. That solution seems impossible, but not necessarily, if the disputants can move on to a different settlement dimension, such as community service instead of prison. On that dimension, they might be able to reach an agreement in which the defendant agrees to serve 10 years in a monastery. From the prosecutor's point of view, that may be better than 5 years in prison. From the defendant's point of view, that might be better than 1 year in prison. Thus, 10 years of monastic community service is an optimizing compromise where both sides feel they have come out ahead of their original optimum positions.

CIVIL CASES

Likewise, in a damages case, the plaintiff may initially demand $100,000, figuring that that amount is substantially higher than the defendant would ever be willing to pay. The defense side, on the other hand, might initially offer $20,000, figuring that that amount is substantially lower than the plaintiff would ever be willing to settle for. An optimizing compromise would be one in which the plaintiff feels that he or she is getting the equivalent of more than $100,000, and the defendant feels he or she is paying the equivalent of less than $20,000. That kind of a settlement also seems impossible, but again, not necessarily so, if the disputants can move on to a different settlement dimension, such as a performance agreement.

Under a performance agreement, the defendant might be willing to promise to comply with certain quality standards in the workplace, in medical practice, or in product manufacturing. The defendant might consider such an agreement a victory because of the favorable publicity that he or she will get by entering into such an agreement. The plaintiff might also consider such an agreement a victory because of the benefits received by the plaintiff's constituents. In that sense, the defendant may feel she or he is getting more than $100,000 worth of benefits. The plaintiff may, however, feel she or he is losing less than $20,000 and is actually gaining something of net value.

USING MICROCOMPUTER SOFTWARE

Table 5-1 shows computer printouts that were generated by a computer program called Best Choice, which, in order to arrive at optimizing or win-plus solutions, can process a set of (1) alternatives being considered; (2)

Table 5-1
Finding a Win-Plus Solution in Civil and Criminal Cases

I. THE CIVIL CASE

A. THE ALTERNATIVES AND THE CRITERIA

Alternative	Criterion	Meas.Unit	Weight
1 P'S BEST >$100,000	1 P'S HAPPINESS	1-5 SCALE	1.00
2 D'S BEST <$20,000	2 D'S HAPPINESS	1-5 SCALE	1.00
3 A WIN+ SOLUTION			

B. SCORING EACH ALTERNATIVE ON EACH CRITERION

	P'S HAPP	D'S HAPP
P'S BEST >$100,000	4.00	1.00
D'S BEST <$20,000	1.00	4.00
A WIN+ SOLUTION	5.00	5.00

C. THE OVERALL SCORES OF EACH ALTERNATIVE

	Combined Raw Scores
P'S BEST >$100,000	5.00
D'S BEST <$20,000	5.00
A WIN+ SOLUTION	10.00

II. THE CRIMINAL CASE

A. THE ALTERNATIVES AND THE CRITERIA

Alternative	Criterion	Meas.Unit	Weight
1 P'S BEST 3 YEARS	1 P'S HAPPINESS	1-5 SCALE	1.00
2 D'S BEST PROBATION	2 D'S HAPPINESS	1-5 SCALE	1.00
3 A WIN+ SOLUTION			

B. SCORING EACH ALTERNATIVE ON EACH CRITERION

	P'S HAPP	D'S HAPP
P'S BEST 3 YEARS	4.00	1.00
D'S BEST PROBATION	1.00	4.00
A WIN+ SOLUTION	5.00	5.00

C. THE OVERALL SCORES OF EACH ALTERNATIVE

	Combined Raw Scores
P'S BEST 3 YEARS	5.00
D'S BEST PROBATION	5.00
A WIN+ SOLUTION	10.00

NOTES:

1. In the civil case, the plaintiff's initial demand is for $100,000. The defendant's initial offer, however, is only $20,000. The win-plus solution involves the defendant giving something to the plaintiff such as a product that the defendant manufactures or sells. Such a product may be worth more than $100,000 to the plaintiff, but worth less than $20,000 to the defendant in terms of the incremental or variable cost.

2. In the criminal case, the prosecutor's initial demand is for the defendant to accept a three-year sentence in order to avoid going to trial. The defendant's initial offer, however, is to plead guilty only if the penalty is no more than probation. The win-plus solutions involves the defendant agreeing to join the Marines in wartime, or agreeing to participate in disease experiments, or agreeing to some other penalty which the prosecutor views as worse than a long prison sentence, but the defendant views as better than pleading guilty and having a record as a convicted felon.

criteria for evaluating them; and (3) relations between alternatives and criteria.

In the civil case, the object is to find a win-plus alternative that will be viewed by the plaintiff as better than receiving $100,000 and by the defendant as better than paying $20,000. In the criminal case, the object is to find a win-plus alternative that will be viewed by the prosecutor as better than a 10-year sentence and by the defendant as better than probation. In both types of cases, the combination of the plaintiff's happiness and the defendant's happiness is the overall goal to be maximized in order to facilitate out-of-court settlements. Both goals are measured on 1–5 scales with equal weight. The plaintiff's original best alternative would make the plaintiff quite happy, but the defendant quite unhappy, whereas the defendant's original best alternative would have the opposite effect in either the civil or the criminal case.

The win-plus solution in the civil case might involve the defendant's insurance company's giving the plaintiff an annuity that pays $10,000 a year for life after age 65:

1. The plaintiff views that solution as worth more than $100,000 because the plaintiff feels he will live to about age 85 and will thus accumulate $200,000.
2. The defendant views that solution as worth less than $20,000 because (a) the plaintiff is only 45 and may never live to 65; (b) the plaintiff may live to 65 but not necessarily to 85, and (c) $20,000 can be invested now at 10% a year, and it will be worth $135,000 by the time the plaintiff reaches age 65 and $405,000 by the time the plaintiff reaches 85, minus the effect of payments of $10,000 per year.

The win-plus solution in the criminal case might involve the defendant's agreeing to commit himself to a long-term nonprison institutionalization, such as being part of a disease research program in a monastery or leper colony:

1. The prosecutor might find that solution to be worth more than three years in prison if there is more than a three-year commitment, especially since a three-year prison sentence may mean release after two years or less with time off. The prosecutor might be especially happy since the state does not pay for monastery incarceration, and the maximum sentence specified in the statute is five years.
2. The defendant might find that solution to be better than probation because there is no plea of guilty, and because the defendant's personality and aspirations may find pleasure in monastery life or even martyrdom to disease research.

SOME CONCLUSIONS

An optimizing solution in this negotiation and mediation context should be distinguished from a Pareto optimum. That goal means that the disputants feel they are coming out ahead of what they would have been willing to settle for. If, for example, in the above criminal case, a plea bargain was struck at 2.5 years, a Pareto optimum would have been reached since the prosecutor was willing to go as low as 2 years, and the defendant was willing to go as high as 3 years. They would then each come out ahead of their worst possible positions, but not ahead of their best possible positions. If negotiators and mediators seek optimizing compromises, they may not succeed. Just trying, however, may result in a more mutually satisfying dispute resolution than merely seeking a Pareto optimum or forcing an agreement. Seeking an optimizing compromise stimulates imaginative solutions that are mutually satisfying to the mediator as well as the disputants.[1]

NOTE

1. For further details on setting and achieving high policy goals, see S. Nagel, *Doing Better than the Best: Higher Goals for America* (Lanham, Md.: University Press of America, 1988). On the application of those ideas to mediating disputes, see S. Nagel and M. Mills, "Microcomputers, P/G%, and Dispute Resolution" 2 *Ohio State Journal on Dispute Resolution* 187–222 (1987).

6

Being a Representative

Ethical constraints are important in public policy evaluation and in the decision-making of policy-makers and administrators. These constraints are to prohibitions or mandates regarding what is considered professionally proper. Perhaps the most common ethical constraint in policy analysis is the constraint that says policy analysts and decision-makers should not personally benefit from their decisions at the expense of their clients or the general public.

THE PROBLEM OF CONFLICTING INTERESTS

Table 6-1 provides an interesting example of a conflict of interest from the field of legal decision-making. The problem involves deciding whether to go to trial or to accept an out-of-court settlement. The attorney could be a government prosecutor, a regulatory agency lawyer, a public defender, or other government lawyer. Assume, though, that this is a private attorney who is paid only if he or she wins the case on behalf of the client. That situation adds extra interest because such a contingency fee arrangement is supposed to put the lawyer and the client on the same side in making decisions. That arrangement is unlike the hourly fee, which may cause the lawyer to want to do too much, or the flat fee, which may cause the lawyer to want to do too little.

In Table 6-1, the best alternative from the lawyer's perspective is to go to trial. That alternative generates benefits of $2,400 minus costs of $1,500 for a net profit of $900, as contrasted to a settlement, which generates $1,000 in benefits and $300 in costs for a net profit of only $700. In Table 6-1 the best alternative from the client's perspective is to settle. That alternative gener-

Table 6-1
Data for Illustrating and Reconciling Some Attorney–Client Conflicts

GOALS / OPTIONS	BENEFIT ITEMS					COST ITEMS			NET ITEMS	
	(1) Average Damages if one Gets Them	(2) Probability of Receiving Damages	(3) Average Damages or Expected Value (1)x(2)	(4) Percentage Fee	(5) Total Benefits (3)x(4)	(6) Number of Hours	(7) Hourly Cost	(8) Total Cost (6)x(7)	(9) Lawyer B/C (5)-(8)	(10) Client B/C (3)x[1-(4)]
A. THE ORIGINAL INPUT VALUES IN THE LITIGATION STRATEGY EXAMPLE										
Settle	$5,000	1.00	$5,000	20%	$1,000	10	$30	$ 300	$ 700	$4,000
Go to Trial	$10,000	.60	$6,000	40%	$2,400	25	$60	$1,500	$ 900	$3,600
B. TIE-CAUSING VALUES FROM THE LAWYER'S PERSPECTIVE										
Settle	$6,000*	1.20	$6,000	24%	$1,200	3.33	$10	$ 100	$ 900	
Go to Trial	$9,167	.55	$5,500	37%	$2,200	28.33	$68	$1,700	$ 700	
C. TIE-CAUSING VALUES FROM THE CLIENT'S PERSPECTIVE										
Settle	$ 4,500	.90	$4,500	28%	$3,600	--	--	--		$3,600
Go to Trial	$11,111	.67	$6,667*	33%	$4,000	--	--	--		$4,000

NOTES:

1. If any of the original input values in Table 6-1A change to its tie-causing value in Table 6-1B then the profit of the lawyer from settling will rise from $700 to $900, or the profit from going to trial will drop from $900 to $700.
2. If any of the original input values in Table 6-1A change to its tie-causing value in 6-2C the profit of the client from settling will drop from $4,000 to $3,600, or the profit from going to trial will rise from $3,600 to $4,000.
3. When one of the basic components changes to its tie-causing value, we assume the other basic components remain constant, although not the products or sums of the basic components. The basic components are shown in columns 1,2,4,6, and 7. The products or sums of the basic components are shown in column 3, 5, 8, 9, and 10.
4. The starred items are those most subject to change in order to bring the lawyer's interest and the client's interest together.

ates $5,000 in damages, of which the client keeps $4,000, whereas going to trial generates, on the average, $6,000 in damages, of which the client keeps only $3,600.

How can those conflicting constraints or conflicting interests be resolved? Perhaps the lawyer resolves them by going to trial. The lawyer may rationalize by saying that the client still comes out $3,600 ahead in comparison to never having filed a claim. The lawyer may also rationalize by saying that by going to trial, the client could come out with $6,000 if the lawyer obtains $10,000 in damages and takes a 40% fee. Perhaps the lawyer resolves the conflicting interests by settling. He or she might then rationalize by saying that he or she still comes out with a $700 profit in comparison to having never taken the case. The lawyer may also rationalize by saying that by settling, he or she avoids the possibility of a total defeat, in which he or she would collect nothing.

MAKING SETTLING MORE PROFITABLE TO BOTH ATTORNEY AND CLIENT

A more meaningful approach to dealing with these conflicting interests is to look for a solution in which both the lawyer and the client will come out ahead by settling rather than going to trial, or by going to trial rather than settling. For example, a sensitivity analysis would quickly show that if the $5,000 settlement could be raised to more than $6,000, both the lawyer and the client would be better off settling. At a settlement offer of over $6,000, the lawyer's net profit moves to over $900, and the client's net profit moves to over $4,800. That solution is shown in the upper-left-hand corner of Table 6-1B.

None of the other tie-causing values in Table 6-1B are as meaningful to change as seeking to get the settlement up from $5,000 to $6,000. Reading across the top row of Table 6-1B, we see that

1. The certainty associated with accepting a settlement cannot go higher than 1.00.
2. The 20% contingency fee for settling cannot be retroactively changed by the lawyer to 24%.
3. The 10 hours probably cannot be easily reduced to 3.33 hours.
4. The hourly value of the lawyer's time in doing nontrial work probably cannot be meaningfully devalued from $30 to $10.
5. Lawyers are not going to deliberately lower the trial damages, probability of victory, or percentage fee in order to decrease their trial profits.
6. Likewise, the lawyer is not going to increase the number of hours to 28.33 or revalue the monetary worth of trial time from $60 to $68 in order to decrease his or her trial profits.

MAKING A TRIAL MORE PROFITABLE TO BOTH

The sensitivity analysis shown in Table 6-1C appears at first glance to provide another meaningful way of resolving the conflicting interests. Table 6-1C shows the tie-causing values from the client's perspective, as contrasted with the lawyer's perspective. The lawyer (in light of Table 6-1A), would like to go to trial, and the problem thus becomes how to get the client to also want to go to trial without hoodwinking the client. That is the reverse of Table 6-1B, where we expressed the problem in terms of how to get the lawyer to want to accept a settlement. The client will want to go to trial if the lawyer will agree to reduce the trial percentage fee from 40% to 33%. Then the client's profit becomes at least as much by going to trial as by accepting the settlement. The client would have no objection to the lawyer's retroactively lowering the contingency fee, rather than raising it. The big defect in this analysis is that if the lawyer lowers the trial percentage fee from 40% to 33%, then the client may want to go to trial, but the lawyer will no longer want to do so. The reason is that at a 33% trial percentage fee, the lawyer would receive only one third of the $6,000 expected value, which would mean only $2,000 in total benefits. The total cost of $1,500 would then be subtracted, leaving the lawyer only $500 in profit. That is worse than the $700 in profit from accepting a $5,000 settlement fee.

The lawyer can make going to trial more attractive to the client than settling for $5,000 by increasing the lawyer's efforts, as measured by the hours expended. One might argue against that approach by saying that increasing the hours expended will increase the total cost and thus wipe out the extra benefits on the increased expected value. The extent to which that is true depends on the relation between the hours expended and the expected value. It is common sense that working harder to prepare the case should result in more damages and a higher probability of victory, but how can one determine the quantitative nature of that relation?

One way to determine the relation is by obtaining information on many previous related cases showing how many hours were devoted to each case and the damages awarded. By putting that information into a statistical calculator or an appropriately programmed microcomputer, one can determine the numerical parameters for a relation of the form $DP = a(H)^b$. In this equation, *DP* is the expected value to be predicted to, *H* is the quantity of hours to be predicted from, *a* is the expected value when *H* is one hour, and *b* measures the degree of diminishing returns in the nonlinear relation between *DP* and *H*. Suppose we have only one case to predict from, like the case shown in row 2 of Table 6-1A. One can assume a value for *b* of .50, since that is the simplest diminishing-returns relation. One can then solve for *a* in the equation, $\$6,000 = a(25)^{.50}$. The value of *a* is thus $6,000 divided by the square root of 25, which simplifies to $6,000/5, or $1,200.

An alternative approach to expressing the relation between expected value and hours is to assume that the elasticity coefficient, b, is .50 and the scale coefficient, a, is 1. Doing so gives a relation of $DP = 1(H)^{.50}$. Thus, when there is a 1% increase in hours, there is a 1/2% increase in expected value. When there is a 100% increase in hours, there is a 50% increase in expected value. The expression $1(H)^{.50}$ also means that when the hours are 1, the expected value is 1 monetary unit or $1,000. Another approach is to insert into a statistical calculator the data point of 25 hours and $6, and a second data point of 1 hour and $1. Doing so yields a production function of $1(H)^{.56}$, after one logs all the numbers. One need not argue over which approach is best, since they all produce approximately the same production functions when 1 monetary unit is $1,000.

By substituting $a(H)^b$ by $1,200 $(H)^{.50}$ for DP, one can then express the lawyer's profit in terms of the hours expended. The relation is $480H^{.5} - 60H$, where $480H^{.5}$ is equal to DPF, and $60H$ is equal to RH, as indicated in note 2 of Table 6-1. Likewise, one can express the client's profit as $720H^{.5}$, where 720 is equal to $DP(1 - F)$. One can then determine the lawyer's profit and the client's profit for a variety of different hours, as is shown in Table 6-2, which indicates that the maximum lawyer's profit is at 16 hours, whereas the maximum client's profit is at infinity. The client does not directly pay any of the lawyer's costs, and thus increased hours mean increased net damages to the client, although at a plateauing rate.

At 31 hours, the lawyer is able to make going to trial more attractive to the client than accepting the $5,000 settlement. At that point, the lawyer's profit of $813 is also greater than the settlement profit of $700. If, however, the lawyer puts in more hours, the high total cost at 64 hours does wipe out the total benefits. The total cost increases at a constant rate of $60 an hour for each additional hour. The total benefits, however, go up only 50% when the hours double or go up 100%. Note the diminishing returns in the sense that from 50 hours to 75 hours, the client's profit goes up by $1,144 (from $5,091 to $6,235), whereas from 75 hours to 100 hours, the client's profit goes up by only $965 (from $6,235 to $7,200).

GENERATING CLEARER ETHICAL PRINCIPLES

The above analysis enables us to clarify better the ethical obligations of a lawyer operating under a contingency fee arrangement. It generates the following principles:

1. If it is more profitable to the lawyer to go to trial, but it is more profitable to the client to settle, or vice versa, the lawyer should seek to increase the settlement to make settling more profitable to both of them. The increase need go only as high as the threshold or tie-causing value of the settlement offer.
2. As an alternative, the lawyer should seek to increase the expected value of going to trial in order to make going to trial more profitable to both of them. The

Table 6-2
The Profits of the Lawyer and the Client at Different Trial Hours

HOURS	LAWYER'S PROFIT	CLIENT PROFIT	COMMENTS
0	0	0	Doing nothing generates nothing.
1	420	720	The starting point.
10	917	2,277	
15	959	2,789	
16	960	2,880	The lawyer's maximum.
20	946	3,210	
25	900	3,600	The trial row of 6-1A.
30	829	3,944	
31	813	4,009	Satisfying one's obligation to the client.
35	740	4,260	
50	394	5,091	
60	118	5,577	
64	0	5,960	Costs begin to exceed benefits for the lawyer.
65	-30	5,805	
75	-343	6,235	
100	-1,200	7,200	Profit is still rising for the client, but more slowly.

NOTES:

1. The average damages or expected value equals $1,200 times the square root of the trial hours. This is determined by observing the trial row of Table 6-1A and observing what has happened in other cases regarding the average damages and the trial hours.

2. The lawyers profit equals DPF - HR, where D = damages, P = probability, F = % fee, H = hours, and R = rate per hour. That equation simplifies to $\$1,200(H)^{.5}(.40) - (H)(\$60)$, where $(H)^{.5}$ is equal to the square root of the trial hours. That equation further simplifies to $480H^{.5} - 60H$.

3. The clients's profit equals DP(1-F). That equation simplifies to $\$1,200(H)^{.5}(.60)$. That equation further simplifies to $720H^{.5}$

4. All the profit figures in Table 6-2 can be calculated with any calculator and can handle exponents or square roots.

5. The optimum number of trial hours can be defined as the quantity that maximized benefits minus costs from the lawyer's perspective, while making going to trial the more attractive alternative to both the client and the lawyer, not just the lawyer.

increase need go only as high as making the trial even more profitable to the client than settling. The lawyer need not push for still more profit for the client when doing so means operating at a decreased profit or even a loss to the lawyer.

3. If, in a rare situation, it is impossible to make settling or going to trial more profitable to both the client and the lawyer, the lawyer should choose between settling and going to trial in light of the client's best interests.
4. Perhaps lawyers of the future should have an ethical obligation to systematically determine the relative profitability to the client and the lawyer of settling and going to trial at differing degrees of effort in order to be able to implement the above ethical principles to their mutual profit.

7

Assigning People to Casetypes

Table 7-1 shows how one can systematically view the problem of assigning lawyers to types of cases as an example of the more general problem of assigning people to tasks. This hypothetical problem involves two lawyers named Able and Baker. It involves the casetypes of criminal and civil cases. Each lawyer is expected to bill 30 hours in an average week. In such a week, there are about 24 criminal hours and 36 civil hours. The problem could be expanded to include more people and more tasks, but two people and two tasks can be used to illustrate the general methodology.

THE INPUT INFORMATION

The partners in the hypothetical law firm decide to score themselves on their degree of interest in each type of case. They do so using a 1–5 scale, where 5 = highly interested, 4 = mildly interested, 3 = neither interested nor uninterested, 2 = mildly uninterested, and 1 = highly uninterested. The partners also decide to anonymously score each other on their degree of ability in each type of case, where 5 = highly capable in this type of case, 4 = mildly incapable, 3 = neither capable nor incapable but just average, 2 = mildly incapable, and 1 = highly incapable. As an alternative to scoring each other on ability, the partners could measure ability in terms of years of experience or quantity of previous cases handled within each casetype. That scoring can also be converted into a 1–5 scale.

Each partner or associate then receives an overall score, which is the sum of the separate scores on interest and ability. Each separate score can be given equal weight, or the ability scores can be doubled to show that they are twice as important. The overall score can then be divided by the number of

Table 7-1
The Problem of Allocating 60 Hours to Two Lawyers for Two Casetypes

CASES / LAWYER	CRIMINAL		CIVIL		Hours per Lawyer
	Quality Score	Hours Assigned	Quality Score	Hours Assigned	
ABLE	4	a	3	b	30
BAKER	2	c	3	d	30
Hours per Casetype		24		36	60

NOTES

1. The allocation system is shown in its simplest form with two lawyers and two casetypes in the law firm.
2. Each lawyer is expected to put in 30 billable hours a week to satisfy the average weekly total of 60 hours of billable time for the firm.
3. Criminal cases constitute 40% of the total or 24 hours, and civil cases constitute 60% or 36 hours in an average week.
4. Lawyer Able receives scores of 4 and 3 on the two casetypes, and Lawyer Baker receives scores of 2 and 3.
5. Hours per casetype and hours per lawyer refer to billable hours, as contrasted to hours that cut across cases and are thus not billable to any specific client, such as general background reading.
6. The problem is to decide approximately how many hours a week Able should do on criminal cases (a) and on civil cases (b), and approximately how many hours Baker should do on criminal cases (c) and on civil cases (d).

scores or the sum of the weights in order to give each person a 1–5 overall score. In the hypothetical data, Lawyer Able receives a score of 4 on criminal cases and 3 on civil cases. Lawyer Baker receives 2 on criminal cases and 3 on civil cases.

THE OVERALL GOAL AND PROCEDURES

The object of the analysis is to determine how to assign the 60 hours to the two lawyers so as to provide the best allocation of the lawyers to the casetypes, or more generally the best allocation of people to tasks. *Best* in this context means an allocation or assignment that will result in a maximum overall quality sum of each product of a lawyer's quality score times the hours assigned for a given casetype. In this context, the overall quality score is equal to $4a + 2c + 3b + 3d$. The object is to solve for a, b, c, and d so as to maximize that overall score while satisfying the constraints.

The best way to proceed, if one does not have a computer, is to give as few hours as possible to those cells which have quality scores of 1 or 2, and as many hours as possible to those cells which have quality scores of 5 or 4, while still satisfying the constraints. Doing so results in an allocation of 0 hours to cell c, 24 hours to a, 6 hours to b, and 30 hours to d. That way, the 24 hours of criminal cases are satisfied (24 plus 0); the 36 hours of civil cases (6 plus 30); the 30 hours for Lawyer A are satisfied (24 plus 6); and the 30 hours for Lawyer B (0 plus 30).

MICROCOMPUTERS AND MODIFICATIONS

That method can be meaningful for a substantial number of lawyers and casetypes. One can, however, solve big assignments faster and with more accuracy by using a linear programming routine. Such routines are easy to use on microcomputers. One simply informs the computer of the row totals, the column totals, and the quality scores. The computer then generates the optimum allocations.

The program will also indicate (1) how much each quality score can vary without affecting the optimum result, (2) how much each row total and column total can vary, and (3) how much of a change in the overall quality score would occur as a result of a one-unit change in the hours assigned or in any of the inputs. In most problems that involve assigning people to tasks, the quality scores can vary substantially without affecting the results, thereby allowing considerable leeway for error. Knowing which changes will have the most effect on the overall output can be helpful in deciding how to change the constraints or other inputs.[1]

OTHER EXAMPLES

This short example involves assigning lawyers to cases. The same kind of analysis, although with different goals, could be used to assign judges to cases to promote courthouse efficiency, or to assign clerical personnel to various tasks to promote law firm efficiency. Rather than assigning lawyers to cases in terms of general ability and interests, one can think in terms of more specific skills, such as ability and interest concerning counseling, negotiating, trial technique, mediating, legal policy evaluation, appellate advocacy, or case analysis and prediction. One can also think in terms of more specific casetypes than simply criminal and civil, such as casetypes which include contracts, property, family disputes, torts, constitutional law, economic regulation, and international law, as well as criminal and civil substance and procedure.

NOTE

1. On computer-aided assignment of people to tasks, see Sang Lee et al., *Management Science* (Dubuque, Iowa: Wm. C. Brown, 1981), 177–235; Samuel Richmond, *Operations Research for Management Decisions* (New York: Ronald, 1967), 277–285; Warren Erikson and Owen Hall, *Computer Models in Management Science* (Reading, Mass.: Addison-Wesley, 1986), 1–86; and S. Nagel and M. Mills, "Allocating Attorneys to Casetypes," 15 *Capital University Law Review* 223–242 (1986).

8

Optimum Sequencing

SEQUENCING ADMINISTRATIVE CASES

The purpose of this chapter is to discuss the application of optimum ordering to the sequencing of governmental activities.

Table 8-1 shows how substantial savings of time per administrative case or application can be obtained by hearing the cases in the order of the shortest cases first. The hypothetical data involve three cases. They are predicted to take 20, 10, and 5 hours to process, respectively.

If they are heard in that order (which is shown in row 1), there will be (1) no waiting time for the first case, which is true for all first cases; (2) 20 hours for the second case to wait for the first one; and (3) 30 hours for the third case to wait for the first two. The total processing time for all three cases or applications is 35 hours or the sum of their separate processing times. If we add 50 hours' waiting time to 35 hours' processing time, we have 85 hours of total time across the three cases. This means an average of 28 hours per case in total time.

If the cases or applications are heard in the order of the shortest cases first (which is shown in row 6), there will be only 5 hours' waiting time for the second case and only 15 hours' waiting time for the third case. That is a total of 20 hours' waiting time to be added to 35 hours' processing time, which comes to an overall time of 55 hours. If we divide 55 by three cases, we have an average of 18 hours per case. That is a savings of 10 hours per case or more than one third by switching from first-come, first-served to shortest-cases-first in the docketing of these cases. Even bigger savings could be shown if the longest cases were relatively longer.

One might question whether such a system is fair and equitable. Table 8-2

Table 8-1
Sequencing Administrative Cases: The Time Criteria

CRITERIA / ALTERNATIVE SEQUENCES	(1) Waiting Time for 1st Case	(2) Waiting Time for 2nd Case	(3) Waiting Time for 3rd Case	(4) Total Processing Time	(5) Total Time (1+2+3+4)	(6) Average Total Time (5)/3
1) 20, 10, 5	0	20	30	35	85	28
2) 20, 5, 10	0	20	25	35	80	27
3) 10, 20, 5	0	10	30	35	75	25
4) 5, 20, 10	0	5	25	35	65	22
5) 10, 5, 20	0	10	15	35	60	20
6) 5, 10, 20	0	5	15	35	55	18
Totals	0	70	140	210	420	140
Averages/6	0	12	23	35	70	23

NOTES:

1. There are three cases. They are predicted to consume in hearing 20 hours, 10 hours, and 5 hours respectively. The problem is determining the optimum order in which to sequence the cases. There are six possible orders or sequence patterns for three cases, as shown in column 1. For the sake of simplicity the analysis assumes only one processor.

2. The waiting time for any case is the sum of the processing times of the cases ahead of it. The total processing time is always the sum of the separate processing times regardless of the order in which the cases are heard. The overall total time is the sum of the waiting times and the processing times.

3. Taking the shortest cases first minimizes the average total time. Taking the longest cases first maximizes the average total time.

4. One can compare the sequence which involves the shortest cases first with (1) the longest cases first, (2) the average sequence, or (3) any sequence that happens to involve first-come, first-served.

Table 8-2
Sequencing Administrative Cases: The Equity Criteria

CRITERIA / ALTERNATIVE SEQUENCES	(7) Sum of Gains	(8) Sum of Losses	(9) Net Gains	(10) Maximum Waiting Time	(11) Maximum Total Time
1) 20, 10, 5	0	0	0	30	35
2) 20, 5, 10	10	-5	5	25	35
3) 10, 20, 5	20	-10	10	30	35
4) 5, 20, 10	30	-10	20	25	35
5) 10, 5, 20	40	-15	25	15	35
6) 5, 10, 20	45	-15	30	15	35
Totals	145	-55	90	140	210
Averages/6	24	-9	15	23	35

NOTES:

1. Equity is generally considered a constraint that is either met or not met, unlike average total time, which is a variable goal to be minimized.
2. The utilitarian measure of equity is whether the greatest good for the greatest number has been promoted. That means whether the sum of the gains outweighs the sum of the losses. This test is not for all the improvements over taking the longest cases first, especially taking the shortest cases first.
3. The Pareto measure of equity is whether those who have losses could be compensated by those who have gains. That test is met here since the losers could be compensated for their losses, and the gainers would still come out ahead. This is especially so if one considers that the losers are the longer cases that are making extra use of tax-supported facilities.
4. The Rawlsian measure of equity is that no case should suffer more than a maximum waiting time. If the maximum waiting time is 60 hours, then that equity criterion is met. Notice that with alternative 6, not only is the average time per case substantially reduced, but also the maximum waiting time. This alternative thus gives both increased efficiency and increased equity.

provides information relevant to that question. It shows how much each case has gained or lost as a result of changing the docketing system. In row 6, for example, the sum of the gains from switching from alternative 1 to alternative 6 is 45 hours. Those 45 hours reflect the fact that the 5-hour case has gained 30 hours, and the 10-hour case has gained 15 hours. Row 6 also shows that the 20-hour case, by being pushed behind the first two cases, has lost 15 hours. The fact that there is a net gain of 30 hours shows that the system does satisfy the utilitarian criterion of fairness by promoting the greatest gain for the greatest number.

Also important in discussing the equity of optimum sequencing is the fact that the gainers could compensate the losers and still come out ahead. Thus, if 1 hour lost is worth 1 monetary unit, the two gainers could collectively give the one loser 15 monetary units and still be 30 monetary units ahead among themselves. That could be done through differential filing fees. It does, however, seem unnecessary, since the "loser" is really gaining by having control over a hearing for so much longer at the taxpayers' expense. More importantly, the system could specify that no case shall have to wait more than 30 or 60 hours. If a long case is approaching that figure, it would be moved to the front of the line. The cases would also be grouped for docketing every one or two weeks so the longest case in any time period would go ahead of the shortest case in the subsequent time period.

One might also note that all the alternative sequences are equal on (1) the cost of the administrative personnel; (2) allowing each set of applicants to have their applications processed; and (3) not reducing the processing time for any applicant. It has also been found meaningful to predict processing time from knowing the subject matter of the applications. Optimum sequencing is politically feasible since there are no elements of unconstitutionality or high expense, and since those who benefit from delay are not likely to be influential enough to block such a system. What is needed is more awareness, experimentation, and implementation.[1]

CASE SEQUENCING AND LAW FIRM EFFICIENCY

The purpose of this material is to describe how the methods of optimum sequencing can improve the efficiency and profits of law practice. Optimum sequencing refers to the order in which cases or other jobs are handled so as to maximize benefits minus costs or income minus expenses. Different arrangements of the cases or jobs can have different degrees of benefits, costs, and profitability.

Table 8-3 shows an example of optimum sequencing applied to law cases. The illustrative problem is: What is the best order in which to handle three cases that involve an estimated 10, 20, and 30 hours and that are predicted to generate $21, $61, and $80, respectively, in billing?

To make the problem more exciting, consider each billing as being mea-

Table 8-3

Law Firm Administration: Sequencing Cases (*Problem*: What is the best order to handle three cases that involve 10, 20, and 30 hours and that generate $21, $61, and $80, respectively, in billing?)

A. THE ALTERNATIVES: FIVE SEQUENCING METHODS

Alternative
1 HIGHEST B'S FIRST
2 LOWEST C'S FIRST
3 1ST COME, 1ST SERVED
4 HIGHEST B-C FIRST
5 HIGHEST B/C FIRST

B. THE CRITERIA: TWO WEEKS OF PROFIT

Criterion	Meas.Unit	Weight
1 1ST WEEK PROFIT	$	2.00
2 2ND WEEK PROFIT	$	1.00

C. THE PROFIT OBTAINED BY EACH ALTERNATIVE FOR EACH WEEK

ALTERNATIVE/CRITERIA SCORING

	1ST WEEK	2ND WEEK
HIGHEST B'S FIRST	70.50	31.50
LOWEST C'S FIRST	68.67	33.33
1ST COME, 1ST SERVED	68.67	33.33
HIGHEST B-C FIRST	70.50	31.50
HIGHEST B/C FIRST	74.33	27.67

D. THE OVERALL SCORE FOR EACH SEQUENCING METHOD

Alternative	Combined Raw Scores
1 HIGHEST B'S FIRST	172.50
2 LOWEST C'S FIRST	170.67
3 1ST COME, 1ST SERVED	170.67
4 HIGHEST B-C FIRST	172.50
5 HIGHEST B/C FIRST	176.33

NOTES:

1. The above computer printout shows that by taking the first three cases in the order of the highest benefit/cost ratio first, one thereby maximizes overall benefits minus costs.
2. This is so because the B/C order results in more profit being earned earlier, and that profit is thus more available to draw interest or to be reinvested more than if it is earned later.
3. In the above example profit from the first week is given twice the weight or importance of profit of the second week. An alternative approach would be to weight the weeks equally, but to time-discount the second week more than the first week.
4. The reasonable assumption is that the 60 hours of work involved in doing the first three cases means 40 hours in the first week and 20 hours in the second week. The assumption is also that there is billing every week, not just at the end of the cases, and that the bills are paid promptly.

sured in $1,000 units, although we will see that optimum sequencing works with any monetary units and any set of hypothetical or real cases. For the sake of simplicity, assume we have a one-lawyer firm, and the lawyer works a 40-hour week. With three cases, labeled A, B, and C, there are six ways in which they can be ordered: ABC, ACB, BAC, BCA, CAB, and CBA. Which is the best order?

The Alternatives and the Criteria

A more general way to view the problem is in terms of five different methods that are frequently proposed for ordering cases in a law firm, a government agency, or elsewhere. Those alternative methods, arranged randomly, are

1. To take the cases in order of the highest benefits first (CBA).
2. To look to the cases with the lowest costs first (ABC).
3. To take them first come, first served (ABC).
4. To prefer the most profitable first, meaning the ones with the highest benefits minus costs: C ($80–30), B ($61–20), and then A ($21–10).
5. To take them in the order of their benefit/cost (B/C) ratios: B ($61/20, or 3.05), C ($80/30, or 2.67), and then A ($21/10, or 2.10).

We want to pick the best ordering criterion in terms of maximizing the profits of the law firm, while operating within ethical constraints. At first glance, one might think that the order of the cases will make no difference in the profit that can be made from these three cases. The cases are going to consume a total of 60 hours regardless of the order in which they are handled. Likewise, the order will not affect the fact that they will collectively bring in $162 in billings. If we assume that one hour is worth $1 or one monetary unit, then their net profit will be $162 minus $60, or $102, regardless of the order in which they are processed.

At second glance, however, we realize that one method may bring in more money earlier than another method. The method that brings in the most money as early as possible is the most profitable because that early money can be invested in the firm or elsewhere, thereby drawing interest which might otherwise be a missed opportunity. Table 8-3B shows that the criterion for judging these methods should be how much profit they generate in the first week, the second week, and so on, with more weight given to the profit of the first week than to that of the second week.

How the Alternatives Compare

Table 8-3 shows for each method how profitable it is in terms of the separate weekly profits, rather than the overall profit, which is the same $102 for all the methods. The winning method is taking the cases in the order of their benefit/cost ratios. That method generates $74.33 in the first week, which is about $4 higher than its nearest competitor. If we assume that these numbers are $1,000 units, then by not taking the cases in their B/C order, the firm may be losing the interest that could have been made on $4,000 invested for one week. If that kind of loss is multiplied by 52 weeks and 30 cases rather than three cases, a lot of money may be needlessly lost.

The $74.33 is calculated by noting that case B has the highest B/C ratio and thus comes first. Case B takes 20 hours and generates a net profit of $41. We then go to case C, which has the second best B/C ratio. It takes 30 hours, but we have only 20 hours left in the week. We therefore do two thirds of the case and thus earn two thirds of the $50 profit, which is $33.33. If we add that to $41, the first week generates $74.33 in profit. The second week brings $27.67 in profit, or the remainder of the $102.

One can contrast that optimally profitable sequencing with any of the other less profitable methods. For example, if the cases are processed in terms of their individual profitability, we would take case C first, rather than case B. Doing so would consume 30 hours for a profit of $50. We would then have time for only 10 of 20 hours of case B, which is the next most profitable case. That would earn half the $41 profit, or $20.50. If we add $50 to $20.50, we get only $70.50, or $70,500, rather than $74.33, or $74,333.

To be more exact, we could time discount the profits of the second week using the time-discounting provisions of the P/G% program. That would give a more accurate overall score than giving the first week's profits a weight of 2. The time discounting, however, would not change the rank order of the best sequencing method.

Implications for Computers and Clients

A computer can aid in implementing the B/C sequencing method by questioning the relevant lawyers as the cases come in as to their estimates of the expenses and income for each case. The computer can then arrange the cases each week in the order of the B/C ratios and then display that order to aid the lawyers in deciding which case to take next. To prevent cases with a low B/C ratio from being unreasonably delayed, the computer can flag cases for immediate processing in time to meet the statute of limitations, other deadlines, or an ethical constraint that says that no case should have to wait more than a given time to reach a certain stage.

By following such procedures, the law firm administration not only will be maximizing the law firm's profits, but will also be maximizing the happiness of the clients collectively. This is so if we assume that $1 in billing activity generates the equivalent of one happiness unit. The B/C method thus generates more client happiness earlier than the alternative methods do. We can calculate the estimated total happiness units per week by adding 40 to the numbers given in the first column of Table 8-3C and adding 20 to the numbers in the second column. The B/C method thus generates 114.33 happiness units, a higher total than any of the other methods. It is pleasing when a law firm's administrative methods can maximize both the interests of the law firm and the interests of the clients.[2]

NOTES

1. For further details on this analysis, see S. Nagel, Mark Beeman, and John Reed, "Optimum Sequencing of Court Cases to Reduce Delay," *Alabama Law Review* (1986); and Richard Conway et al., *Theory of Scheduling* (Reading, Mass.: Addison-Wesley, 1967).

2. On computer-aided sequencing (CAS) of law firm cases and other jobs, see S. Nagel, "Sequencing and Allocating Attorney Time to Cases," 13 *Pepperdine Law Review* 1021–1039 (1986); and S. Nagel, Mark Beeman, and John Reed, "Optimum Sequencing of Court Cases to Reduce Delay," 37 *Alabama Law Review* 583–638 (1986). Also see the more general literature on efficient sequencing, such as Richard Conway et al., *Theory of Scheduling* (Reading, Mass.: Addison-Wesley, 1967). On allocating time per case regardless of the order of the cases, see S. Nagel, "Attorney Time Per Case: Finding an Optimum Level," 32 *University of Florida Law Review* 424–441 (1980). For general materials on computer-aided law decisions (CALD), see S. Nagel, *Using Personal Computers for Decision-Making in Law Practice* (Westport, Conn.: Greenwood-Quorum, 1986). An earlier version is available from the Committee on Continuing Professional Education of the American Law Institute and the American Bar Association.

9

SOS Evaluation

One of the most exciting waves of the future in human interaction is the movement that relates to alternative dispute resolution. That movement began with the rather mundane purpose of decreasing delay in resolving disputes. It has now shifted toward the more important purpose of resolving disputes in mutually beneficial ways, or even in ways in which all sides come out ahead of their best expectations.

To put the subject into a broader historical context, one might note that human beings have been having and resolving disputes since prehistoric times. The traditional method of resolving disputes (as with other primates and mammals) is for one side to dominate the other either by brute force or by verbal argument. A higher form of dispute resolution is to arrive at a compromise whereby there is a splitting of the difference between the two sides either with or without the aid of a neutral third party. Compromising is considered a more civilized form of human interaction, at least where it does not involve retreating from fundamental principles.

In recent times, there has been a growing literature advocating dispute resolution in which all sides come out ahead. Such solutions are associated with the concept of settlement through mediation or through win–win negotiation, as contrasted to the adversary determination of who is right and who is wrong. Win–win negotiation, however, may merely involve each side's coming out ahead of their worst expectations.

The concept of the super-optimum solution (SOS) goes beyond settlement mediation and win–win negotiation by emphasizing the possibility and desirability of each side in a dispute coming out ahead of their best expectations. That kind of dispute resolution partly stems from new philosophies that relate to supply-side economics, industrial policy, and other forms of expansionist thinking, rather than zero-sum or fixed-pie thinking.

The purpose of this chapter is to discuss the new, almost futuristic concept of achieving super-optimum solutions in public controversies. The discussion covers (1) the essence of super-optimum solutions; (2) examples from dispute resolution; (3) examples from policy-making; (4) contrasts with other types of solutions; (5) procedures for arriving at super-optimum solutions; (6) the helpfulness of decision-aiding software; (7) the generic super-optimum solution from a spreadsheet perspective; (8) classifying super-optimum solutions; and (9) streams of relevant ideas and literature.

In addition to discussing super-optimum solutions, this chapter also helps add to the bridge-building between futures research and policy studies. Futures research tends to emphasize describing what the future is likely to be. Policy studies emphasizes the development of public policies for achieving a desired future. Both futures research and policy studies are currently undergoing change in the direction of becoming more global geographically, more long-term in the time dimension, and more interdisciplinary or cross-cutting regarding traditional fields of knowledge.

THE ESSENCE OF SUPER-OPTIMUM SOLUTIONS

In general terms, a super-optimum solution is a solution to a decision-making problem that is considered objectively better than the previous best possible solution to that type of problem.

One type of super-optimum solution is a solution that achieves a super-optimum goal. A super-optimum goal is one that is far higher than has traditionally been considered the best attainable. An example would be doing better than 0% unemployment by simultaneously eliminating or reducing traditional unemployment and greatly increasing job opportunities for those who are willing and able to work more, but who were formerly regarded as being outside the labor force or as being fully employed.

A second type of super-optimum solution occurs in resolving public policy disputes. Such a solution provides a way of satisfying liberals and conservatives in a policy dispute so that both the liberals and the conservatives view the solution as better than their original best expectations for their own respective goals and priorities. The attached minimum-wage-policy dispute is an example.

A third type of solution occurs in resolving adjudicative or rule-applying controversies, rather than policy-making disputes. It is a solution that provides a way of satisfying the disputants that is better than their respective best expectations. An example is where a plaintiff demands $900,000, the defendant refuses to pay more than $300,000, and they agree that the defendant will turn over merchandise which the defendant manufactures that is worth more than $1 million to the plaintiff, but whose variable cost is worth less than $200,000 to the defendant.

A fourth type of solution enables all sides in a dispute to add substantially to their original net worth. An example would be in the same litigation, where the defendant agrees to give the plaintiff a franchise for selling the defendant's products and the franchise brings in a net of $1 million a year, with $500,000 a year for the plaintiff and $500,000 a year for the defendant. This type of expanded-sum solution would still be met if the total net worth of the participants substantially increased and even if the net worth of some of the participants slightly decreased, provided that decrease did not cause those participants to go below a minimum level of satisfaction.

Whatever solution is reached, it not only should be optimum in one or more of the above four ways but should also enable affected outsiders who are not parties to the dispute or the negotiations to come out ahead. That criterion excludes any agreement which greatly benefits the immediate parties, but at the substantial expense of others.

AN EXAMPLE FROM DISPUTE RESOLUTION

The Situation

A good example from the field of resolving litigation disputes is one in which the plaintiff demands $800 as a minimum to avoid going to trial or resorting to other nonsettlement action. The defendant insists that it will not part with more than $200. As long as the dispute remains in that single dimension, there is no way that both sides can come out ahead. Whatever the plaintiff gains, the defendant loses, and vice versa. A traditional compromise would involve splitting the difference and settling for $500, or else going to trial. The plaintiff might console herself or himself by saying that it could have been worse if liability were rejected at trial, since the plaintiff would then get $0. The defendant might console herself or himself by saying that it could have been worse if liability were established at trial, since the defendant might then wind up paying $800 or more. In reality, the plaintiff has lost $300 if she or he really thought that $800 was what she or he deserved to get, and the defendant has also lost $300 if she or he really thought that $200 was what she or he deserved to pay.

The Solution of Small Costs and Big Benefits

The same problem might be approached from a multicriteria perspective by adding one or more additional criteria to the plaintiff's goal of maximizing the money paid. The additional criteria could include products of the defendant. Those products might include insurance annuities, manufactured goods, or free transportation. Those criteria have in common that they cost relatively little per incremental unit for the defendant to produce if he or she is already in the business of producing them. However, they may have considerable value to the plaintiff in view of their market price, even with liberal discounts.

For example, in the case just mentioned, suppose the defendant manufactures electronic equipment, including television sets or other electronic equipment worth over $800 to the plaintiff. The same equipment might be worth less than $200 to the defendant, since the equipment has already been manufactured by the defendant. An exchange of a product is possible, maybe along with some cash to pay the plaintiff's attorney. This solution could result in the plaintiff's gaining more than $800 in terms of the plaintiff's values and in the defendant's losing less than $200 in terms of the defendant's values. That is a multicriterion dispute resolution in a litigation or rule-applying situation with mutually beneficial results. The best expectation of the plaintiff in the litigation example was probably to collect $800, since the plaintiff's initial demand tends to reflect an exaggeratedly high starting point. Likewise, the best expectation of the defendant was probably to have to pay only $200, since the defendant's initial offer tends to reflect an exaggeratedly low starting point. Solutions like these can be referred to as super-optimum solutions because they are above the optimum or best that each side was initially expecting to achieve. An example of this kind of case is summarized in Table 9-1.

EXAMPLES FROM POLICY-MAKING

The Outside Offer

The minimum wage dispute could be used as an example to arrive at a potential super-optimum solution. The liberals in Congress are arguing for a minimum wage of approximately $4.50 an hour. The conservatives are arguing for approximately $4.00 an hour. A traditional compromise would be $4.25 an hour. That might be greeted as a victory by liberals, since it is $0.90 more than the current $3.35. It might be greeted as a victory by conservatives since it is $.25 less than what the liberals are seeking.

A wage of $4.25 an hour, though, could be considered a loss for both sides. It is a loss to liberals if $4.50 an hour is necessary for minimum food, shelter, clothing, and other necessities for an average family of four. The $4.25 is a loss to conservatives if $4.00 an hour is the maximum that business firms can afford to pay to minimum wage employees and thus anything higher than $4.00 an hour will mean laying off workers who will then suffer a lack of minimum food, shelter, clothing, and other necessities.

A super-optimum solution might involve the minimum wage's being

Table 9-1
A Super-Optimum Solution to Settling versus Going to Trial

A. FROM THE PLAINTIFF'S PERSPECTIVE

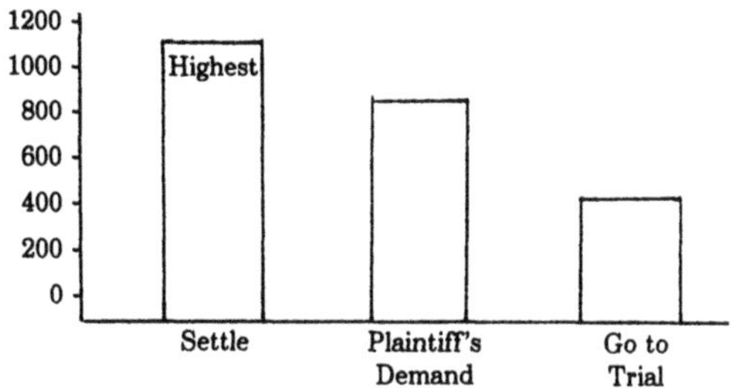

B. FROM THE DEFENDANT'S PERSPECTIVE

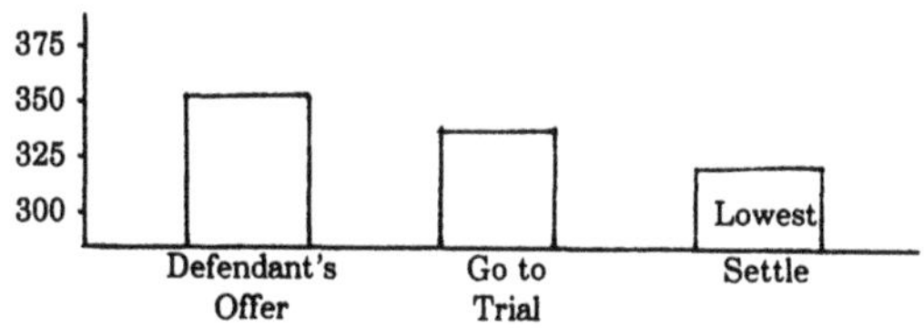

NOTES TO TABLE 9-1A

1. The expected value of settling from the plaintiff's perspective is $1,099,000, as described in the text (the first bar)

2. The middle bar shows that the plaintiff's first demand or best expectation was $700,000.

3. The expected value of going to trial from the plaintiff's perspective is only $290,000, as described in the text (the third bar)

NOTES TO TABLE 9-1B

1. The defendant's first offer or best expectation is $350,000 (the first bar).

2. The expected value of going to trial from the defendant's perspective is $330,000 (the second bar).

3. The expected value of settling from the defendant's perspective is only $326,000 (the third bar).

4. Note the settlement is lower and thus better than the defendant's best expectation from the defendant's perspective.

5. The $326,000 settlement could be substantially lower and still bring the plaintiff to a settlement in view of the big gap between the settlement value and the trial value from the plaintiff's perspective.

raised to $4.75 an hour in terms of what each worker would receive, but simultaneously requiring each employer to pay only $3.75 an hour. The $1.00 difference would be paid by the government for every minimum wage worker who would otherwise be unemployed either because the firm could not afford to hire the worker, or because the worker would not be sufficiently inspired to take the job at less than the increased minimum wage.

Under such an arrangement the liberals come out ahead of their initial bargaining position of $4.50 and probably ahead of their best expectations. Likewise, the conservatives come out ahead of their initial bargaining position of $4.00 and probably ahead of their best expectations.

The government and the taxpayers might especially come out ahead by virtue of (1) the money saved in terms of public aid, public housing, Medicaid, and unemployment compensation; (2) the decreased cost of antisocial behavior associated with people who are embittered by unemployment or who resort to criminal sources of income; (3) the increase in the gross national product (GNP) as a result of the products these people produce and the accompanying increase in the taxes they pay; and (4) the better role models they now provide for their children and grandchildren, who might otherwise be caught in a cycle of unemployment, public aid, criminal activity, and lack of productivity.

As an additional requirement for a business firm to be eligible to pay only $3.75 an hour, the firm would be expected to provide on-the-job training so the workers would become even more productive to the firm, the economy, and themselves. One salient point of this example is that by getting off the single track of the exchange of dollars between an employer and an employee, one can arrive not only at mutually beneficial solutions, but also at solutions that exceed the initial best expectations of both sides.

This example is summarized in Table 9-2. Table 9-2A shows the liberal, neutral, and conservative alternatives, as well as the super-optimum solution. Table 9-2B shows six criteria for judging among the alternatives, although, for the sake of simplicity, the emphasis in the subsequent analysis is on just the first two criteria. Table 9-2B also shows that liberals place a higher weight than conservatives on paying a decent wage. On the other hand, conservatives place a higher weight than liberals on avoiding overpayment. The other criteria are given middle weights on a 1–3 weighting scale for the criteria, where a 3 means relatively big importance, 2 means middling importance, and 1 means relatively low importance.

Table 9-2C shows how each alternative is scored on each criterion by means of a 1–5 scoring scale for the relations. A 5 means that the alternative is highly conducive to the goal, relatively speaking; a 4 means mildly conducive; a 3 means neither conducive nor adverse; a 2 means mildly adverse; and a 1 means highly adverse. Thus the liberal solution has at least a mildly conducive effect on paying a decent wage, but a rather neutral effect on avoiding overpayment. The conservative solution is rather neutral on paying a decent wage, but mildly conducive on avoiding overpayment.

Table 9-2D shows the total scores for the liberal, neutral, and conservative alternatives. The first total column involves the liberal weights or multipliers of a 3 for paying a decent wage and a 1 for avoiding overpayment. With those weights, the liberal alternative gets a total score of 15, which is 3×4 plus 1×3. The conservative alternative gets a total score of 13, which is 3×3 plus 1×4. The second total column involves the neutral weights of a middle 2 for each goal. With those weights, the liberal alternative gets a total score of 14, which is 2×4 plus 2×3. The third total column involves the conservative weights of a 1 for paying a decent wage and a 3 for avoiding overpayment. With those weights, the liberal alternative gets a relatively low score of 13, which is 1×4 plus 3×3.

Combining Alternatives into a Creative Synthesis

The kind of dispute resolution with which this chapter is especially concerned applies to disputes over public policies for dealing with various social problems. For example, in the controversy over how to provide legal services for the poor, liberals and Congress advocate salaried government lawyers by way of the Legal Services Corporation. Conservatives and the Reagan White House advocated a program of volunteer lawyers serving the poor. Both sides agreed that the key criteria for deciding among the alternative delivery systems are (1) inexpensiveness; (2) accessibility; (3) political feasibility; and (4) competence. There was also rough agreement that volunteers are better on inexpensiveness and political feasibility, whereas salaried government lawyers are better on accessibility and competence. The big dispute about the inputs for arriving at a conclusion was over the relative weights of the goals. The liberals placed a higher weight on accessibility and competence, whereas the conservatives placed a higher weight on inexpensiveness and political feasibility.

Perhaps the best way to resolve disputes over the relative weights of the goals (or, for that matter, over any disputed policy problem) is to try to find a new alternative that will please both sides in light of their differing weights, goals, perceptions, constraints, or other inputs. An example is working with the existing Legal Services Corporation, but requiring all legal services agencies to use 10% of their budgets to improve the accessibility and competence of volunteer lawyers. Accessibility can be improved by bringing the volunteer lawyers to the agency offices to meet with relevant clients. Competence can be improved through training manuals, training workshops, and matching specialist lawyers with clients who relate to their specialties. Such a 10% system may be better than a pure Legal Services Corporation, even for those with liberal weights, because it provides a better

Table 9-2
Minimum Wages as a Super-Optimum Solution Policy Example Involving a Third-Party Offer

2A. THE ALTERNATIVES

Alternative	
1 SOS WAGE SUPP.	($4.75) (To Workers)
2 +SUBSTANTIAL	($4.50) (Liberal)
3 COMPROMISE	($4.25) (Neutral)
4 +SLIGHT	($4.00) (Conservative)
5 SOS WAGE SUPP.	($3.75) (From Employers)

2B. THE CRITERIA

Criterion	Meas. Unit	Liberal Weights	Neutral Weights	Conserv. Weights
1 PAY DECENT WAGE	1-5 Scale	3.00	2.00	1.00
2 AVOID OVERPAYMENT		1.00	2.00	3.00
3 SAVE TAXES		2.00	2.00	2.00
4 EMPLOY UNEMPLOYED		2.00	2.00	2.00
5 ON-JOB TRAINING		2.00	2.00	2.00
6 +ROLE MODELS		2.00	2.00	2.00

2C. SCORES OF ALTERNATIVES ON CRITERIA

	Pay Decent	Avoid Over	Save Taxes	Employ Unemp	On-Job Train	+Role Model
+SUBSTANTIAL	4.00	3.00	3.00	2.00	2.00	2.00
COMPROMISE	3.50	3.50	3.00	2.50	2.50	2.50
+SLIGHT	3.00	4.00	3.00	3.00	3.00	3.00
SOS WAGE SUPP.	5.00	5.00	4.00	4.00	4.00	4.00

2D. INITIAL ANALYSES

Alternative	Liberal Combined Raw Scores	Neutral Combined Raw Scores	Conserv. Combined Raw Scores
1 +SUBSTANTIAL	15.00	14.00	13.00
2 COMPROMISE	14.00	14.00	14.00
3 +SLIGHT	13.00	14.00	15.00
4 SOS WAGE SUPP.	20.00	20.00	20.00

NOTES ON HOW THE WAGE SUPPLEMENT OPERATES:

1. The minimum wage gets raised to $4.75 per hour.
2. Employers need pay only $3.75 per hour for workers who were otherwise unemployed and who are provided with on-the-job training.
3. Those workers receive a wage supplement of $1 per hour from the government, bringing their total wage up to the $4.75 per hour new minimum wage.
4. The government provides the $1 per hour supplement to the employer to cover the minimum wage as an incentive to get the employer to hire an unemployed worker and to provide on-the-job training.

(*Continued*)

Table 9-2 (continued)

5. The government provides the $1 per hour supplement to the worker to cover the minimum wage as an incentive to get the worker to accept the job and to provide the worker with a decent wage to cover necessities.
6. The government provides the $1 per hour supplement which helps both the employer and the worker partly because
   (1) It relieves the taxpayer from various welfare burdens such as Medicaid, food stamps, unemployment compensation, public housing, aid to dependent children, social security, disability aid, etc.
   (2) It facilitates better role models thereby relieving the taxpayer of the welfare burdens of future generations.
   (3) The new employment lessens costly antisocial behavior and attitudes such as crime, drugs, vice, bitterness, and depression.
   (4) The employment adds to the gross national product, helps create jobs for others, and adds to the tax base.

NOTES ON THE GENERAL ANALYSIS:

1. The alternatives can be generalized into the four basic alternatives of liberal, neutral, conservative, and super-optimum alternatives. (Table -2A)
2. The dollar amounts of $4.75, $4.50, $4.25, $4.00, and $3.75 are approximations partly to facilitate easy arithmetic. They do, however, approximate the actual minimum wage amounts over which liberals and conservatives were arguing in Congress as of 1989. (Table -2A)
3. Liberals and conservatives both place a positive weight on paying a decent wage and avoiding overpayment. They differ, however, in the relative weights which they are likely to assign to those two key criteria. (Table -2B)
4. The alternatives are scored on the criteria using a 1-5 scale where 5 means highly conducive to the goal, 4 means mildly conducive, 3 means neither conducive nor adverse, 2 means mildly adverse, and 1 means highly adverse to the goal. (Table -2C)
5. Liberals and conservatives tend to be roughly in agreement on the scores relating the alternatives to the criteria even though they disagree on the relative importance of the key criteria. (Table 2C)
6. The combined raw scores are determined by adding the weighted relation scores together. For example, a substantial increase receives 15 points in the liberal total by adding (3 times 4) to (1 times 3). For the sake of simplicity in this introductory analysis, only the two key criteria are used of paying a decent wage and avoiding overpayment. (Table -2D)
7. The wage supplement comes out so far ahead of the second-place alternative on each of the three totals that the only way the second-place alternative could be a winner is (1) if one or more of the goals were to be given a negative weight, or (2) if one or more of the relation scores were to go above 5, below 1, or otherwise be unreasonable. (Table -2D)

benefit/cost ratio and greater political feasibility without decreasing accessibility or competence. Such a system is also better than the existing Legal Services Corporation from a perspective with conservative weights because it represents an improvement on all four goals over the existing system. Also, if volunteering becomes mandatory for license renewal, then the volunteers are likely to dominate the system.

The computer output for the legal service example is given in Table 9-3. The first part of the table shows how the two original alternatives and the new alternative score on the four criteria on a scale of 1–2, corresponding to "relatively no" and "relatively yes." The second part of the table shows the same data, but with the scores on inexpensiveness and political feasibility doubled to reflect conservative values. The third part shows the same data as

Table 9-3
An Example of Computer-Aided Mediation

	Inexpen-siveness	Accessibility	Political Feasibility	Competence
3A. WITH UNWEIGHTED CRITERIA				
Volunteer	2.00	1.00	2.00	1.00
Salaried	1.00	2.00	1.00	2.00
SOS	1.50	2.00	2.00	2.00
3B. WITH CONSERVATIVE VALUES				
Volunteer	4.00	1.00	4.00	1.00
Salaried	2.00	2.00	2.00	2.00
SOS	3.00	2.00	4.00	2.00
3C. WITH LIBERAL VALUES				
Volunteer	2.00	2.00	2.00	2.00
Salaried	1.00	4.00	1.00	4.00
SOS	1.50	4.00	2.00	4.00

NOTES:

1. The alternative ways of providing legal counsel to the poor include:
   (1) Volunteer attorneys, favored by the White House.
   (2) Salaried government attorneys, favored by the Congress.
   (3) A compromise that involves continuing the salaried system, but requiring that 10% of its funding go to making volunteers more accessible and competent (table rows).
2. The criteria are inexpensiveness, accessibility, political feasibility, and competence. Each alternative is scored on each criterion on a scale from 1.00 to 2.00 (table columns and cells).
3. Conservative values involve giving a weight of 2 to inexpensiveness and political feasibility when the other criteria receive a weight of 1. (Table -3B) Liberal values involve giving a weight of 2 to accessibility and competence when the other criteria receive a weight of 1. (Table -3C)
4. With conservative values, the volunteer system wins over the salaried system 10 points to 8. The compromise is an overall winner with 11 1/2 points. (Table -3B)
5. With liberal values, the salaried system wins over the volunteer system 10 points to 8. The compromise is an overall winner with 11 1/2 points. (Table -3C)
6. The "10% compromise" is thus a super winner in being better than the original best solution of both the conservatives and the liberals. (The third row in tables -3A, -3B, and -3C)

the first part, but with the scores doubled on accessibility and competence to reflect the liberal emphasis. The key is that the optimizing compromise scores better than the favored alternative of either side based on each side's own value system. Finding such optimizing compromises is facilitated by this kind of analysis.

CONTRASTED WITH OTHER TYPES OF SOLUTIONS

Disputes in adjudication or policy-making can take various forms. Perhaps the most basic form relates to the winning and losing dimension. In that regard, the solutions to disputes can be classified as follows:

1. Super-optimum solutions, in which all sides come out ahead of their initial best expectations, as described above. At the opposite extreme is a super-malimum solution, in which all sides come out worse than their initial worst expectations. That can be the case in a mutually destructive war, a labor strike, or a highly expensive litigation.
2. Pareto optimum solutions, in which nobody comes out worse off and at least one side comes out better off. That is not a very favorable solution compared to a super-optimum solution. A Pareto malimum solution would be one in which nobody is better off and at least one side is worse off.
3. A win–lose solution, in which what one side wins the other side loses. The net effect is zero when the losses are subtracted from the gains. This is the typical litigation dispute when one ignores the litigation costs.
4. A lose–lose solution, in which both sides are worse off than they were before the dispute began. This may often be the typical litigation dispute, or close to it, when one includes litigation costs. Those costs are often so high that the so-called winner is also a loser. That is also often the case in labor–management disputes that result in a strike, and even more so in international disputes that result in a war.
5. The so-called win–win solution. At first glance this sounds like a solution in which everybody comes out ahead. What it typically refers to, though, is an illusion, since the parties are coming out ahead only relative to their worst expectations. In this sense, the plaintiff is a winner no matter what the settlement is because the plaintiff could have won nothing if liability had been rejected at trial. Likewise, the defendant is a winner no matter what the settlement is because the defendant could have lost everything the plaintiff was asking for if liability had been established at trial. The parties are only fooling themselves, in the same sense that someone who is obviously a loser believes she or he won because she or he could have done worse.

Another common way of classifying dispute resolutions is in terms of whether there is a third party present. In that sense, adjudication, arbitration, and mediation are frequently referred to as forms of three-party dispute resolution, and negotiation refers to two-party dispute resolution. Adjudication tends to mean a court or an administrative agency that resolves disputes, usually in a win–lose way. Arbitration tends to involve an ad hoc third party who is hired or obtained just for the immediate dispute, but who also tends to operate from a win–lose perspective. A mediator, like an arbitrator, tends to be ad hoc but seeks to have the sides arrive at a mutually beneficial settlement which could be win–win, Pareto optimum, or even super-optimum, but not win–lose, or lose–lose. That distinction between three-party and two-party dispute resolutions may be undesirable because it encourages two-party negotiation to go for a win–lose solution. When two negotiators are present, it is possible for one or both of them to have a mediation perspective in the sense of truly seeking to bring about a super-optimum or Pareto optimum solution.

Another way of classifying dispute resolutions or policy solutions is in terms of the substance or subject matter, including such categories as disputes involving family members, neighbors, merchant–consumer situations, management–labor situations, litigation or rule-applying, legislation or rule-making, and international disputes. Those categories are meaningful in the sense that it is possible to tell a family dispute from an international dispute. Emphasizing those distinctions, however, may be undesirable because the same underlying principles may apply regardless of the subject matter. Those principles include (1) the desirability of getting off a single dimension into multiple criteria; (2) the desirability of generally seeking super-optimum solutions in which all sides, including society, come out ahead of their best expectations; and (3) the usefulness of decision-aiding software for dealing with multicriteria dispute resolution toward achieving super-optimum solutions.

Still another way of classifying solutions to policy controversies is in terms of the directions in which benefits and costs move. In a super-optimum solution, the benefits go up, and the costs go down. In a traditional solution, the benefits may go up, but at the expense of increased costs; or the costs may go down, but at the expense of decreased benefits. In a super-malimum solution, which is the opposite of a super-optimum solution, the benefits go down and the costs go up. Drug crackdowns can have that effect by being highly expensive, and yet encouraging more suppliers to enter the market by raising the sales price of drugs.

PROCEDURES FOR ARRIVING AT SUPER-OPTIMUM SOLUTIONS

New Alternatives

One procedure for arriving at a super-optimum solution is to think in terms of what is in the conservative alternative that liberals might like and, likewise, what is in the liberal alternative that conservatives might like, and then to think whether it is possible to make a new alternative that will emphasize those two aspects.

Another technique is to emphasize the opposite. It involves saying what is in a conservative alternative that liberals especially dislike and what is in the liberal alternative that conservatives especially dislike, and then to think about making a new alternative that eliminates those two aspects.

In arriving at super-optimum solutions in litigation settlements, one should especially try to find something that the defendant can give to the plaintiff that is not worth very much to the defendant but is worth a lot to the plaintiff. This may be a product that the defendant manufactures or sells which has a low variable cost to the defendant but a high market value to the plaintiff. An example is the defendant insurance company giving a valuable annuity to the plaintiff. Another example is the defendant manufacturer giving manufactured products to the plaintiff which the plaintiff can use. That kind of trade can be generalized to policy-making situations as well as litigation situations.

New Goals

Another technique is not to concentrate on the alternatives, as the above procedures do, but instead to concentrate on the goals. One approach is to ask what goals are especially important to liberals, and what goals are especially important to conservatives. Then try to find alternatives that can simultaneously satisfy both of those goals. This technique is illustrated by the minimum wage example, in which the goals do not change at all. Conservatives endorse the goal of low wages, and liberals endorse the goal of high wages. Or to put it differently, conservatives endorse the goal of providing a stimulating environment for business, and liberals endorse the goal of preventing the abuse of workers. The minimum wage supplement allows a business to pay as little as $4.00 per hour while the worker receives $4.50 per hour as a result of the voucher supplement.

A variation is to add new goals. The usual procedure starts with the conservative goals as givens in light of how they justify their current best alternative, and it starts with the liberal goals as givens in light of how they justify their current best alternative. This technique advocates thinking about the goals that conservatives tend to endorse that are not currently involved in the controversy, but that could be brought in to justify a new alternative. Likewise, what goals do liberals tend to endorse that are not currently involved in the controversy, but that could also be brought in? For this technique, a good example is the free speech controversy, in which liberals want virtually unrestricted free speech in order to stimulate creativity, and conservatives want restrictions on free speech in order to have more order in the legal system. However, liberals also like due process, equal protection, and the right to privacy. That raises questions about whether it might be permissible to restrict free speech in order to satisfy those constitutional rights, where the restrictions are not so great, but the jeopardy of those other rights might be great. Likewise, conservatives like policies that are good for business. They might therefore readily endorse permissive free speech that relates to advertising, that tries to convince workers that they should not join unions, or that relates to lobbying.

Combining Alternatives

An important technique is to find a policy that, in effect, combines two policies into one. On the first policy, liberals receive a lot, and conservatives give up relatively little. On the second policy, conservatives receive a lot, and liberals give up relatively little.

Bringing in a Third Party

In the minimum wage example, conservatives get more than they want, and liberals also get more than they want. The important thing is that conservatives do not get by taking it from liberals, and liberals do not get by taking from conservatives. Instead, at least on the surface, they are both taking from a third party. In this context, the third party, in the short run, is the federal government and the American taxpayer. In the long run, though, the taxpayer benefits if subsidizing the minimum wage results in putting to work people who otherwise would be receiving public aid or would be engaging in antisocial behavior. The taxpayer especially benefits if, combined with that minimum wage, there is an on-the-job training requirement that upgrades the skills of the workers so they substantially add to national productivity.

Getting the Solution Adopted

One problem with super-optimum solutions is that they look so good that they may cause some people to think they might be some kind of a trap. An example is the Camp David Accords. That example is a classic super-optimum solution where Israel, Egypt, the United States, and everybody involved came out ahead of their original best expectations. According to the *New York Times* of March 26, 1989, however, Israeli intelligence, at least at first, opposed Anwar Sadat's visit to Israel and the Camp David Accords until close to the signing on the grounds that it all sounded so good that it must be a trap. The Israeli intelligence felt that Israel was being set up for a variation on the Yom Kippur War, when Israel got into trouble by relaxing its guard because of the holidays. They viewed the peace overtures as an attempt to get them to relax their guard again and predicted that any minute the attack would begin. They were on a more intense alert at the time of the Camp David negotiations than they had been at any other time during Israel's history. That example nicely illustrates how easily super-optimum solutions can be viewed by people as a trap because they look so good that they are unbelievable. Traditional solutions are not so likely to be viewed as traps, and they are taken more at their face value, which is generally not much.

THE HELPFULNESS OF DECISION-AIDING SOFTWARE

Super-optimum solutions are facilitated not only by multicriteria thinking, but also by decision-aiding software that is based on multicriteria spreadsheets. A spreadsheet is nothing more than a table, matrix, or chart that has rows, columns, and cells which can be manipulated in various ways.

The goals of each side are put in the columns. The alternatives available to them are put in the rows. The cells show how each alternative scores on each goal. A column at the far right shows the total scores for each alternative, when added across to take into consideration that the goals may be measured in different ways. The whole system is subjected to what-if analysis, which can be especially useful for dealing with missing information.

Each side has its own spreadsheet perspective on the dispute that needs to be resolved. A super-optimum solution has been achieved if settling becomes the most desired alternative on each of those spreadsheets, and if such settling results in more net benefit to each side than each side's original favored alternative.

THE GENERIC SUPER-OPTIMUM SOLUTION FROM A SPREADSHEET PERSPECTIVE

From the examples that have been given thus far (especially Tables 9-1, 9-2, and 9-3), we can talk about the generic super-optimum solution from a spreadsheet perspective. Table 9-4 is designed to achieve that purpose. Using general language, it shows the alternatives, the criteria, the scores of the alternatives on the criteria, and the initial analyses. The alternatives are referred to as the conservative, compromise, liberal, or super-optimum alternatives. The criteria are referred to as the conservative, liberal, or neutral goals.

Each goal has a conservative weight and a liberal weight, since the conservatives and liberals differ especially in terms of the relative weights they assign to goals. The scores are expressed on a 1–5 scale to bring out the relations more clearly. The initial analysis shows how well each alternative scores overall in terms of the conservative weights and then in terms of the liberal weights.

Among the three basic alternatives, the conservative alternative, as expected, is the winner when the conservative weights are used. The liberal alternative is then the loser, with the compromise in-between. The opposite is true when the liberal weights are used. The super-optimum solution does better than any of the three basic alternatives when the conservative weights are used. It also does better than any of the three alternatives when the liberal weights are used. That is the essence of a super-optimum solution.

Table 9-4
The Generic Super-Optimum Solution from a Spreadsheet Perspective

A. THE ALTERNATIVES

Alternatives
1 CONSERVATIVE ALT.
2 COMPROMISE
3 LIBERAL ALT.
4 SOS1 (Dominating SOS)
5 SOS2 (Non-Dominating SOS)
6 SOS3 (New-Goal SOS)

B. THE CRITERIA

Criterion	Meas. Unit	Conserv. Weights	Liberal Weights
1*CONSERVATIVE GOAL	1-5 Scale	3.00	1.00
2*LIBERAL GOAL		1.00	3.00
3 NEUTRAL GOAL		2.00	2.00

C. SCORES OF ALTERNATIVES ON CRITERIA

	CONS.GOAL	LIB.GOAL	NEUT.GOAL
CONSERVATIVE ALT.	5.00	1.00	3.00
COMPROMISE	3.10	3.10	3.00
LIBERAL ALT.	1.00	5.00	3.00
SOS1	5.10	5.10	3.10
SOS2	4.50	4.50	2.90
SOS3	4.00	4.00	4.00

D. INITIAL ANALYSES

Alternative	Conserv. Combined Rawscores	Liberal Combined Rawscores
1 CONSERVATIVE ALT.	16.00	8.00
2 COMPROMISE	12.40	12.40
3 LIBERAL ALT.	8.00	16.00
4 SOS1	20.40	20.40
5 SOS2	18.00	18.00
6 SOS3	16.00	16.00

NOTES TO THE ALTERNATIVES:

1. The conservative alternative is shown first because it tends to be the current alternative on which we would like to improve. The conservative alternative or set of alternatives in a policy problem tends to differ from the liberal alternatives in the relative extent to which it favors those who are relatively well off in a society, whereas the liberal alternative tends to favor those who are not so relatively well off.

2. The first super-optimum solution (and the most difficult to achieve) is to find an alternative that is better than the conservative, liberal, and compromise alternatives on all the goals. The second super-optimum solution is an alternative that is not better on all the goals than the other alternatives, but it is better on the overall

(*Continued*)

Table 9-4 (continued)

or combined score adding across the goals. The third super-optimum solution is not better on all the goals and is not better on the overall score with the initial goals, but it is better on the overall score than the non-SOS alternatives when another goal is added.

NOTES TO THE CRITERIA:

3. The conservative goal or goals in this context are by definition goals that conservatives disproportionately favor, as indicated by the fact that those goals are given relatively high weight by conservatives. The liberal goals are likewise given relatively high weight by liberals. Note however that in a typical policy problem, conservatives tend to give positive weight to liberal goals (although relatively less weight than to conservative goals), and vice versa with liberals.

4. The scores of the alternatives on the criteria are based on a 1-5 scale for the sake of simplicity, although that does not have to be. Under a 1-5 scale, 5 means highly conducive to the goal, 4 means mildly conducive, 3 means neither conducive nor adverse, 2 means mildly adverse, and 1 means the alternative is highly adverse to the goal.

NOTES TO THE RELATION SCORES:

5. The conservative alternatives logically score high on the conservative goals and low on the liberal goals, and vice versa for the liberal alternatives. The compromise alternative scores slightly above the middle on each goal. That avoids ties in this analysis, and that is the general nature of compromises.

6. The scores of the super-optimum solutions on the conservative, liberal, and neutral goals are consistent with their definitions. Likewise the scores of the alternatives on the neutral goal are consistent with the definition of the neutral goal as being between the conservative goal and the liberal goal in its normative direction.

NOTES TO THE INITIAL ANALYSES:

7. The combined raw scores are determined by adding the weighted relation scores together. For example, the conservative alternative receives 16 points using the conservative weights by adding (3 times 5) to (1 times 1). Using the liberal weights, the conservative alternative receives only 8 points by adding (1 times 5) to (3 times 1). For the sake of simplicity in this generic analysis, only the conservative goal and the liberal goal are used. The neutral goal has to be activated to enable the "New Goal SOS" to be a super-optimum solution.

8. Using the conservative weights, the conservative alternative logically comes out ahead of the liberal alternative, and vice versa using the liberal weights. The compromise alternative is the winner among those three alternatives with an aggregate score of 24.80 versus 24.00 for either the conservative or the liberal alternative, but the compromise alternative is only the second choice of both groups.

9. The three super-optimum alternatives all do better than the traditional compromise. What is more important, the three super-optimum alternatives all simultaneously do better than the conservative alternative using the conservative weights and they do better than the liberal alternative using the liberal weights. That is the essential characteristics of a super-optimum alternative. It is the new first choice of both groups.

10. Even the worst of the three super-optimum solutions comes out so far ahead of the traditional compromise that the only way the traditional compromise could be a winner is (1) if one or more of the goals were to be given a negative weight, or (2) if one or more of the relation scores were to go above 5, below 1, or otherwise be unreasonable.

Three different types of super-optimum solutions are presented, but they all have that essential characteristic of being simultaneously better than the conservative first choice in light of the conservative goals and better than the liberal first choice in light of the liberal goals. Further details are given in the notes to the table corresponding to the sections of the table dealing with the alternatives, the criteria, the relation scores, and the initial analyses.

CLASSIFYING SUPER-OPTIMUM SOLUTIONS

Dimensions for classifying super-optimum solutions are

1. Whether or not super-optimum goals are involved.
2. Whether we are talking about dispute resolution or policy-making.
3. Whether we are talking about all sides coming out ahead of their best expectations, or coming out ahead in a more absolute sense.
4. A typology that emphasizes the ways of arriving at super-optimum solutions, including:
   a. An alternative that involves small costs to one side and big benefits to the other.
   b. The outside offer.
   c. The combination alternative that does well on everybody's goals.
   d. A package of items that does not simply involve combining the liberal and conservative alternatives into a new synthesis. An example would be the Vera system for dealing with pretrial release so as to simultaneously increase the probability of released defendants' showing up without committing crimes (in order to please conservatives) while increasing the percentages of defendants who are released before trial (in order to please liberals). The Vera package of items includes screening for good risks, having released defendants report to the courthouse periodically before trial, notification immediately before trial, prosecution of no-shows, and reduction of delay between arrest and trial.
   e. A super-optimum solution which involves removing the problem rather than trying to synthesize the liberal and conservative solutions. An example would be better birth control to deal with the abortion problem.
5. Whether or not a third party is present as a mediator, arbitrator, or adjudicator.
6. Classification of the situation by its substance or subject matter.
7. Whether or not decision-aiding software is present.
8. Ways of arriving at super-optimum solutions in terms of concentrating on the alternatives, the goals, or a better subclassification might be:
   a. Developing a new alternative that is not a combination of the old alternatives.
   b. Developing a new alternative that is a combination of the old alternatives.
   c. Bringing in a new goal which enables an old or new alternative to become super-optimum, which it would not be without the new goal.
9. Classifying the super-optimum solutions in terms of:
   a. Whether the solution is better than or at least as good as the original alternatives on all goals. This is a solution that is dominating.
   b. Whether the solution is better than all the original alternatives on the summation score but not necessarily on every criterion. This is the nondominating super-optimum solution.
   c. The nondominating super-optimum solution that requires an additional goal to receive the highest summation score.

MUTUALLY BENEFICIAL TRENDS

Table 9-5 summarizes some of the trends in specific policy fields. The overall idea is that there have been increased benefits for people who had few rights as of the base years of 1910, 1930, or 1950. These people have been the immediate beneficiaries of the policy changes. It is, however, unduly narrow to limit the analysis to those immediate effects. The longer term and broader effects have also been to benefit the dominant groups and the total society. This is shown, for example, in the top row. Labor has benefited from better wages, shorter hours, better working conditions, the ending of child labor, and the lessening of race and sex discrimination. Also highly important is the stimulus that those labor policies have had on encouraging the development and adoption of labor-saving technology. As of 1980, the United States might still have been using slave labor or cheap immigrant labor and have been a backward, low-technology country if it had not been for the successful efforts of labor unions and working-class people to increase the cost of their labor. A third-level result is that the labor-saving technology has made labor more productive and more skilled. This has had the effect of increasing wages still further, thereby stimulating greater consumption and the creation of new jobs, especially in service fields.

Likewise, one can go through each of the 11 policy fields and see that the initial policy changes have tended in a direction of increasing the rights of the have-nots. Those increases have in turn stimulated benefits for the total society, regardless of whether one is talking about consumer rights, free speech, criminal justice, equal treatment, government reform, world peace and trade, poverty, education, the environment, or health.

STREAMS OF RELEVANT IDEAS AND LITERATURE

A number of relevant ideas and much literature have played an important part in the development of the concept of achieving super-optimum solutions. One stream of ideas relates to the use of computers to facilitate systematic, evaluative, and explanatory reasoning.[1] The second stream of inspiration has come from people in the field of mediation and alternative dispute resolution.[2]

The third stream of inspiration has come from people who are expansionist thinkers. These include the conservative economist Arthur Laffer and the liberal economist Robert Reich. They have in common a belief that policy problems can be resolved by expanding the total pie of resources or other things of value available to be distributed to disputants. The expansion can come from well-placed subsidies and tax breaks with strings attached to increase national productivity. That kind of thinking can be applied to disputes involving blacks and whites, rich and poor, males and

Table 9-5
Some Trends in Specific Policy Fields

POLICY FIELDS	BENEFITS FOR THE HAVE NOTS	BENEFITS FOR THE HAVES OR ALL
ECONOMIC POLICY		
Labor	Better wages, hours, working conditions. No child labor. Less discrimination.	Stimulus to labor-saving technology. Happier and more productive workers.
Consumer	More rights concerning product liability.	Stimulus to providing better products & greater sales.
POLITICAL-LEGAL POLICY		
Free Speech	More rights in politics, art, and commerce	Stimulus to creativity.
Due process & criminal justice	More rights to counsel, notice, hearings.	More respect for the law.
Equal treatment	More rights to blacks, women, & the poor on voting, criminal justice, schools, employment, housing, & consumer.	More equality of opportunity and allocation on the basis of merit.
Government reform	Less corruption, intimidation, & incompetence.	More effectiveness & efficiency.
World peace & trade	Increased standards of living for developing countries.	Uplifted countries become good trading partners.
SOCIAL POLICY		
Poverty	More rights as employees, consumers, tenants, welfare recipients, & family members.	The same rights apply to middle-class employees, consumers, tenants, & family members.
Education	More access to more education.	More efficient economy from better training. Less welfare.
SCIENCE POLICY		
Environment	More rights to cleaner air, water, solid waste, noise, radiation, and conservation.	The same rights are important to all people.
Health	More access to medical help.	That includes catastrophic help from which even the rich benefit.

females, North and South, urban and rural, and other categories of societal disputants.[3]

In addition to decision-aiding software with an MCDM spreadsheet base, win–win dispute resolution, and expansionist growth economics, one might also find origins of SOS thinking in the dialectic analysis of Hegel and Marx. The essence of the dialectic is that progress or change tends to proceed from a status quo thesis, to a conflicting antithesis, and then toward a higher level synthesis. For Marx, the main thesis was the existing capitalism, which emphasized private ownership and distribution in accordance with supply, demand, and inheritance. The antithesis was a form of socialism that emphasized government ownership and distribution in accordance with one's contribution. The synthesis was a form of ideal communism that emphasized a withering away of the state and distribution in accordance with need. The implicit and sometimes explicit goals were greater national productivity and fairness in providing opportunities regardless of class, ethnic group, or other nonmerit considerations.

There is some question about whether Marx's ideal communism would be highly productive in comparison with a state that provides well-placed subsidies and tax breaks. There is also some question about whether Marx's ideal communism would be equitable in allocating in proportion to need rather than allocating to encourage socially desired behavior, with a minimum constraint that considers need. The important point regarding the predecessors of super-optimum analysis is that the dialectical materialism of Karl Marx was partly meant to achieve a synthesis that would enable advocates of capitalism and socialism both to come out ahead of their best initial expectations. It was largely SOS thinking in purpose, although not necessarily in effect.[4]

NOTES

1. Some of the key literature about the use of computers in the area of reasoning includes Patrick Humphreys and Ayleen Wisudha, *Methods and Tools for Structuring and Analyzing Decision Problems* (London: London School of Economics and Political Science, 1987); Saul Gass et al. (eds.), *Impacts of Microcomputers on Operatings Research* (Amsterdam: North-Holland, 1986); and S. Nagel, *Evaluation Analysis with Microcomputers* (Greenwich, Conn.: JAI Press, 1989).

2. Some of the key literature in the field of mediation and dispute resolution includes Lawrence Susskind and Jeffrey Cruikshank, *Breaking the Impasse: Consensual Approaches to Resolving Disputes* (New York: Basic Books, 1987); Stephen Goldberg, Eric Green, and Frank Sander (eds.), *Dispute Resolution* (Boston: Little, Brown, 1984); and S. Nagel and M. Mills, "Microcomputers, P/G%, and Dispute Resolution," 2 *Ohio State Journal on Dispute Resolution* 187–223 (1987).

3. Some of the key expansionist literature includes Ira Magaziner and Robert Reich, *Minding America's Business: The Decline and Rise of the American Economy* (New York: Harcourt, Brace, 1982); and Paul Roberts, *The Supply Side Revolution* (Cambridge: Harvard University Press, 1984).

4. For further details on SOS evaluation, see such books by S. Nagel as *Policy Analysis Methods and Super-Optimum Solutions* (Ann Arbor: University of Michigan Press, 1991); *Public Policy Substance and Super-Optimum Solutions* (Ann Arbor: University of Michigan Press, 1992); and *Legal Process Controversies and Super-Optimum Solutions* (New York: Quorum Books, 1992). For the use of SOS analysis by a variety of other people, see *Super-Optimum Solutions* (symposium issue of *Public Budget and Financial Management,* 1991); and *Applications of Super-Optimizing Analysis* (Westport, Conn.: Greenwood, 1992).

PART II

Explanatory or Predictive Reasoning

10

Explaining Public Policy-Making

A fundamental distinction in public policy analysis is the distinction between policy formation and policy implementation, or the distinction between policy causes and policy effects. That distinction is relevant to the concept of policy failure and policy success. Policies can thus be failures in the sense of never being adopted, or in the sense of being adopted but having unsatisfactory effects. The failure to get a policy adopted is a subject of particular relevance to political science, since adoption failure is almost always due to a lack of interest group support, whereas the opposition to the policy being considered is strong. Studying the interaction of interest groups is an important part of the mainstream of political science. Such study may be helpful in developing policies that are more likely to be adopted. Numerous examples can be given of highly praised policies that were adoption failures because of interest group opposition, such as tariff removal in the 1930s, free-market farm pricing in the 1950s, and pollution taxes in the 1970s.

There are a variety of ways of classifying postadoption policy failures. One dimension is the subjective intent of the decision-makers versus the objective reality. In terms of *intent*, a policy is a success if it achieves its goals, and a failure if it does not. In terms of *reality*, a policy is a success if its benefits minus its costs are maximized, or are at least positive, regardless of whether the benefits or costs were intended. A second dimension is quantity and quality. A policy is a *quantitative* failure if its achievement units fall below an intended or objective standard, even though there is some net achievement. A policy is a *qualitative* failure if it produces more undesirable than desirable results, as measured either by the intentions of the decision-makers or by the objective effects, regardless of intent. Since each of these two dimensions involves two categories, one could combine the two pairs of categories into a four-cell table to yield four types of policy failures.

A good set of categories, however, is one that suggests meaningful ways of reducing policy failure. The above categories may lack that characteristic. Showing too much concern about the intent of decision-makers may, for example, lead one to suggest reducing policy failure by lowering one's goals, which is analogous to reducing crime by legalizing all activities that were formerly classified as criminal. Postadoption failure might be more usefully classified in terms of policies that prohibit or legitimize certain activities and policies that involve allocating resources or effort. Prohibition or legitimation policies can relate to criminal activities, negligent behavior, breach of contract, economic regulation, transferring property, unconstitutional administrative practices, or other activities in which legal policies specify what is right and what is wrong. In that context, postadoption failure is measured by noncomplying behavior, behavior that does the wrong thing in spite of the prohibition or nonlegal recognition. Compliance is likely to be facilitated when (1) the legal policies are clearly specified and represent a minimum deviation from custom; (2) the policy-makers are highly regarded and maintain a unity of support for the legal policies; (3) the policy-appliers have the time, financial resources, expertise, positive incentives, and negative sanctions to administer the policies; (4) the policy recipients have attitudes and backgrounds that favorably dispose them toward the policies; and (5) environmental conditions are conducive to compliance, including the communications media, the education facilities, and the business conditions.

The opposite kinds of policies on the prohibition–allocation dimension are ones that involve decisions to generate various inputs in order to achieve various outputs. These policies include allocating resources to places or activities, deciding the degree of enforcement for given policies, or deciding how much due process to provide in order to protect the innocent from being treated as if they were guilty while apprehending and negatively sanctioning the guilty. At least in theory, such policies lend themselves to arriving at an optimum allocation of resources in which the nonlinear marginal rates of return are equalized across places or activities, or to arriving at an optimum level at which the marginal benefits equal the marginal costs. In practice, it is often quite difficult to use the methods of operations research or related fields to arrive at those optimum figures because of the difficulty of measuring the benefits and costs, and of relating them to varying inputs. To the extent that one can at least roughly arrive at a notion of a policy optimum, one can measure failure of a policy as the difference between the optimum and the actual. Thus, if the optimum allocation of a budget to a given anticrime activity is $1,000 and the actual allocation is $800, the anticrime allocation is $200 off what it should be. If the $1,000 allocation would produce 50 crimes and the $800 allocation would produce 60 crimes, the anticrime allocation is suffering an opportunity cost of 10 crimes. Perhaps one should generally measure policy failure in terms of the degree of noncompliance, the deviation of the actual from the optimum, and opportunity costs, rather than in terms of the dichotomy of failure and success.

The deviation of the actual from the optimum can generally be explained in two ways. The researcher may be wrongly attributing values or intended goals to the decision-makers, or the decision-makers may be misperceiving the relations between their decisions and their goals. For example, if the optimum percentage of defendants to hold in jail before trial is 4%, and the actual percentage is 27%, the deviation may be explained by the fact that the optimum was arrived at by using societal costs such as the costs of incarceration and lost gross national product. The actual decision-makers do not bear those holding costs, but they may be quite sensitive to the personal embarrassment of releasing a defendant who fails to appear in court or who commits a crime while released. The problem in these common circumstances is how to internalize the external costs that the decision-makers generate. Doing so may involve trying to generate some offsetting embarrassment by publicizing the holding costs that the high holders incur without a commensurate improvement over the lower bail costs in getting defendants to appear. "High holders" in this context refers to judges who set bail on arrested defendants in such a way that a substantially above-average percentage of the defendants are held in jail pending trial, rather than are released on bail.

The alternative or supplementary explanation is that the decision-makers do have the goals that the researchers attribute to them, but the decision-makers in this context do not have the facts regarding how their behavior relates to their goals. More specifically, the legal policy-makers may lack information on the high percentage of released defendants who appear in court without committing crimes while released, and they may lack the information to predict more accurately the probability that various defendants will appear. There are numerous policy situations in which policy-makers could have their degree of failure decreased or their degree of success increased by having additional social science information. When one talks in terms of the deviation of the actual from the optimum, one can readily see that social science and policy analysis can play a useful role in attempting to determine the optimum, and how the actual can be moved closer to the optimum.

11

Explaining Individual Decision-Making

The purpose of this chapter is mainly to discuss how one can determine the motives, goals, or values of past decision-makers by knowing what decisions they have reached and their perceptions of the relevant facts. One may also be able to deduce their perceptions from their decisions and goals.

The chapter is divided into three parts. The first part deals with the decision-making of Chief Justice John Marshall in deciding the case of *Marbury v. Madison*. That case established the principle that U.S. courts could declare unconstitutional the acts of legislatures or administrators. The second part deals with the decision-making of President Franklin Roosevelt in deciding to go ahead with the development of the atomic bomb. The *Marbury* case involves deducing goals from decisions on specific issues and from likely perceptions. The atomic bomb case involves deducing the goals and the process by which the decision was reached even though the benefits, the probability of success, and the costs were highly unclear.

The third part of the chapter deals with general principles suggested partly by the examples of the first two parts. Those general principles lead to a conclusion that it is possible to deduce decision-makers' values and perceptions from past decisions. One must, however, be alert to the possibility of alternative motives and perceptions, which might also be consistent with the decisions reached and other aspects of the decision-making situation.

This chapter has important theoretical significance. It deals with the deduction of values and perceptions from past decisions, regardless of the subject matter or the source of the decisions. The analysis applies equally well to decisions that are legislative, executive, judicial, administrative, or voting and is relevant to all fields of political science, including decision-making at the international, national, regional, state, or local level on any subject matter.

APPLYING A SPREADSHEET PERSPECTIVE TO DEDUCING MOTIVES

One of the most useful innovations associated with the advent of microcomputers is the development of spreadsheet analysis, especially by the use of Lotus 1-2-3. A spreadsheet is simply a table with columns and rows. Lotus 1-2-3 is brand name software which enables one to easily enter data into a spreadsheet table and manipulate the data. The manipulation can produce a variety of insights into what might happen to the conclusions if some of the input data were changed.

One especially useful purpose of the spreadsheet analysis is to aid in making decisions. In that regard, a spreadsheet can be used to process a set of (1) goals to be achieved in the columns; (2) available alternatives for achieving them in the rows; (3) relations between the goals and the alternatives in the cells; and (4) overall scores for each alternative at the far right, as well as the capability of determining what it would take to bring a second-place or other-place alternative up to first place.

A variation on this decision-making use is to work backward from the decisions reached to the hypothesized goals of the decision-maker or decision-makers. This process assumes that we know the alternatives that were available. It also assumes that we know how the decision-makers probably would have perceived the relations between the hypothesized goals and the alternatives if those really were their goals. Another variation is to work backward from the decisions reached to the hypothesized perceived relations, rather than to the goals. However, social scientists are usually more interested in deducing goals or motives than in deducing perceptions.

For example, if we know that the decision-makers have chosen alternative 1 over alternative 2, we might hypothesize that the decision-makers were seeking goal A or goal B. To test that hypothesis, we ask how the decision-makers would be likely to score alternatives 1 and 2 on goals A and B if those were the true goals of the decision-makers. If alternative 1 receives high scores on both goals and alternative 2 receives low scores on both goals, this result is partial confirmation that those were the goals of the decision-makers.

This kind of testing, however, is only a partial confirmation because it is somewhat like a blood test for paternity. If the baby and the alleged father have very different blood types, the alleged father is not likely to be the real father. If they have the same blood type, the alleged father may or may not be the real father. Likewise, if alternative 2 scores higher than alternative 1 on both goals, it is not likely that decision-makers who chose alternative 1 were pursuing those goals. However, if alternative 1 scores higher on both goals, then the decision-makers may or may not have been pursuing those goals because other goals might also have been consistent with the decision.

This kind of testing can be greatly facilitated with modern spreadsheet software because one can so easily try out many different goals and different perceptions to see how well alternative explanations hold up in comparison with the hypothesized goals and the assumed perceptions. The advent of "what-if" analysis in social science has been beneficial in that regard. Such analysis includes related concepts like breakeven, threshold, and critical value analysis. The reader should bear in mind the broadness of these perspectives.

DEDUCING GOALS IN *MARBURY V. MADISON*

Table 11-1 applies a spreadsheet or matrix perspective to analyzing the case of *Marbury v. Madison*. Each row represents a separate issue in the case or a subdecision involved in arriving at the overall decision. Each column represents a likely goal of the decision-maker. The cells in the matrix show how a yes answer on each issue relates to each goal. The column at the far right shows how many overall points each yes answer would receive by summing the points per goal. The far right also shows the decision-maker's actual decisions on each issue. If the goals have been properly determined and weighted, then all the issues on which a no answer was reached should each have fewer total points than the issues on which a yes answer was reached. The data have been analyzed by means of the policy/goal percentaging software. It processes the goals to be achieved, the policies to be used to achieve them, and the relations between the goals and the policies in order to arrive at a best policy, decision, or combination.

The Issues and the Goals

More specifically, the separate issues in the *Marbury* case were:

1. Should John Marshall disqualify himself in view of his not delivering the commission to William Marbury while Marshall was secretary of state, which commission Marbury is now seeking?
2. Should John Marshall find that the court has no jurisdiction to hear the case but still discuss whether Marbury deserves the commission?
3. Should he uphold the statute which authorizes the Supreme Court to issue writs of mandamus in cases warranted by the law by saying that the statute does not apply in this case since hearing the case is not warranted by Article III of the Constitution?
4. Should he uphold the statute by saying that the Constitution requires the Su-

Table 11-1
Briefing by Analyzing Multiple Issues: The *Marbury* Case

A. THE ISSUES AND OUTCOMES

Alternative	Previous Outcome
1 DISQUALIFY ONESELF	NO
2 NO JURIS/W.MERITS	YES
3 UPHOLD/S.NOT APPLY	NO
4 UPHOLD/CONST.ALLOW	NO
5 APPT.CONTINUITY	YES
6 JUDICIAL SUPREMACY	YES
7 JR JUDICIAL ONLY	NO
8 JP IS PUB.MINISTER	NO
9 CONG.CHANGE JURIS.	NO
10 GRANT APPOINTMENT	NO

B. THE GOALS, SCALES, AND WEIGHTS

Criterion	Meas.Unit	Weight
1 ATTACK JEFFERSON	1-3 SCALE	3.00
2 AVOID NONCOMPLY		2.00
3 JR ESTABLISH.		4.00
4 LEGAL CONSISTENT.		1.00

C. HOW SAYING YES ON EACH ISSUE SCORES ON THE GOALS

	ATTACK J	AVOID NO	JR ESTAB	LEGAL CO
DISQUALIFY ONESELF	1.00	3.00	1.00	3.00
NO JURIS/W.MERITS	3.00	2.00	2.00	1.00
UPHOLD/S.NOT APPLY	1.00	3.00	2.00	3.00
UPHOLD/CONST.ALLOW	2.00	2.00	2.00	2.00
APPT.CONTINUITY	2.00	2.00	2.00	3.00
JUDICIAL SUPREM.	2.00	2.00	3.00	2.00
JR JUDICIAL ONLY	2.00	2.00	2.00	2.00
JP IS PUB.MIN.	2.00	2.00	2.00	1.00
CONG.CHANGE JURIS.	2.00	2.00	1.00	1.00
GRANT APPOINTMENT	3.00	1.00	1.00	2.00

D. TOTAL SCORES OF SAYING YES ON EACH GOAL

Alternative	Combined Raw Scores	Previous Outcome
1 DISQUALIFY ONESELF	16.00	NO
2 NO JURIS/W.MERITS	22.00	YES
3 UPHOLD/S.NOT APPLY	20.00	NO
4 UPHOLD/CONST.ALLOW	20.00	NO
5 APPT.CONTINUITY	21.00	YES
6 JUDICIAL SUPREMACY	24.00	YES
7 JR JUDICIAL ONLY	20.00	NO
8 JP IS PUB.MINISTER	19.00	NO
9 CONG.CHANGE JURIS.	15.00	NO
10 GRANT APPOINTMENT	17.00	NO

preme Court to grant original jurisdiction in cases involving diplomats or states as a party, but that Congress can add to that list as long as Congress does not decrease the list?

5. Is an appointment to a nonpolitical office by a previous president binding on the subsequent president?
6. Should the Supreme Court have the final word on what the Constitution means?

7. Should the Supreme Court exercise judicial review only in matters involving the judicial process?
8. Is a justice of the peace a public minister who can seek the original jurisdiction of the U.S. Supreme Court?
9. Can Congress by ordinary statute change the jurisdiction of the Supreme Court?
10. Should Marbury be granted his appointment by the Supreme Court?

The criteria that John Marshall may have had in mind in answering yes or no to these 10 questions or issues include:

1. Attacking Jefferson in view of the fact that he is the leader of the Jeffersonian party, and Marshall is one of the leaders of the Federalists, and Marbury is a Federalist appointee.
2. Avoiding issuing a court order that will result in noncompliance and embarrass the Supreme Court.
3. Establishing the principle that the Supreme Court and other courts have the power to review the constitutionality of acts of Congress and the president.
4. Being legally consistent with prior precedents and procedures.

These four criteria or goals are weighted 3, 2, 4, and 1, respectively, to show their possible relative importance in John Marshall's hierarchy of values in this case. A good proof that those weights make sense is the fact that they are the only set of weights which explain all the no's and yes's in the prior outcome column of Table 11-1A.

Relating Yes Answers to the Goals and the Overall Scores

Table 11-1C shows how each of the 10 decisions scores on each of the four criteria. The scoring is on a 1–3 scale where 3 = conducive to the criterion, 2 = neither conducive nor adverse, and 1 = adverse to the criteria. For example, disqualifying oneself would be adverse to providing John Marshall with the opportunity to attack Jefferson or to establish judicial review. It would, however, avoid noncompliance and would be legally consistent with accepted judicial practice under those disqualifying circumstances.

Table 11-1D shows the total scores for each of the 10 decisions. These total scores involve adding the weighted relation scores across each decision. For example, disqualifying oneself receives a 16, which equals $(1 \times 3) + (3 \times 2) + (1 \times 4) + (3 \times 1)$. The computer quickly calculates an overall weighted relation score for each alternative decision. Any decision which receives 21 or more points is answered yes, and any decision which receives 20 or fewer points is answered no. That perfect consistency gives support to the idea that we have captured the essence of John Marshall's goals, his relative weights, and his perceptions of how the alternative decisions relate to the goals.[1]

DEDUCING THE REASONING IN THE MANHATTAN PROJECT DECISION

The Nature of the Problem

The concrete example is President Roosevelt's 1941 decision on whether to develop an atomic bomb. The basic alternatives were either to develop an atomic bomb or not to develop an atomic bomb. Three criteria were especially important. One was the quantity of lives that would be saved if the atomic bomb was successfully developed before the war was over. A second criterion was the probability that an atomic bomb could be successfully developed before the end of the war. The third criterion was the cost of developing an atomic bomb.

Information was almost totally missing on all three criteria. On the first criterion (the quantity of lives that might be saved), there were conflicting opinions. One opinion was that the Japanese would fight to the last person and that there would be a tremendous loss of both American and Japanese lives in the attempt to occupy the Japanese islands. That opinion tended to argue that an atomic bomb would make little difference in American lives saved while conquering Japan. The only way that a large number of American lives could be saved was if millions of Japanese lives were taken by the dropping of numerous atomic bombs. On the other hand, the more optimistic opinion was that one or two atomic bombs would be so devastating that Japan might surrender without requiring an invasion of the home islands. That opinion turned out to be the more accurate in 1945, but the prevailing opinion in 1941 was that the Japanese would be unlikely to surrender without an invasion.

On the second criterion (the probability of success), opinions also differed greatly. The prevailing opinion was that it would probably take many years to develop an atomic bomb since it was such a revolutionary concept in warfare, physics, and human thinking. Research on atomic energy had barely begun in 1941. Thus the project had to be started almost completely from scratch, with basic research as well as applied research. The more skeptical opinion had a double argument. First, the idea of an atomic bomb might be an impossible idea. Second, even if it were possible, there was not enough time to develop it before the war was over. Those who argued in favor of a higher probability of success may have been partly motivated by wishful thinking and partly by a feeling that something had to be done along these lines for fear that Nazi Germany might develop an atomic bomb first.

On the third criterion (cost), there may have been even less information than on the other criteria. The cost could range so high as to cripple the defense effort and the domestic economy. On the other hand, the cost could actually be low since once the research and development were completed, the production costs were not likely to be very high. However, a big question on cost was how many billions of dollars it would take to complete the research and development. The important point here is that there was virtually no reliable information on the quantity of lives likely to be saved, the probability of timely success, and the annual or total cost.

In spite of that unclear situation, the literature describing the decision-making process indicates that President Roosevelt was not the least bit hesitant. He was not in a brain-wracking quandary, and he never indicated any serious second thoughts about the decision he reached. The literature is scant, but one can read between the lines that President Roosevelt may have used a best–worst analysis in reaching his decision.

Such an analysis involves saying that although we cannot determine the benefits, the probability of success, or the costs, we can know the range of possibilities. This is true in relation to the subject matter of any decision. It is, for example, obviously easier to say that the worst probability is zero and the best probability is 1.00 than it is to say what the exact probability is.

Scoring the Alternatives on the Criteria

Applying that approach to the atomic bomb problem, Table 11-2 seeks to reconstruct what may have been in President Roosevelt's mind. On the quantity of lives saved, Table 11-2B shows that the best figure would be about 500,000 lives that might otherwise be lost. The worst figure would be to save only about 60,000 lives. Those figures are hypothetical since we do not have any exact records of President Roosevelt's calculations. Whatever figures we use, however, can be helpful in illustrating how best–worst analysis operates.

In a go/no-go decision like this, the no-go alternative has no benefits and no costs. In other words, if the atomic bomb is not developed, that alternative results in no lives saved because of the use of the atomic bomb. (The lives saved in this context are American lives. The nondevelopment of the atomic bomb would have saved some Japanese lives which were lost at Hiroshima and Nagasaki, but still more Japanese might have been lost to conventional bombing and warfare if the war had been prolonged.) Likewise, if the atomic bomb is not developed, no costs will be incurred as part of the development. If nondevelopment results in a net gain of nothing, then the question can be thought of as determining whether the development of the atomic bomb will produce a positive net gain with the benefits exceeding the costs, or a negative net gain with the costs exceeding the benefits.

The best probability of success is given as .70. The worst probability of success is given as only .10. In theory, the probability could go as high as 1.00, but that is obviously an unrealistic best in this context. Likewise, a zero probability is obviously an unrealistic worst in this context. The best cost is $10 billion a year, whereas the worst cost with these hypothetical data is $100 billion a year.

Table 11-2
Best–Worst Analysis: Deciding Whether to Develop the Atomic Bomb in 1941

A. THE ALTERNATIVES AND THE EVALUATIVE CRITERIA

Alternative	Criterion	Meas.Unit	Weight
1 DEVELOP ATOM BOMB	1 WORST Q SAVED	1000 LIVES	0.10
2 DO NOT DEVELOP	2 BEST Q SAVED	1000 LIVES	0.70
	3 WORST $ COST	$ 1 BILLION	1.00
	4 BEST $ COST	$ 1 BILLION	1.00

B. HOW THE ALTERNATIVES SCORE ON THE CRITERIA

	BEST Q	BEST $	WORST Q	WORST $
DEVELOP ATOM BOMB	500.00	10.00	60.00	100.00
DO NOT DEVELOP	0.00	0.00	0.00	0.00

C. THE OVERALL SCORES OF EACH ALTERNATIVE

	BEST Q	BEST $	WORST Q	WORST $	MIDPT.Q	MIDPT.$
DEVELOP ATOM BOMB	350.00	10.00	6.00	100.00	178.00	55.50
DO NOT DEVELOP	0.00	0.00	0.00	0.00	0.00	0.00

NOTES:

1. The basic criteria are benefits to be received and costs to be incurred in this and in most go/no-go decisions or conflicting choice decisions.

2. The benefits here are the quantity of lives saved measured in thousands of lives. The costs are the billions of dollars which the development might cost.

3. The weights of the benefits and costs reflect the idea that the worst scenario provides for a .10 probability that the atomic bomb development will be successful before the war is over. The best scenario provides for .70 probability.

4. The best scenario provides for a saving of 500,000 lives if the atom bomb succeeds before the war is over, and a worst scenario of only 60,000 lives saved.

5. The best scenario provides for a cost of only $10 billion, and the worst scenario provides for a cost of $100 billion.

6. The midpoint refers to the average between the best and the worst.

7. The issue boils down to which is better: to save approximately 112,000 lives or to save $5.5 billion. President Roosevelt chose the lives saved over the dollars saved and ordered the atomic bomb developed. He might have decided otherwise if there had been fewer lives involved and more dollars.

How does one aggregate that information? The most logical way is to calculate the overall score for each alternative, using the best scores and the worst scores on lives saved, probability, and cost. That is what is shown in Table 11-2C. At its best, developing the atomic bomb will save 350,000 lives. That figure is calculated by discounting the 500,000 lives by the high .70 probability of success. At its best, the cost will be $10 billion. The cost does not depend on whether the bomb works or not, whereas the total of lives saved because of the bomb does require that it be successful. At its worst, developing the atomic bomb has an expected value of only 6,000 lives saved. That figure is calculated by discounting the 60,000 lives by the low .10 probability of success. At its worst, the cost will be $100 billion, as mentioned above.

Deciding with Best, Worst, and Midpoint Scores

With that aggregated information, how does one reach a decision? There are basically three approaches: looking at the best scores, looking at the worst scores, or looking at the midpoints between the best and worst scores. If we look at the best scores, the problem becomes one of deciding which is the better of (1) saving 350,000 lives or (2) saving $10 billion. Because these are the best scores, we could rephrase the problem as being one of deciding between (1) saving as many as 350,000 lives or (2) saving only $10 billion. Since President Roosevelt decided to go ahead with the atomic bomb, his reaction would have been favorable to the development alternative presented in its best possible light, although not necessarily more favorable than to the nondevelopment alternative at its best.

If we look at the worst scores, the problem becomes one of deciding which is the better of (1) saving only 6,000 lives or (2) saving as much as $100 billion. If President Roosevelt considered development the best alternative even with the worst possible scores for that alternative, then he surely would have decided in favor of going ahead. In other words, if an alternative is the better alternative both at its best and at its worst, then it is clearly the better alternative.

We must look to the midpoints between the best and the worst overall scores if developing the atomic bomb is the better alternative at its best, but not the better alternative at its worst, or vice versa. The midpoints take both the best and the worst into consideration. They represent averages between the possible best and the possible worst. In this case, the problem becomes one of deciding which is the better of (1) saving about 178,000 lives or (2) saving $55.5 billion. The total of 178,000 lives is the midpoint between 350,000 and 6,000. The $55.5 billion is the midpoint between $10 billion and $100 billion.

One might ask: Why not obtain one overall score for each alternative? The overall score for not developing the atomic bomb is zero, as mentioned above. There is no meaningful overall score for developing the atomic bomb in the sense of subtracting costs from benefits. The costs are measured in billions of dollars, and the benefits are measured in thousands of lives. Creating one overall score might require (1) converting lives into dollars; (2) converting dollars into lives; or (3) converting both lives and dollars into a common unit. There is unlikely to be agreement on how to make such a conversion. Another alternative would be to transform both sets of scores into part/whole percentages or some other dimensionless numbers. That approach would not be meaningful here. All the development scores would be transformed into 100% because each one is both the part and the total in its respective column. Part/whole percentages also lose some information and imagery that is preserved by working with the raw scores in a paired-comparison manner as has been done here.

In general, the best decision-making approach in this context is to work with the midpoints between the best and the worst overall benefits and between the best and the worst overall costs. That approach gives both perspectives equal weight on the assumption that the truth usually tends to be somewhere between the best and the worst possible outcomes. One would, however, choose the alternative that does better on the worst scores if the alternative that does worse does unacceptably worse. For example, if $100 billion is a totally impossible loss, the development alternative might have to be rejected. An analogous example would be two possible investments, one likely to be far more profitable than the other, but the more profitable investment involving a high risk of losing one's right arm. Under those circumstances, one might readily choose the less profitable investment. The atomic bomb example would be more analogous if it involved choosing between two or more weapons systems, rather than making a go/no-go decision. It was, however, basically a go/no-go decision.

Likewise, one would pick the alternative that does better on the best scores even if it does poorly on the worst scores but not unacceptably poorly, where the other alternative does not satisfy a minimum degree of benefit. For example, if at least 20,000 lives must be saved to justify any development, an alternative weapons system must be ruled out if it cannot save that many lives no matter how well it does when one looks at the worst scores. Along related lines, one can ignore the best scores of an alternative if the benefits are beyond the maximum needed. For example, any investment that would provide an individual with $1 million per year might be no more valuable than an investment that would provide $50,000 per year, since $50,000 a year should be enough to cover virtually everything that one might need.

Consistency with Other Values or Perceptions

As for how President Roosevelt aggregated the best and worst overall scores for each alternative, all we know is that his decision was to develop the atomic bomb. That decision would be consistent with any one of the following aggregations:

1. The development alternative won on the best scenario and won on the worst scenario.
2. The development alternative won on the best scenario and lost on the worst scenario but won on the midpoints scenario.

3. The development alternative won only on the best scenario and lost on both the worst and the midpoints scenarios, but President Roosevelt gave extra weight to the best scenario because
   a. He felt an obligation to save a lot of lives and this was the only weapons system that could satisfy that obligation.
   b. He worried that if he rejected the development alternative and it would have worked, then his regret would be overwhelming, whereas he would not regret trying the development alternative even if it failed.
   c. His personality was highly optimistic, so that he felt the best outcomes were much more likely to occur than the worst outcomes.
4. The development alternative lost on the best scenario but won on the worst and midpoint scenarios.
5. The development alternative won on the worst scenario and lost on the best but won on the midpoints.
6. The development alternative won only on the worst scenario and lost on the other two, but President Roosevelt gave extra weight to the worst scenario because
   a. He felt an obligation not to spend wastefully and the competing alternative would violate that obligation.
   b. He worried that if he accepted the competing alternative and it failed, his regret would be overwhelming, but he would not regret accepting the development alternative. Points 6a and 6b assume a competing alternative, not just a no-go decision.
   c. His personality was highly pessimistic, at least on this issue, so that he felt the worst outcomes were more likely to occur than the best outcomes.

GENERAL PRINCIPLES IN DEDUCING MOTIVES AND PERCEPTIONS FROM DECISIONS

An optimum decision-making model takes the basic syllogistic form of (1) *Y* is good; (2) *X* causes *Y*; (3) therefore adopt *X*. An alternative form is (1) it is optimum to maximize benefits minus costs; (2) *X* will maximize benefits minus costs; (3) therefore adopt *X*. The first premises can be symbolized *V* for value judgment; the second premises can be symbolized *P* for perception or *R* for reality; and the conclusion can be symbolized *D* for decision.

Such models have many uses. The most common use is for making decisions. Another use is for influencing decisions. The second use recognizes that if we want decision-makers to adopt *X*, we should influence their perceptions of what *X* causes and encourage them to have a favorable attitude toward what *X* causes. Another use is for predicting decisions. That use recognizes that if we know that the values or perceptions of a decision-maker have changed in the first or second premise, we may be able to predict how the decision-maker will change his or her decisions. Another use is for measuring decisional propensities. That use recognizes that asking decision-makers what their decisional propensities are is likely to lead to answers that they think will make them look good. To prevent that, one can ask about their values and perceptions and then deduce from those more reliable answers what their decisional propensities are likely to be.

One Goal and One Choice

The key question in this analysis is: What can we deduce about *V, P,* and/or *R* by knowing *D* with or without additional information? If we merely know that *X* was adopted, we cannot know that *Y* is valued even if we know that *X* causes *Y*. The reason is that *X* may also cause *Z*, which the decision-maker may be seeking. The judicial system presumes that a decision-maker intends to cause *Y* when he or she does *X* if it is common knowledge that *X* causes *Y*. That presumption, however, is rebuttable if the decision-maker has a satisfactory alternative explanation. Likewise, if *X* is adopted, we cannot know that the decision-maker perceives that *X* causes *Y*, even if it does so. If virtually everyone knows that *X* causes *Y*, then, from that inductive generalization, we can deduce that the decision-maker also knows that *X* causes *Y*, but that is not a deduction from the decision to do *X*.

One might, however, think that if we know the decision plus one of the premises, we should be able to deduce the other premise. That is also not necessarily so. For example, if we know that the decision-maker adopted *X*, and that he or she perceives that *X* causes *Y*, this does not necessarily mean that *Y* is being sought as a goal since the decision-maker may also perceive that *X* causes *Z*, which is what he or she may really want. The decision-maker may even adopt *X*, recognizing that *X* causes *Y*, and yet consider *Y* undesirable. That would be so if he or she recognizes that the amount of *Z* which *X* causes is enough to offset the undesirable *Y*.

On the other hand, if we know that the decision-maker adopted *X*, and that he or she positively values *Y*, we might think that we could deduce that the decision-maker must perceive that *X* causes *Y*. That, however, does not necessarily follow since the decision-maker may think that there is an inverse relation between *X* and *Y*, but may still adopt *X* because it produces the *Z* effect, which he or she may also desire. Thus, knowing the *D* conclusions and the *P* or *V* premise does not necessarily enable us to deduce the other premise.

A key reason why one cannot easily work backward from decisions and perceptions to the motives or the goals sought (or backward from the decisions and the goals sought to the perceptions) is that the second premise is an asymmetrical causal statement, rather than a symmetrical equality statement. If, for example, the syllogism were (1) *Y* is good, (2) *X* equals *Y*, (3) therefore adopt *X*, the situation would be different. With that kind of syllogism, we can deduce the first premise if we know the second and the third. However, we cannot deduce the second premise if we know the first and the third. This is especially so when we are working with abstract symbols, rather than with facts.

Multiple Goals and/or Choices

To clarify further the need for careful thinking in optimizing models, we might note that if (1) *Y* is good and (2) *X* causes *Y*, it does not necessarily follow that *X* should be adopted. The reason is that *X* may also cause *Z*, which may be more bad than *Y* is good. In other words, one should adopt *X* only if it has no offsetting adverse side effects. In effect, the one-goal syllogism assumes that there are no relevant goals other than *Y*.

One can extend the above analysis to deal with multiple goals and multiple policies. Doing so involves a basic syllogism like (1) Y_1 and Y_2 are good; (2) X_1 and X_2 have relations with Y_1 and Y_2, respectively; and (3) therefore adopt X_1 rather than X_2 because X_1 generates a greater sum of Y_1 and Y_2 than X_2 does. We could also talk about a weighted sum, like a weighted average in which each goal is given a relative weight for its measurement units and its normative value. With a syllogism like that, knowing which *X* has been adopted tells us little about the perceived relations of the second premise or the normative values of the first premise for the same reasons that apply to the simpler syllogism, which involves only one goal and one policy. Even with many decisions, we cannot inductively or deductively arrive at the motives of a decision-maker, although we may be able to make general statements about patterns of behavior, which we cannot do with only one decision.

Although we may not be able to deduce specific goals or perceptions from decisions, we can deduce highly general goals and perceptions from decisions. For example, if the U.S. Supreme Court allowed segregation in 1896 and disallowed it in 1954, we can conclude that the Court found the benefits minus the costs of segregation to be positive in 1896 and to be negative in 1954. That does not tell us what the Court found the benefits or the costs to be, unless the Court explicitly said what they were and we accepted their statements. Merely saying that the net benefits shifted is true by definition, since all decisions seek to maximize benefits minus costs, or net satisfaction, and net satisfaction is what decisions seek to maximize. Thinking in terms of benefits minus costs of the decision-makers can, however, help stimulate a more systematic evaluation of the decisions.[2]

SOME CONCLUSIONS

There are many uses for optimizing models for P/G% spreadsheet matrices, such as making, influencing, predicting, and measuring decisions. An additional use is deducing motives and perceptions from decisions and other aspects of decision-making situations. One might think that use is easier in a situation involving only abstract symbols, which clarify the decision-making situation and eliminate muddying facts. On the contrary, deducing motives and reconstructing decision-making are easier in a factual situation. In these circumstances, we can eliminate alternative explanations that make no factual sense in light of what we know about the situation, even though these alternative explanations may be consistent with abstract symbolic logic.

Deducing motives from decisions and likely perceptions is very much like determining causation in social science. *X* is viewed as causing *Y* if (1) *X* and *Y* vary together; (2) *X* precedes *Y* in time; and (3) there is no third variable, *Z*, which when held constant will cause the covariation between *X* and *Y* to disappear or substantially lessen. A typical way of determining causation in social science is to develop a causal model in which some variables are hypothesized to be the cause or a cause of other variables, while other relations are noncausal covariations or are nonrelations. Parts of the model are then tested for the influence of *Z* variables.

When one or more *Z* variables are held constant, the relation between *X* and *Y* may not substantially lessen. We therefore tentatively accept the relation as being a causal relation until a new explanation or *Z* variable is adequately offered for the covariation. Likewise, in determining motives, if a *Y* goal or a *V* value does explain an *X* or *D* choice and a *P* perception, it makes sense to accept the *Y* goal as at least one of the decision-maker's true goals until an adequate alternative explanation is offered. Offering an adequate alternative explanation means showing it to be as consistent or more consistent with the *X* or *D* choice and the *P* perception than the original explanation.

Deducing motives has been a fascinating concern for people in history, psychology, law, and other fields. Historians do it by compiling circumstantial evidence. Psychologists do it by working with theories in human behavior, including theories that relate to sex, power, and biological needs. Lawyers do it partly by operating with a variety of rebuttable presumptions. Policy analysts do it by, in effect, reversing the policy evaluation process. The normal order is to go from values and facts to decisions or policy recommendations. Motivational analysis works backward, from policies to hypothesized values. Working backward, however, requires special caution where asymmetrical reasoning is involved, as previously mentioned.

The main benefit of determining motives and reconstructing past reasoning processes may be to obtain a better understanding of how people who are acknowledged to be good decision-makers reach their decisions. These include a highly revered Supreme Court Chief Justice like John Marshall and a President like Franklin Roosevelt. The essence of expert systems software is the idea of emulating what experts do in a given field of analysis, rather than trying to impose an abstract model on future decision-makers that may bear no relation to how experts actually decide. Thus, seeking deduced values and perceptions in past decisions is consistent with an expert systems approach to developing principles of effective and efficient decision-making.

In that regard, it is hoped that this chapter will contribute to the development of the principles of decision-making, including the idea of weighted goals and summation scores which we attributed to John Marshall, or the idea of best-worst analysis which we attributed to Franklin Roosevelt. It is also hoped that this chapter will contribute to the development of principles that relate to deducing values and perceptions from past policy decisions.[3]

NOTES

1. For further details on deducing goals in *Marbury v. Madison*, see Charles Warren, *The Supreme Court in United States History* (Boston: Little, Brown, 1935); Charles G. Haines, *The Role of the Supreme Court in American Government and Politics, 1789-1835* (Berkeley: University of California Press, 1944); and Robert Carr, *The Supreme Court and Judicial Review* (New York: Rinehart, 1942), 57-74. On deducing goals in judicial decisions in general, see Glendon Schubert, *Quantitative Analysis of Judicial Behavior* (New York: Free Press, 1959), 173-268.

2. For further details on the Roosevelt decision to proceed with the development of the atomic bomb, see H. Smyth, *Atomic Energy for Military Purposes: The Official Report on the Development of the Atomic Bomb* (Princeton, N.J.: Princeton University Press, 1947); Arthur Compton, *Atomic Quest* (New York: Oxford University Press, 1956); and R. Clark, *The Birth of the Bomb* (New York: Horizon, 1961). On decision-making under conditions of uncertainty including best-worst analysis, see Edward Quade, *Analysis for Public Decisions* (Amsterdam: North-Holland, 1982), 33-42; and Samuel Richmond, *Operations Research for Management Decisions* (New York: Ronald, 1968), 487-492.

3. On the determination of motives in history, see Jacques Barzun and Henry Graff, *The Modern Researcher* (New York: Harcourt, Brace, 1957), 115-130. On determining motives in psychology, see Peter Lindsay and Donald Norman, *Human Information Processing* (New York: Academic Press, 1972), 592-639; and Gardner Lindzey (ed.), *Handbook of Social Psychology: Theory and Method* (Reading, Mass.: Addison-Wesley, 1954), 57-258. On determining motives in law, see Wayne LaFave and Austin Scott, *Handbook on Criminal Law* (St. Paul: West, 1972), 191-218.

12

Generalizing from Cases

The purpose of this chapter is to describe how microcomputers can be helpful in analyzing the characteristics of a set of cases in order to generate a decision rule about how related future cases are likely to be decided.

APPELLATE CASES

A simple form of computer-aided case prediction involves the following steps:

1. One obtains a set of past cases that deal with whatever subject or issues one is interested in.
2. One counts how many of the cases resulted in victory for the plaintiff or a given position, and how many resulted in victory for the defendant or the other position. The plaintiff victories divided by the total number of cases is the probability of plaintiff victory.
3. Working just with the plaintiff victory cases, one determines the average amount of the damages awarded or the average sentence received by the defendant.
4. By multiplying the probability from Step 2 by the average from Step 3, one can determine the expected value for the type of case involved.

That kind of prediction may, however, often be insufficient. For example, the prior set of cases may have yielded a probability of .70 and average damages of $100,000. However, one may be reluctant to predict that the next case is likely to be worth $70,000 because one knows that it has some characteristics that give it a higher or lower probability or larger or smaller predicted damages. One may therefore prefer a method that takes the relevant characteristics of the cases into consideration, rather than just the general type that the cases fit into.

The essence of multicriteria decision prediction (MCDP) is the idea of working with two or more predictive criteria, rather than just looking at overall probabilities and averages for a given type of case. More specifically, MCDP involves the processing of a set of (1) alternative cases, casetypes, or other occurrences, (2) various predictive or explanatory criteria, and (3) relations between the alternatives and the criteria, in order to develop a decision rule that will accurately predict or explain 100% of the past decisions so as to facilitate predicting future decisions.

There are two especially effective ways of developing a predictive decision rule with no inconsistencies. One involves changing the weights of the predictive criteria, and the other involves changing the measurement of the relations between the cases and the predictive criteria. The first method can be illustrated with legislative redistricting cases and the second with welfare proceedings.[1]

Changing the Weights of the Predictive Criteria

Table 12-1 provides an example of synthesizing a set of appellate cases by using the P/G% software. The appellate cases consist of nine cases dealing with legislative redistricting from *Colegrove v. Green* in 1948 to *Baker v. Carr* in 1962. Each case is scored yes with a 2 and no with a 1 on each of the four predictive criteria. The criteria include (1) whether equality is explicitly required by the relevant federal or state constitution; (2) whether a state or federal legislature is involved; (3) whether the degree of equality violation is big or little; and (4) whether a federal or state court is involved. The yes answer is the one that favors a decision for the side that is attacking the existing redistricting system.

The last column shows how each case was decided in terms of whether the winner was the defender or the attacker of the existing redistricting system. The second to last column shows the sum of the raw scores. It leads to a decision rule that says, "If there is a total raw score of 7 or above, then the attacker wins; and if there is a total raw score of 6 or below, then the defender wins." That decision rule, however, has one inconsistency. It is the *Grills* case, in which there were only 6 points, but the attacker still won.

To eliminate such inconsistencies, one can do a variety of legitimate things, as indicated in the notes below the table. The most meaningful approach is generally to give the predictive criteria different weights to indicate their relative importance. In this context, the most important criteria are the first criterion (which deals with the nature of the law) and the third criterion (which deals with the key facts). Of the two, the equality requirement is the most important, since the degree of equality violation would

Table 12-1

Data for Predicting Redistricting Cases

Criteria / Cases	Equality Requirement W = 1 (or 2)	State Legislature W = 1	Equality Violation W = 1	Federal Court W = 1	SUM (Weighted)	OUTCOME	
						Winner	Award
Colegrove	1 (2)	1	1	2	5 (6)	D	$0
Grills	2 (4)	2	1	1	6 (8)	A	2
Maryland	1 (2)	2	2	1	6 (7)	D	0
Scholle	1 (2)	2	2	1	6 (7)	D	0
WMCA	1 (2)	2	1	2	6 (7)	D	0
Asbury	2 (4)	2	2	1	7 (9)	A	6
Dyer	2 (4)	1	2	2	7 (9)	A	8
Baker	2 (4)	2	2	2	8(10)	A	9
Magraw	2 (4)	2	2	2	8(10)	A	10

NOTES:

1. A 1 in columns 1 to 4 means No. A 2 means Yes. An "A" in the outcome column means that the attacker wins. A "D" means that the defender wins.

2. The decision rule that the above data initially generates is the following:
   (1) If a redistricting case during the time period covered has a summation score of 7 or above, the attacker wins.
   (2) With a summation score of 6 or below, the defender wins.

3. That decision rule generates one inconsistent case. The inconsistency can be eliminated by (1) changing the decision rule to say that a summation score of 6 leads to an unclear outcome; (2) giving the first variable a weight of 2, which would be consistent with the importance of requiring equality; (3) adding a fifth variable called "Deciding after the Maryland Case"; (4) eliminating the Grills case, but that does not seem justifiable; (5) changing the measurement on the first variable from no-yes to a 1-3 scale and giving Grills a score of 3; (6) finding that Grills really deserves a relation score of 2 on the third of the four variables.

4. Each predicted criterion is initially given an equal weight of 1. If the equality requirement is given a weight of 2 in view of its substantive importance, then the Grills case would no longer be an inconsistently low-scoring case in which the attacker won. The new predictive decision rule would be the following:
   (1) If a redistricting case has a weighted summation score of 8 or above, the attacker wins.
   (2) If the weighted summation score is 7 or below, the attacker loses.

5. The dollar amounts in the last column represent hypothetical data showing how many thousands of dollars the successful attacker received in the form of damages. That information is useful for illustrating how the methodology can predict a continuum outcome as contrasted to a dichotomous outcome of winning versus losing.

mean little if there were no equality requirement. Giving the equality requirement a weight of 2 doubles all the numbers in the first column. Doing so changes the summation scores. The new weighted summation scores now lead to a decision rule that says, "If there is a total raw score of 8 or above, then the attacker wins; and if there is a total raw score of 7 or below, then the defender wins." That new decision rule results in no inconsistencies. The set of cases has thus been synthesized into a meaningful decision rule.

The data shown in Table 12-1 are useful not only in illustrating how to develop a decision rule for predicting who will win in a set of cases, but also in developing a decision rule for predicting what the damages or other judgment will be. The last column is called "Award." It contains hypothetical data for the nine cases. Using a two-variable regression analysis program, one can easily develop a predictive equation of the form, Award = $A + B$(Sum). That equation says that the predicted award will be equal to a base amount (when the summation score is zero) plus the summation score times a computer-generated multiplier. The computer generates a numerical value for both A and B in order to maximize the accuracy of one's ability to predict awards from summation scores, given the data available. That kind of software is included with the P/G% program.

Changing the Measurement of the Relations

Table 12-2 provides an example of how the P/G% software can be used to synthesize a set of cases. This example differs from the previous one in the following ways:

1. The alternatives are not specific cases, but casetypes or sets of facts that may or may not have actually occurred.
2. Inconsistencies are eliminated by changing the measurement of the relations between the casetypes and the predictive criteria, rather than changing the relative weights of the predictive criteria.
3. The example is substantively different; it deals with welfare cases, rather than with redistricting cases.

There are 12 alternative casetypes in these welfare cases. One dimension for the casetypes relates to whether the welfare recipient was denied eligibility, subjected to reduced benefits, terminated, or criminally prosecuted. A second dimension relates to whether the welfare recipient was denied a free attorney, a hearing with direct and cross examination, or reasons for the administrative treatment. The first dimension relates to substance, and the second relates to procedure. The first dimension has four categories, and the second has three. Thus there are 12 alternative casetypes.

There are two predictive criteria. One criterion relates to what the case

Table 12-2
Changing the Measurement of the Relations Predicting Welfare Cases

A. THE ORIGINAL 1-3 MEASUREMENT ON THE PROCEDURAL CRITERION

Alternative	SUBSTANCE	PROCEDURE	Combined Raw Scores	Previous Outcome
ELIGIBLE-LAWYER	1.00	1.00	2.00	L
BENEFITS-LAWYER	2.00	1.00	3.00	L
ELIGIBLE-HEARING	1.00	2.00	3.00	L
TERMINATE-LAWYER	3.00	1.00	4.00	L
BENEFITS-HEARING	2.00	2.00	4.00	?
ELIGIBLE-REASONS	1.00	3.00	4.00	W
CRIM.PROS.-LAWYERS	4.00	1.00	5.00	W
TERMINATE-HEARING	3.00	2.00	5.00	W
BENEFITS-REASONS	2.00	3.00	5.00	W
CRIM.PROS.-HEARING	4.00	2.00	6.00	W
TERMINATE-REASONS	3.00	3.00	6.00	W
CRIM.PROS.-REASONS	4.00	3.00	7.00	W

B. THE NEW .99-3.01 MEASUREMENT ON THE PROCEDURAL CRITERION

Alternatives	SUBSTANCE	PROCEDURE	Combined Raw Scores	Previous Outcome
ELIGIBLE-LAWYER	1.00	0.99	1.99	L
BENEFITS-LAWYER	2.00	0.99	2.99	L
ELIGIBLE-HEARING	1.00	2.00	3.00	L
TERMINATE-LAWYER	3.00	0.99	3.99	L
BENEFITS-HEARING	2.00	2.00	4.00	?
ELIGIBLE-REASONS	1.00	3.01	4.01	W
CRIM.PROS.-LAWYER	4.00	0.99	4.99	W
TERMINATE-HEARING	3.00	2.00	5.00	W
BENEFITS-REASONS	2.00	3.01	5.01	W
CRIM.PROS.-HEARING	4.00	2.00	6.00	W
TERMINATE-REASONS	3.00	3.01	6.01	W
CRIM.PROS.REASONS	4.00	3.01	7.01	W

NOTES

1. A "W" in the outcome column means that the welfare recipient wins. An "L" means that the welfare recipient loses.

2. The decision rule that the above data generate is the following:
   (1) If a welfare case involves a summation score of 4.01 or above, the welfare recipient wins.
   (2) With a summation score of 3.99 or below, the welfare recipient loses.
   (3) With a score of 4.00, the outcome is unclear.

3. The leading case is Goldberg v. Kelly, (casetype 8). It involved a summation score of 5.00, and the welfare recipient won. Therefore, one would expect the welfare recipient to win even more with scores higher than 5.00. That covers casetypes 9, 10, 11, 12. The outcome of case 7 is known from the Argersinger case. The outcomes of casetypes 1, 2, 3, 4, and 6 are known from things said in the Goldberg case, not from a fortiori deduction.

4. With the 1-3 measurement, there are three inconsistent cases, all of which received an overall score of 4.00. One case was a loser; one was a winner; and the outcome of the third is unknown. With the .99-3.01 measurement, there are no inconsistencies. The losing case gets a score of 3.99; the winning case gets a score of 4.01; and the questionable case gets a score of 4.00.

5. The justification for changing the scale from 1-3 to .99-3.01 is secondarily to remove the inconsistencies. The primary justification is because the changes make substantive sense. Giving no reasons is practically the ultimate in deprivation of procedural due process. It should therefore score higher than 3 on a 1-3 scale. Not having an attorney in a civil matter is relatively minor compared to not having reasons or a hearing. It should therefore score lower than a 1 on a 1-3 scale.

involves in terms of procedure. A simple way of scoring each casetype on each criterion is a rank order. We can obtain widespread agreement that the worst treatment is criminal prosecution and the least severe is eligibility denial. Next to the worst is termination, and next to the least severe is benefits reduction. That means a 1–4 scale. Likewise, we can obtain widespread agreement that the worst procedural treatment is to be denied reasons. The least severe procedural treatment is to be denied a free attorney. Between these two is being denied a hearing. A 1–3 scale is called for.

If we use a simple rank-order scoring and then sum the two ranks across each casetype, we find a set of inconsistencies. There are three cases that score 4.00. They include termination without a lawyer, in which the welfare recipient is likely to lose unless there are other considerations. The three cases also include denial of eligibility without giving reasons, in which the welfare recipient is likely to win unless there are other considerations. The third case involves a benefits reduction without a hearing; at the time of this analysis, it was questionable how the courts were likely to decide such a case. If three cases receive the same score and are decided in three different ways, then two out of the three cases are being inconsistently handled in the synthesis. The summation column and the previous outcome column do not generate a decision rule that predicts or explains the cases.

If, however, we change the simplistic 1–3 scoring on the procedural dimension to a scale that considers the subject matter more validly, then the inconsistencies and mispredictions can be eliminated. In revising the scale, we find that giving no reasons is such an abuse of procedural due process that it deserves a score higher than 3 on a 1–3 scale where no lawyer receives a 1, and no hearing receives a 2. Likewise, not being given a free lawyer in a civil case deserves a score lower than a 1 if no hearing receives a 2, and no reasons receives a 3.

If we work with a .99 to 3.01 scale, rather than a 1–3 scale, we can get perfect prediction in this context. That means that alternative 5 receives a summation score of 3.99 and loses. Alternative 7 receives a summation score of 4.01 and wins. Alternative 6 still receives a score of 4.00, which is fitting, given its questionable outcome. Thus we have a good illustration of how changing the measurement can convert a 10 out of 12 prediction to 100% accuracy.[2]

CRIMINAL TRIAL CASES

Table 12-3 contains data for predicting criminal cases. These data are hypothetical, but for methodological purposes such data should be just as usable as real data. There are five cases. Table 12-3A shows how they were decided. It also shows the four predictive criteria used to separate the conviction cases from the acquittal cases. The predictive criteria are given equal weight to begin with.

Table 12-3
Data for Predicting Conviction or Acquittal

A. THE CASES AND THE PREDICTIVE CRITERIA

Alternative	Previous Outcome	Criterion	Meas.Unit	Weight
1 JONES (C)	CONVICT	1 MISD.V.FELONY	2/YES-1/NO	1.00
2 SMITH (C)	CONVICT	2 LOW GNP V.HIGH		1.00
3 BROWN (A)	ACQUIT	3 REP.JUDGE V.DEM		1.00
4 GREEN (A)	ACQUIT	4 BLACK DEF.V.WHITE		1.00
5 MILLER (A)	ACQUIT			

B. HOW THE CASES SCORE ON THE PREDICTIVE CRITERIA

	MISD.	LOW GNP	REP.JUDGE	BLACK DEF.
JONES (C)	2.00	2.00	2.00	1.00
SMITH (C)	2.00	2.00	1.00	1.00
BROWN (A)	1.00	1.00	1.00	1.00
GREEN (A)	2.00	1.00	1.00	2.00
MILLER(A)	1.00	1.00	1.00	2.00

C. THE OVERALL SCORES OF THE CASES BEFORE AND AFTER ADJUSTING THE WEIGHTS

Alternative	Combined Raw Scores	Previous Outcome	Alternative	Combined Raw Scores	Previous Outcome
1 JONES (C)	7.00	CONVICT	1 JONES (C)	9.00	CONVICT
2 SMITH (C)	6.00	CONVICT	2 SMITH (C)	8.00	CONVICT
3 BROWN (A)	4.00	ACQUIT	3 BROWN (A)	5.00	ACQUIT
4 GREEN (A)	6.00	ACQUIT	4 GREEN (A)	7.00	ACQUIT
5 MILLER (A)	5.00	ACQUIT	5 MILLER (A)	6.00	ACQUIT

D. REVERSING THE WEAKEST ACQUITTAL OR CONVICTION

	GREEN (A)	SMITH (C)	Weight
MISD.V.FELONY	3.00	1.00	??
LOW GNP V.HIGH	1.50	1.50	1.000
REP.JUDGE V.DEM	2.00	0.00	??
BLACK DEF.V.WHITE	3.00	0.00	2.000

NOTES:

1. The case names, predictive criteria, and the scores of the cases on the criteria are hypothetical. These hypothetical data first appeared in S. Nagel, "Using Simple Calculations to Predict Judicial Decisions," 4 *American Behavioral Scientist* 24-28 (1960) and 7 *Practical Lawyer* 68-74 (1961).

2. If the predictive criteria are given equal weight, then inconsistent predictions occur. There are two cases with total scores of 6, but one resulted in a conviction and one in an acquittal. If, however, area income is given extra weight as a predictive criterion, then the inconsistencies are eliminated.

3. The decision rule generated by these data is that if there are 8 or more points,there will be a conviction, but if there are 7 or fewer points, there will be an acquittal.

Convict or Acquit

Table 12-3B shows how the cases score on the predictive criteria. The scoring is on a 1–2 scale, with 2 meaning relatively high and 1 meaning relatively low. The predictive criteria relate to:

1. Whether the charge was a misdemeanor or a felony.
2. Whether the geographical area of the courthouse involved people with a low gross national product (GNP) per capita or a high GNP per capita.
3. Whether a Republican or Democratic judge heard the case.
4. Whether the defendant was black or white.

Table 12-3C shows the summation scores per case when the weights were all set at 1.00. The *Smith* case and the *Green* case both received 6 points. Smith was convicted, however, and Green was acquitted, so that they are an inconsistent pair. However, if the income variable is given a little extra weight, the inconsistencies are eliminated. The new decision rule becomes that if there are 8 or more points, there will be a conviction. If there are 7 or fewer points, there will be an acquittal.

Extra weight should be given to a predictive criterion whose scores have an especially close relation to case outcome. Area income has a perfect relation. Wherever income was relatively high, there was an acquittal. Wherever income was relatively low, there was a conviction.

Possible explanations for the relations between the predictive criteria and the case outcomes are that

1. Misdemeanors may be more likely to result in convictions than felonies, because felony defendants fight harder, and more due process is provided in felony trials.
2. Poorer jurisdictions may have higher conviction rates, because they cannot afford to provide as good right to counsel as wealthier jurisdictions do.
3. Republican judges may have higher conviction rates, because they tend to believe more than Democratic judges in individual (rather than social) responsibility, and they are more likely to place a higher value on avoiding acquittal errors.
4. Black defendants may be more likely to be convicted than white defendants, because they are more likely to be poor and to have less expensive counsel. They may also have less sympathetic judges and juries, especially if white victims are involved.

Table 12-3D shows that the *Green* case might get as high a score toward conviction as the *Smith* case if Green were tried by a Republican judge; the *Smith* case might get as low a score toward acquittal as the *Green* case if Smith were charged with a felony rather than misdemeanor; and the cases would be tied if the income of the area were given a weight of 1, rather than a weight of 2.

Length of Sentence

Table 12-4 contains the data for predicting the length of sentence from a small sample of only three cases. Two of the three cases are the *Jones* and *Smith* cases from Table 12-3. Both resulted in a conviction. Jones had an adjusted summation score of 9, and Smith had a score of 8. A third case was added; its summation score of 10 means it had a yes answer on all four predictive criteria. As part of the hypothetical data, Smith received a 10-year prison sentence, Jones received 10.5 years, and the third case received 10.75 years. Those data are given in Table 12-4A.

In order to convert these data into a decision rule, they are put into a simple linear and nonlinear regression analysis program called Regress. The program is an example of public domain software. It is now available as part of the P/G% package. A future version of P/G% will enable the regression analysis to be automatic if requested. One will thereby avoid having to type the P/G% output in order to provide the regression input.

The decision rule (as determined by the linear regression analysis) is expressed in the equation $Y = 7.04 + .375(X)$. The equation means that when the summation score is zero, the predicted sentence is 7 years. As the summation score goes up one unit, the predicted sentence goes up three eighths of a year. The decision rule (as determined by the diminishing-returns analysis) is expressed in the equation $Y = 5.09(X)^{.33}$. The equation means that when the summation score is 1, the predicted sentence is 5 years. As the summation score goes up 100%, or doubles, the predicted sentence goes up 33%, or up by one third.

Table 12-4C applies the two equations to various values of X. That aspect of the program is useful for making fast predictions in light of either equation. Those predictions can include summation scores which do not correspond to any of the actual cases. The predictions are designed to minimize the sum of the squared deviations between the predicted sentences and the actual sentences for the three cases in the data set, while preserving a straight-line relation in the linear regression and a smooth curve in the nonlinear regression.

In addition to providing the information for the predictive equations, Table 12-4B also shows that there is almost a perfect fit between the linear regression line and the three points, and likewise between the nonlinear regression line and the three points. The nonlinear fit is slightly higher, as indicated by the R^2 value. There is not much room for improvement in the goodness of fit here. In other situations, the goodness of fit can be improved by changing the weights of the predictive criteria, adding predictive criteria, changing the measurement units, or doing other things that make substantive sense and bring the changes in the X scores even more in line with changes in the Y scores. This is much easier to do when all the predictive criteria have been combined into a summation score, rather than left separate.

Table 12-4
Data for Predicting Length of Sentence

A. THREE CONVICTION CASES, THEIR SUMMATION SCORES AND THEIR SENTENCES

I	X	Y
Point 1	8	10.00
Point 2	9	10.50
Point 3	10	10.75

B. THE PREDICTION EQUATION COEFFICIENTS

LINEAR REGRESSION

$$Y = 7.04 + .38(X)$$

Coefficient of Determiniation (R^2) = .96
Coefficient of Correlation (R) = .98

GEOMETRIC REGRESSION

$$Y = 5.09(X)^{.33}$$

Coefficient of Determination (R^2) = .97
Coefficient of Correlation (R) = .99

C. APPLYING THE EQUATION TO POSSIBLE SUMMATION SCORES

X	Y1	Yg
5	8.92	8.61
6	9.20	9.14
7	9.67	9.61
8	10.04	10.03
9	10.42	10.43
10	10.79	10.79

NOTES:

1. The data are hypothetical. Points 1 and 2 are the Smith and Jones cases from Table 12-3. Point 3 is a new case called the Atkins case. The X variable is their summation scores, and the Y variable is their sentences expressed in years.

2. The above output was generated by working with a public domain program called Regress, which is part of the Math/Stat package of PC-SIC group of 1556 Halford Avenue, Santa Clara, CA 95051. The program is now available as part of the P/G% Disk #1.

3. Table 12-4B shows the prediction equations. They are $Y = 7.04 + .375(X)$, and $Y = 5.09(X)^{.33}$. The linear equation means that with a summation score of 0, the predicted sentence is 7 years. As the summation score goes up one unit, the predicted sentence goes up 3/8 of a year. The nonlinear equation means that with a summation score of 1, the predicted sentence is 5 years. As the summation score goes up 100%, the predicted sentence goes up 33%.

Sensitivity analysis in predicting sentence length or some other continuum outcome is different from predicting conviction–acquittal or some other dichotomous outcome. If we want to know how much a prediction concerning sentence length is likely to change as a result of changes in the characteristics of the defendant or the case, we go through the following three steps:

1. We apply the predictive equation $Y = a + bX$ or $Y = aX^b$ to the case using its original characteristics.
2. We apply the predictive equation $Y = a + bX$ or $Y = aX^b$ to the case using its new characteristics.
3. We determine the difference between Y_1 and Y_2. That difference shows how much the prediction is likely to change as a result of the changes in the characteristics.[2]

We might note that the Y variable we are trying to predict is sentence length, damages, winning or losing (expressed as a 1 or a 0), or some other decisional outcome. The X variable that we are trying to predict from is the summation score of the case at hand. This process is different from traditional prediction from cases, which is called *multivariate regression analysis*. It involves predicting from the scores of the case at hand on each of the individual criteria, rather than from a summation score. Such a method tends to be more complicated and less valid. The greater complexity is due to trying to predict from so many variables at the same time without first aggregating them. The lowered validity is due mainly to the fact that the separate variables tend to interact with each other in ways that hide or accentuate spurious causation, reciprocal causation, and other confounding interactions. The P/G% prediction system decreases those occurrences by encouraging the user of the method to adjust the weights in light of his or her knowledge of the subject matter.[3]

CIVIL TRIAL CASES

A Distinctive System

This kind of prediction has certain distinctive characteristics. It is *multi-criteria*, as contrasted to

1. Merely predicting the basis of the victory percentage in previous related cases, such as 6 out of 10, or 60%.
2. Merely predicting the average previous damage reward in related cases, such as $75,000.
3. Merely predicting from a single criterion or a single composite criterion like three times the out-of-pocket medical costs plus the lost wages.

The system makes use of a spreadsheet base with the following *inputs:*

1. The predictive criteria are shown in the columns.
2. The prior cases are shown in the rows.
3. How each prior case scored on each predictive criterion is shown in the cells.

At the far right of each spreadsheet matrix is a total score for each case and how it was decided. This information facilitates the development of a *decision rule,* which takes the form:

1. If the total points are at or above a certain amount, the plaintiff is likely to win.
2. If the total points are at or below a certain amount, the defendant is likely to win.

The system makes considerable use of the "what-if" analysis associated with spreadsheets in order:

1. To determine the effects on the decision rule of various changes, including the relative weights of the criteria.
2. To determine how the prediction of the case at hand would change as a result of changes in the perceived characteristics of the case.

The Key Elements or Inputs

Table 12-5 deals with predicting who will win in civil cases and with what damages. For illustrative purposes, the table shows data from five hypothetical *cases*. The defendant won in two of the five cases, and the plaintiff won in three, for amounts of $70, $65, and $78.

For the sake of discussion, four *predictive criteria* are shown:

1. Whether the judge is elected or appointed. It is hypothesized that elected judges are more likely to side with the plaintiff in damage suits when political party is held constant. The reason is that elected judges are more likely to rise up within the party ranks as doorbell ringers and as lawyers with small practices. Appointed judges may be more likely to be chosen for their financial contributions to the party and to come from larger law firms.
2. Whether the area provides for no-fault liability or for liability only if the plaintiff is completely or substantially free from contributory negligence.
3. Whether the place where the case is heard is urban or rural.
4. Whether the plaintiff is male or female. Elected judges, no-fault liability, and urban places tend to be associated with plaintiffs' winning. Male plaintiffs are not more likely to win than female plaintiffs, but they are likely to be awarded higher damages if they do win.

Table 12-5B shows the *scores* of hypothetical cases on these four criteria. One could use any set of criteria that are meaningful in light of the specific

Table 12-5
Predicting Who Will Win in Civil Cases

A. THE PREVIOUS CASES, THEIR OUTCOMES, AND THE PREDICTIVE CRITERIA

ALTERNATIVES	PREVIOUS OUTCOME	CRITERIA	MEAS. UNIT	WEIGHT
1 Johnson (D)	D - $0	1 Elected Judge	1/No - 2/Yes	1.00
2 Park (P)	P - $70	2 No Fault Law		1.00
3 Dixon (D)	D - $0	3 Urban Place		1.00
4 Crawford (P)	P - $65	4 Male Plaintiff		1.00
5 Hudson (P)	P - $78			

B. HOW THE CASES SCORE ON EACH OF THE PREDICTIVE CRITERIA

ALTERNATIVES	CRITERIA			
	Elected Judge	No Fault Law	Urban Place	Male Plaintiff
Johnson (D)	1.00	1.00	1.00	1.00
Park (P)	2.00	1.00	2.00	2.00
Dixon (D)	2.00	1.00	1.00	1.00
Crawford (P)	2.00	2.00	2.00	1.00
Hudson (P)	2.00	2.00	2.00	2.00

C. THE OVERALL SCORES OF THE CASES

ALTERNATIVES	COMBINED RAWSCORES	PREVIOUS OUTCOME
1 Johnson (D)	4.00	D -$0
2 Park (P)	7.00	P -$70
3 Dixon (D)	5.00	D -$0
4 Crawford (P)	7.00	P -$65
5 Hudson (P)	8.00	P -$78

D. BRINGING THE HIGHEST LOSER UP TO THE LEVEL OF THE LOWEST WINNER

CRITERIA	ALTERNATIVES		WEIGHT
	Dixon (D)	Park (P)	
Elected Judge	4.00	0.00	??
No Fault Law	3.00	-1.00	??
Urban Place	3.00	0.00	-1.000
Male Plaintiff	3.00	0.00	-1.000

subject matter of the cases being analyzed. These four criteria are representative of the four types of predictive criteria that are frequently referred to in the judicial decision analyses of social scientists. The first criterion relates to who the decision-makers are. The second criterion relates to what the law is. The third relates to a factual element, although not necessarily an evidentiary one. The fourth criterion relates to who the litigants are. Normally the law and the facts are by far the most important, but when they are held constant, the nature of the decision-makers and the litigants may have some predictive value.

Major Uses or Outputs

Table 12-5C shows the overall results. These results lead to a *decision rule* that says if the total score of a case is 7 or more, the plaintiff is likely to win. If the total score is 5 or less, the defendant is likely to win. Table 12-5C also leads to saying that if the plaintiff wins with 7 points, the average damages are likely to be about $67.50. If the plaintiff wins with 8 points, the average damages are likely to be about $78. That kind of reasoning can be extended to a much larger sample of cases. In order to get good separation between the winners and the losers, it may be necessary to give different weights to the predictive criteria. To obtain better precision in predicting the amount of damages from the total scores, it may also be helpful to have the computer develop an equation in which damages are shown as a function of the total scores.

This kind of analysis can be useful not only for predictive purposes, but also for *advocacy* purposes. Suppose, for example, that a lawyer is representing the plaintiff in the *Dixon* case, and suppose the *Dixon* case is not included in the set of cases that have already been decided. Table 12-5D shows what changes it would take to bring the *Dixon* case up to the level of the *Park* case, which was one of the winning cases with a relatively low score. The answers include:

1. If the lawyer for Dixon could convince the court that the urban place factor or the male plaintiff factor deserves less importance, that could help the *Dixon* case since it does not do well on those two criteria, assuming those are relevant criteria to argue in court as contrasted to nonevidentiary predictive criteria.
2. The lawyer for Dixon might try to convince the court to perceive that the *Dixon* case deserves a higher score on each of the predictive criteria. In this situation, that might be difficult to do since the cases are just scored no or yes. Moving some of the no answers in the *Dixon* case up to yes answers could bring Dixon up to the level of Park.
3. One should note that Park received a score of 7, and Dixon receives a score of 5. We are thus looking for ways to raise the overall score of the *Dixon* case by 2 points. We can do this by (a) raising the weight or importance of the criteria on which Dixon does well or (b) lowering the weight or importance of the criteria on which Dixon does poorly. We can also do it by (c) increasing the scores of the *Dixon* case on the criteria.
4. The *Park* column of Table 12-5D shows that by lowering the scores in the *Park* case, we can generate a tie between Park and Dixon. It may be possible to convince the court that the *Park* case did not score very well but still deserved to win. One normally does better, though, by arguing that one's client deserves to win than by arguing that some previous plaintiff who was a winner was really not very deserving.
5. The question marks in the upper-right-hand corner of Table 12-5D show that no changes in the relative importance or weight of the elected-judge factor or the no-fault law factor will make any difference, since both the *Dixon* and the *Park* cases received the same scores of yes on elected judge and no on no-fault liability.

The threshold or breakeven analysis in Table 12-5D can also be helpful in *eliminating inconsistencies* when we are developing a predictive decision rule. Suppose, for example, that there was a sixth case that had only five points, and yet the plaintiff won. One can do threshold analysis between the sixth case and either the *Park* or the *Crawford* case, since those were the lowest scoring cases in which the prosecution won. The threshold analysis should indicate what predictive criteria would need to have extra weight in order to bring the total number of points of the sixth case up to the same total score as either *Park* or *Crawford*. In some situations, having differential weighting would make good substantive sense. Thus the analysis would eliminate the inconsistency of two cases' having the same total scores and being decided oppositely and would at the same time add to the substantive meaningfulness of the analysis, since predictive criteria are usually not of equal weight.

There are many *variations* on this basic analysis, including how to deal with (1) predictive criteria that are measured differently, like miles and hours, rather than just yes or no; (2) multiple missing information; (3) criminal or other cases in which the outcomes are nonmonetary; and (4) more complex situations that involve many more cases and many predictive criteria.[4]

NOTES

1. For further details on this analysis, see S. Nagel, "Using Microcomputers and P/G% to Predict Court Cases," 18 *Akron Law Review* 541–574 (1985), and S. Nagel, *Causation, Prediction, and Legal Analysis* (Westport, Conn.: Greenwood-Quorum, 1986). On the P/G% software applied to case prediction and other law practice matters, see S. Nagel, *Microcomputers as Decision Aids in Law Practice* (Westport, Conn.: Greenwood-Quorum, 1987), and S. Nagel, "Case Prediction by Staircase Tables and Percentaging," 25 *Jurimetrics Journal* 169–196 (1985). Also see Karl Llewelleyn, *The Common Law Tradition: Deciding Appeals* (Boston: Little, Brown, 1960). Relevant software for inductively synthesizing appellate cases includes statistical analysis software such as SPSS-PC, 444 N. Michigan Avenue, Chicago, Ill. 60611.

2. On predicting decisions from the characteristics of a situation, see Harold Spaeth, *Supreme Court Policy Making: Explanation and Prediction* (San Francisco: Freeman, 1979); Glendon Schubert (ed.), *Judicial Behavior: A Reader in Theory and Research* (Chicago: Rand McNally, 1964); Harry Jones, John Kernochan, and Arthur Murphy (eds.), *Legal Method: Cases and Text Materials* (Mineola, N.Y.: Foundation Press, 1980); and S. Nagel, "Microcomputers and Improving Social Science Prediction," 10 *Evaluation Review* 635–660 (1986). Notice that if one merely predicts the average outcome for the data in Table 12-4, then one would always predict an acquittal, and one would be wrong two out of five times. Predicting from the characteristics of the cases leads to being wrong zero out of five times for the sample of five cases. Likewise, predicting the average outcome would lead to predicting that all convicted defendants would receive a sentence of 10.42 years, since that is the average of the three conviction cases. Doing so would lead to bigger differences

between the actual years and the predicted years in the three cases than predicting from the summation scores of the cases, which take the case characteristics into consideration.

3. The P/G% prediction from cases produces approximately the same results as multivariate regression analysis if there is little overlap among the predictive criteria or if one assigns multiplier weights to take the overlap into consideration. If two predictive criteria have virtually no overlap and are equally important, they can be assigned weights of 1.00 apiece. If they have highly redundant overlap, they should be assigned weights of about .50 apiece. If there is a small amount of overlapping correlation between the two predictive criteria, they should be assigned weights of about .90 apiece. The overlap problem also occurs in the next chapter on predicting from facts. The problem can be handled in a simple commonsense manner or in a complicated mechanistic manner that has greater objectivity but less meaningfulness and validity.

4. These matters are discussed in the chapters on judicial prediction in S. Nagel, *Microcomputers as Decision Aids in Law Practice* (Westport, Conn.: Greenwood-Quorum, 1987), and S. Nagel, *Decision-Aiding Software and Legal Decision-Making* (Westport, Conn.: Greenwood-Quorum, 1989).

13

Generalizing from Facts

The purpose of this chapter is to describe an alternative prediction system called generalizing from facts. It may be even more applicable to lawyers and others than generalizing from cases.

The essence of the procedures is estimating probabilities of victory for each important factual matter, and then averaging the probabilities to arrive at an overall probability of victory. Likewise, one can estimate the likely damages in light of various factual elements and then average those estimates to arrive at an overall prediction of the amount of damages likely to be awarded. The system can take into consideration the relative importance of different factual elements by giving the elements different relative weights or multipliers, so that a weighted overall average can be calculated.

The methods are illustrated with an actual product liability case from the federal district court of the Northern District of Illinois. In this case, an American insurance company sued a foreign electronics manufacturer for damages which allegedly occurred when an appliance caught fire. The resulting fire caused approximately $950,000 in damages to a restaurant and other business establishments that were insured by the American insurance company and other insurance companies. They had already paid the injured parties, and they were now seeking to be reimbursed by the foreign manufacturer.

DETERMINING THE PROBABILITY OF LIABILITY

Averaging Separate Probabilities

A key issue in this case and in a high percentage of civil cases was whether liability would be established. Basically, the court could take two alternative positions on this issue, as is shown in the alternatives column of Table 13-1B.

Table 13-1
Determining Liability in a Civil Case

A. THE PREDICTIVE CRITERIA

CRITERIA	MEAS.UNIT	WEIGHT
1 P's Prediction	Prob. Win	1.00
2 D's Prediction	"	1.00
3 Combustible?	"	1.00
4 No Break Circuit?	"	1.00
5 Prior Occurrence?	"	2.00

B. THE PROBABILITY OF LIABILITY IF EACH PREDICTIVE CRITERION WERE THE ONLY ONE

ALTERNATIVES	CRITERIA				
	P's Predict.	D's Predict.	Combustible?	No Break?	Prior?
D Liable (Pro P)	0.70	0.10	0.40	0.40	0.30
No Liable (Pro D)	0.30	0.90	0.60	0.60	0.70

C. COMBINING THE PROBABILITIES OF THE PREDICTING CRITERIA

ALTERNATIVES	COMBINED WTD. P/W%'s	Percentages
1 D Liable (Pro P)	220.00	36.67
2 No Liable (Pro D)	380.00	63.33

Either the defendant would be found liable, the decision that would favor the plaintiff, or the defendant would be found not liable, the decision that would favor the defendant.

Five predictive criteria are shown in Table 13-1A:

1. The plaintiff's prediction of the probability of victory is shown in Table 13-1B as a .70 probability that the plaintiff would win. Thus the plaintiff was predicting that there was a .30 probability that the defendant would win. Those probabilities were determined by talking with the plaintiff's attorneys and translating their words, gestures, and emotions into predictive probabilities.

2. The defendant's prediction of the probability of victory is shown as a .10 probability that the plaintiff would win and thus a .90 probability that the defendant would win. All the probabilities are expressed in the top row of Table 13-1B in terms of plaintiff victory and in the bottom row in terms of defendant victory. The defendant was more confident of victory in this case than the plaintiff, as indicated by the .90 and .70 probabilities.

3. A key subissue or predictive criterion within the larger issue of liability probability was a question of whether the appliance was combustible, that is, whether it was capable of burning. The plaintiff argued that it was, but the defendant argued that it was not. Their arguments translated into a .40 probability that the plaintiff would win and a .60 probability that the defendant would win on the overall liability issue if combustibility were the only factual element. Note that the .40 does not say that there was a .40 probability that the appliance was combustible. Instead, it says that if the only evidence present in this case were combustibility evidence, then the plaintiff would have about a .40 probability of winning the case.

4. A related subissue was whether the circuit breaker in the appliance might not have worked as it was supposed to do in the presence of intense heat. The plaintiff argued that it was possible that the electrical circuit did not immediately break when it was supposed to. The defendant argued that such a failure was virtually impossible. Their respective arguments led to the mediator's saying in his analysis that if there was evidence only on the circuit breaker, the plaintiff would also have just a .40 probability of winning.

5. The last factual element or predictive criterion on this list is the question of whether there had been a prior occurrence of this type, in which the appliance had caused a fire. The plaintiff's lawyers argued that they were in the process of showing that there had been a prior occurrence, but they were reluctant to be specific in the pretrial proceedings, claiming that they wanted to save the evidence for trial. The defendant's lawyers argued that the company records and a thorough search of prior court cases showed no such prior occurrence. The plaintiff's lawyers were less convincing on this issue than on the two issues of combustibility and circuit breaking. Thus it was reasoned that if this were the only predictive criterion, the plaintiff would have only a .30 probability of winning. There seemed to be a consensus, however, that this was an especially important issue deserving more weight than the others. The first two predictive criteria were considered less weighty in view of the expected biases of the plaintiff's and defendant's predictions. The factual elements in points 3 and 4 above are not very crucial, since even if it could be shown that it was physically possible for the appliance to burn and physically possible for the circuit breaker not to work, it would not indicate that these events occurred in this instance or had ever occurred in any previous instance. However, if a pattern of previous fires due to this appliance could be shown, that would be devastating to the product and would practically ensure the victory of the plaintiff.

Table 13-1C shows how the probabilities of the predictive criteria are combined. If each criterion was equally important, then we could add .70 + .10 + .40 + .40 + .30 and obtain a total of 1.90. We could then divide by five predictive criteria and get an average of .38. We would thus be saying that if any one predictive criterion (such as the third) yields a .40 probability of plaintiff victory and if we add a second predictive criterion (like the defendant's prediction) which is only .10, it seems logical to average the two for an average of .25. In this approach, we assume that both predictions are equally important and accurate. This method is like averaging the allocation percentages of two different allocation criteria. If, however, one criterion such as the fifth criterion, is twice as important as the others, we should logically count it twice or give it a weight or multiplier of 2. Thus we add another .30 to the 1.90 and obtain a total of 2.20. We then divide that weighted total by the sum of the weights, which is 6, and we obtain a probability of .37, the 36.67% in the bottom line.[1]

What It Would Take to Make the Loser into a Winner

For any given predictive criterion, we might ask: How do the probabilities have to change to bring the victory probability for the plaintiff up to, for example, .50? The algebra that answers that question is relatively simple and can be explicitly programmed as part of the P/G% threshold analysis, although this process has not yet been used. Suppose that we want to know how much the plaintiff victory probability has to be increased on the combustibility criterion in order to make the plaintiff a winner, given the scores and weights on the other four criteria. Being a winner in this context means having an overall probability of more than .50. An easy way to answer that question is by summing $.70 + .10 + X + .40 + .30 + .30$, for a total of $1.80 + X$. Notice that we added the .30 twice because the fifth criterion has a weight of 2. The next step is to divide that sum by the sum of the weights, which is 6. We then solve for X in the equation $(1.80 + X)/6 = .50$. The solution is $1.80 + X = 3.00$, and thus $X = 3.00 - 1.80$, which is 1.20.

As an alternative to this algebraic approach, we could use a reiterative guessing approach to arrive at the same result:

1. The initial pair of probabilities on the third criterion are .40 and .60. In order for the plaintiff to tie with the defendant at 50-50, the .40 probability would have to be raised.
2. We might therefore try .80 and .20 as a new pair of probabilities. We would insert them into the data matrix in place of the .40 and .60 and then ask for a new primary analysis.
3. The new primary analysis, however, would still show less than .50 for the victory probability of the plaintiff. We might then substitute a pair of probabilities equal to 1.00 and 0 and ask to see the new primary analysis.
4. As the overall plaintiff victory probability is still less than .50, we might try 1.20 and −.20, in which case the overall or averaged probabilities are .50 and .50. Thus we have found the threshold probabilities for the combustibility predictive criterion.
5. At step 4, we might easily have overshot the mark by trying 1.30 and −.30, which would yield an overall plaintiff probability higher than .50. On the next step, we would come back down a bit from 1.30 toward 1.00 and move up a bit from −.30 toward 0. In doing so, we would eventually converge on 1.20 and −.20.

6. Some people would consider this kind of reiterative guessing rather inelegant compared to the algebraic method, which immediately gives the right answer. It is partly a matter of taste. The reiterative guessing method is quite fast with the P/G% program, which allows the user to see experimental changes quickly. It also has the advantage of preventing the clerical errors that are made in algebra and arithmetic. It has the further advantage of making it easier to conceptualize what is happening, and it quickly shows that the alleged threshold values really are tie-causing values.

As for interpreting the 1.20, it tells us that the combustibility issue would have to generate a plaintiff victory probability of 1.20 in order for the overall probability to be .50, given all the other numbers, so that, in effect, there is no way that the plaintiff can win in terms of the overall probability only by increasing the combustibility evidence, since no probability can be higher than 1.00. The threshold analysis can give us a threshold probability for every cell and every weight so we can see what combinations of changes might lead to victory for the second-place alternative, which is the plaintiff's winning. We know that if the threshold probability in the top row under combustibility is 1.20, then the threshold probability immediately beneath it must be −.20, since the two probabilities have to add to 1.00, although the current computer program does not know that. A probability of −.20 is just as impossible as a probability of 1.20. We can easily see that 1.20 makes sense because if we substitute 1.20 for the .40 which is now in that cell and add across, we then obtain a figure of .70 + .10 + 1.20 + .40 + .30 + .30, or 3.00. If we then divide by 6, we obtain .50. We would also see proof if we substituted a −.20 for .60 in the second row and then added across, since we would then also obtain a sum of 3.00. If we think that merely getting a probability above .50 is not sufficient insurance, we can change the equation we are working with to $(1.80 + X)/6 = .60$, rather than .50, or we can change the right-hand side to whatever high or low probability we are interested in.

This discussion helps to clarify how the idea of threshold analysis applies to generalizing from facts by aggregating probabilities.

Building on Past Averages

Lawyers most commonly determine victory probabilities by starting with an average figure like .65 in a personal injury case, and then asking whether the case is above, below, or at the average regarding the probability that the plaintiff will win. If the lawyer finds that this is an average or below-average case, he or she has to decide roughly how much above or below .65. That method is cruder than either predicting from cases or predicting from facts. It does not explicitly consider prior cases, although it may do so implicitly.

It does not explicitly consider the factual elements that go into determining liability, although it may implicitly do that, too.

One interesting and useful aspect of this approach is that .65 seems to be the average probability of plaintiff victory regardless of the type of case involved. It is the average probability by which the prosecutor wins in criminal cases, according to the University of Chicago Jury Project. It is the average probability by which plaintiffs win in personal injury cases, according to the Jury Verdict Research Service. It is also the percentage of international law cases that the United States wins according to an analysis which will be described shortly. The explanation of why .65 is such a common victory probability or percentage, regardless of subject matter, is that

1. If the victory probability is substantially below .50, the plaintiff is not likely to go to trial and will be willing to settle or to withdraw.
2. If the victory probability is substantially above .75, the defendant is not likely to go to trial and will be willing to settle.
3. If the victory probability is between .50 and .75, the case is more likely to go to trial. A typical case in that set is likely to have a .65 victory probability.

DETERMINING THE DAMAGES LIKELY TO BE AWARDED

Traditional Methods

The most common way of predicting damages is probably through various rules of thumb, like multiplying the "specials" by 5, 10, or some other figure, depending on whom one talks to. The specials consist of the out-of-pocket medical expenses and the lost wages. Thus, if the out-of-pocket medical expenses are $2,000, the lost wages are $8,000, and the multiplier is 5, the predicted damages would be $50,000 if the case is won. This method is also cruder than predicting from prior cases, although the multiplier may be based implicitly on prior cases. It is also cruder than predicting from specific facts, which may include more relevant items than just the specials.

When one systematically predicts damages from prior cases, the most common approach is to average the damages from similar cases. Thus, if in two similar cases one was awarded $40,000 in damages, and the other was awarded $30,000, one might predict that the damages in the case at hand will be $35,000. That approach has the fault of relying on a sample that may be unrepresentative. It also has the fault that the concept of "similar cases" may be highly subjective. In addition, it does not explicitly consider any facts that go into determining damages, although something about what facts are relevant may be implicit in the definition of the similarity of the cases chosen.

A higher step in the quantitative prediction of damages is a statistical regression analysis like that based on prior cases. The big drawback of this method is that it depends on the variables specific to those prior cases and may exclude important variables in the case at hand that do not occur very often or that are difficult to measure quantitatively when they do occur. Predicting or generalizing from facts has an advantage since this method does not depend on what is in the prior cases or on what is conveniently measurable.

Averaging across Factual Elements

Table 13-2 provides an illustration of generalizing from facts in order to determine the damages that are likely to be awarded. The left side of Table 13-2A shows alternative damage amounts for the case concerning the American insurance company and the foreign electronics manufacturer. Seven rows of alternatives are listed. The first alternative is from $600,00 to $700,000, and so on up to the fifth alternative, which is $1 million. The sixth row is blank. The seventh row refers to damages without providing for intervals. It is only the seventh alternative in which we are interested in this context.

Table 13-2
Determining Damages Likely to Be Awarded

A. THE DAMAGES ALTERNATIVES AND THE PREDICTIVE CRITERIA

Alternative	Criterion	Meas.Unit	Weight
1 $600,000	1 P'S LOW PRED.	$1,000'S	1.00
2 $700,000	2 P'S HIGH PRED.	$1,000'S	1.00
3 $800,000	3 P'S MOST LIKELY	"	2.00
4 $900,000	4 D'S LOW PRED.	"	1.00
5 $1,000,000	5 D'S HIGH PRED.	"	1.00
6	6 D'S MOST LIKELY	"	2.00
7*DAMAGES			

B. SCORES OF THE KEY ALTERNATIVE ON THE CRITERIA

ALTERNATIVE/CRITERIA SCORING

	P'S LOW	P'S HIGH	P'S MOST	D'S LOW	D'S HIGH	D'S MOST
DAMAGES	600.00	950.00	750.00	600.00	900.00	750.00

C. THE OVERALL OR AGGREGATE SCORE OF THE KEY ALTERNATIVE

Alternative	Combined Raw Scores	%
7 DAMAGES	6050.00	100.00

The right side of Table 13-2A shows the predictive criteria with which the mediator was actually working in this case. The predictive criteria did not include medical expenses or lost wages, since this was a property damage case. The main damages involved a burned-out restaurant and some burned-out offices. Thus a rule of thumb for predicting damages based on medical specials and lost wages would not apply to this relatively common type of property damage case. The most important predictive criteria were considered the estimates of the knowledgeable lawyers on both sides of the case. They were not only knowledgeable in the sense of being specialists in product liability cases, including appliance-fire cases, but also were knowledgeable about the facts of this specific case. The mediator discussed the likely damages with the lawyers separately, together, and together with their clients. From these discussions one could roughly determine (1) the plaintiff's lowest prediction of the damages likely to be awarded if the plaintiff won; (2) the plaintiff's highest prediction; (3) the plaintiff's most likely prediction; (4) the defendant's lowest prediction; (5) the defendant's highest prediction; and (6) the defendant's most likely prediction. The measurement unit column in the table shows that these predictions are measured in $1,000 units to keep the numbers small and manageable. The weight column shows that extra weight is logically given to the plaintiff's most likely prediction and the defendant's most likely prediction, rather than to their lowest or highest predictions. We could also adjust the weights for the relative credibility of each side if one side seemed to be perceiving the damages more accurately than the other side, possibly based on more experience or inside information. In this case, there was no reason to give more weight to one side than to the other.

Table 13-2B shows how the key alternative of "Damages" scored on each of the six criteria. The plaintiff's lowest prediction was about $600,000, and the highest was about $950,000. The plaintiff's most likely prediction was about $750,000. The most likely prediction is not necessarily the midpoint between the lowest and the highest. A person can estimate that somebody could be as young as 20 and as old as 50 but is probably 30. The defendant's lowest prediction was about $600,000 and the highest about $900,000, with the most likely prediction also at $750,000. One might wonder why the plaintiff's and the defendant's predictions of damages were so close when their predictions were so far apart regarding the victory probabilities. The answer is that victory probabilities are much more subjective. That was especially so in this case, where the insurance company had already made payments to the injured parties. Those payments constituted liquidated damages and therefore reduced some of the subjectivity which otherwise would have been present if the plaintiff's insurance company was still arguing with the injured parties over the amount of the property damage they had suffered.

Table 13-2C provides an overall figure by summing eight separate figures. The eight figures come from the six basic figures shown in Table 13-2B, plus the plaintiff's and the defendant's most likely predictions, each multiplied by

2 since both those criteria are given extra weights of 2. The sum of those eight figures is $6,050,000. That figure is then divided by 8, which is the sum of the weights, to yield an overall prediction of $756,250. That is the figure with which the mediator worked in seeking to bring about a fair settlement. The settlement involved considering more than just the damages. It also involved taking into consideration the possibility that the electronics manufacturer would give computers to the insurance company for use by its agents, TV sets as sales bonuses, and claims against Americans which the manufacturer's foreign insurance company was willing to part with. In seeking a settlement, the mediator tended to emphasize the plaintiff's lowest prediction when dealing with the plaintiff, and the defendant's highest prediction when dealing with the defendant.[2]

SOME CONCLUSIONS

The methods for predicting liability and damages discussed in this chapter emphasize averaging across probability estimates and averaging across damage estimates. That approach can be contrasted with methods that involve making predictions about a future case from a set of past cases. The crudest way of doing that is simply to note the percentage of the past cases that were decided in favor of the plaintiff and the average damages awarded in the cases in which the plaintiff won. A more sophisticated analysis might attempt to determine the characteristics in the past cases that were associated with victory for the plaintiff or high damages, as well as the characteristics associated with victory for the defendant or low damages. Those methods are unnecessarily complicated, and they may not be as valid as averaging a set of probability estimates and damage estimates based on various factual elements.

Either approach can be facilitated by spreadsheet-based software. For prediction from cases, the cases can be shown in the rows, and the predictive criteria in the columns. How each case is scored for each criterion can be shown in the cells, with overall scores for each case at the far right. One can then observe how many points are associated with victory for the plaintiff, and how many points are associated with victory for the defendant. For prediction from facts, the possible outcomes can be shown in the rows, and the predictive criteria or facts in the columns. The probability estimates (like .70 and .30) or damage estimates (like $100,000) can be shown in the cells, as in Tables 13-1 and 13-2. Summation scores can be shown at the far right. Those scores can then be divided by the sum of the weights of the criteria to yield a weighted average for each potential outcome.

Predicting from cases has the advantage of explicitly drawing on prior precedents, and predicting from facts has the advantage of freeing one from the constraint of having to work with a limited sample of prior cases. One can combine the two approaches by doing each analysis separately. One can also combine the approaches by working with a set of cases to generate probabilities for facts or predictive criteria. The probabilities can then be averaged for the case at hand.

Perhaps the most important point is that both methods (predicting either from cases or from facts) by using the P/G% system (or related spreadsheet-based systems) are simple and valid enough for lawyers to use without any technical training in statistics or mathematical probability. Both methods reflect a kind of common sense among lawyers regarding how case outcomes are to be predicted. In that sense, P/G% prediction seeks to reflect what good decision-makers implicitly do. This approach contrasts with telling lawyers what statisticians or mathematicians think they ought to do, as if they were operating in a world in which there are only algebraic symbols, hypothetical numbers, or complete information on all variables and cases. We need predictive methods for operating in a real world of multidimensionality and limited information to make predictions that relate to important decisions.

NOTES

1. The traditional approach to aggregating probabilities is to use the formulas associated with Bayesian probability calculations. Those calculations are extremely complicated, especially when there is more than one predictive criterion. An analysis of what those calculations require in the context of predicting case outcomes is given in "Alternative Predictive and Analytic Techniques Applicable to Multiple-Category Variables" in S. Nagel, *The Legal Process from a Behavioral Perspective* (Homewood, Ill.: Dorsey Press, 1969), 169–171, and S. Nagel, D. Lamm, and M. Neef, "Decision Theory and Juror Decision-Making," in Bruce Sales (ed.), *The Trial Process* (New York: Plenum Press, 1981), 373–376.

Averaging the probabilities will yield exactly the same result if there is only one predictive criterion. Averaging the probabilities will also give approximately the same result no matter how many predictive criteria there are if there is little overlap among the predictive criteria or if the overlap is taken into consideration in how the criteria are weighted. For example, if two criteria are highly redundant, then instead of each criterion being given a weight of 1.00, they should be given a weight of .50 apiece. If they are mildly redundant, .90 apiece might be appropriate. Assigning weights does have an element of subjectivity, although there may be reasonable agreement among knowledgeable people. More importantly, averaging weighted probabilities is possible, whereas obtaining information on the degree of overlap by using the Bayesian approach is virtually impossible in any real-world problem, given the Bayesian emphasis on odds, likelihood ratios, priors, and conditional probabilities.

2. On the systematic synthesizing of facts in trial decisions, see Jerome Frank, *Courts on Trial: Myth and Reality in American Justice* (Princeton, N.J.: Princeton University Press, 1950); Bruce Sales (ed.), *The Trial Process* (New York: Plenum Press, 1981); and Norbert Kerr and Robert Bray (eds.), *The Psychology of the Courtroom* (New York: Academic Press, 1982). Relevant software for calculating probabilities includes the Bayesian probabilities program in the package called Computer Models for Management Science, Addison-Wesley, Reading, Mass.

14

Relational Analysis

This chapter illustrates how multicriterion decision analysis and P/G% decision-aiding software can be applied to the two most important problems in statistical relation analysis. The first problem is determining the direction and magnitude of the relations and whether they are causal or only correlative. The second problem is determining how reliable the relations are in terms of how easily they could be changed by chance sampling error or by wrongly measuring how some of the persons, places, or things are scored on the variables that are being related.

DIRECTION, MAGNITUDE, AND CAUSATION IN RELATIONS

To illustrate this use of P/G% for prediction purposes, we use the example of trying to *predict the decisional propensities of judges from their background and attitudinal characteristics*. When Disk #1 is in Drive A and Disk #2 is in Drive B, access the Predict master file and the JC&JDM data file on Drive B. *JC&JDM* stands for "judicial characteristics and judicial decision-making." Hit F9 to go to the main menu, 2 for the data management menu, and 2 for the alternatives display. The key decisional propensity we are interested in here is being worker-oriented or employer-oriented in disputes that involve an employer–employee relation. Most of these disputes relate to on-the-job injuries at the state supreme court level. Table 14-1 shows that we are concerned with the decisional propensity of being employee-oriented or employer-oriented, although the same data file can be used to do a predictive analysis on being defense-oriented or prosecution-oriented in criminal cases.

Table 14-1
The Possible Case Outcomes in Employment Disputes

Alternative	Previous Outcome
1 DEFENSE ORIENTED	
2 PROSECUTION ORIENTED	
3*EMPLOYEE ORIENTED	
4*EMPLOYER ORIENTED	
5	
6	

Hit Return twice. Go to the data management menu, and press 3 for the criteria. Table 14-2 shows that *10 characteristics of the judges* are used as predictive criteria. The 10 characteristics can be arranged in four groups.

1. *Political party*. Was the judge a Republican or a Democrat? These are all state supreme court judges serving as of 1955.
2. *Religion*. Was the judge a Protestant or a Catholic?
3. *Ideology*. Was the judge a conservative or a liberal? This was determined by a mail questionnaire survey of the judges asking questions about controversial political issues. The previous characteristics were determined from various *Who's Who* directories.
4. *Combining party and ideology*. Was the judge a conservative Republican, a conservative Democrat, a liberal Republican, or a liberal Democrat? Every odd-numbered criterion is hypothesized to be more employer-oriented than the corresponding even-numbered criterion. All the criteria are given equal weight. The minus signs just show that we might like to know the difference between the paired categories if we do a separate primary analysis on each pair.

Table 14-2
Characteristics of the Judges Relevant to the Possible Outcomes

Criterion	Meas.Unit	Weight
1*REPUBLICAN JUDGES	TALLIES	-1.00
2*DEMOCRATIC JUDGES	"	1.00
3*PROTESTANT JUDGES	"	-1.00
4*CATHOLIC JUDGES	"	1.00
5*CONSERVATIVE		-1.00
6*LIBERAL		1.00
7*REP.CONS.		-1.00
8*DEM.CONS.		1.00
9*REP.LIBERAL		-1.00
10*DEM.LIBERAL		1.00

Table 14-3
How the Judicial Characteristics Relate to the Case Outcomes, Showing Tallies on the First Five Characteristics

	ALTERNATIVE / CRITERIA SCORING				
	REPUBLICAN	DEMOCRAT	PROTESTANT	CATHOLIC	CONSERVATIVE
EMPLOYEE ORIENT	12.00	19.00	8.00	8.00	9.00
EMPLOYER ORIENT	22.00	9.00	19.00	4.00	23.00

Hit Return twice to go to the data management menu, and press 4 to see the data matrix. Tables 14-3 and 14-4 show tallies indicating the *relations between the judicial characteristics and being worker- or employer-oriented.* For example, of the 34 Republican judges in the sample, 12 scored as being employee-oriented, and 22 scored as being employer-oriented. An employee-oriented judge was one who was above the average of his or her respective court in terms of the percentage of times that he or she decided in favor of the employee in employee injury or dispute cases. Of the 28 "usable" Democrats in the sample, 19 scored as being employee-oriented, and 9 scored as being employer-oriented. A usable judge was one serving on a 1955 state supreme court who could be positioned as a Republican or a Democrat and who heard some nonunanimous employee cases.

Hit F9 twice to go back to the main menu, and hit 3 for the primary analysis. Then hit Shift-Return to see the *part/whole percentages.* The primary analysis itself is not meaningful, since there is so much multidimensionality across the criteria. Tables 14-5 and 14-6 show percentages indicating the relations between the judicial characteristics and being employee-oriented. For example:

1. Of the Democrats, 68% are above the average of their respective courts on deciding for the employee, but only 35% of the Republicans.
2. The percentages are about the same for Catholics and Protestants as for Democrats and Republicans, probably because of the high relation between being a Catholic judge and being a Democrat, and being a Protestant judge and a Republican.

Table 14-4
How the Judicial Characteristics Relate to the Case Outcomes, Showing Tallies on the Second Five Characteristics

	ALTERNATIVE / CRITERIA SCORING				
	LIBERAL	REP.CONS.	DEM.CONS.	REP.LIB.	DEM.LIB.
EMPLOYEE ORIENT	22.00	6.00	3.00	6.00	16.00
EMPLOYER ORIENT	8.00	18.00	5.00	4.00	4.00

3. The percentage split between liberal judges and conservative judges is stronger than between Democrats and Republicans, showing that ideology is a more important predictor than party.
4. If ideology is held constant, much of the difference between the parties lessens. Thus there is only a 12% point difference between Republican and Democratic conservatives as contrasted to a 32% difference between Republicans and Democrats. There is also only a 20% point difference between Republican liberals and Democratic liberals. Note that each column in Tables 14-5 and 14-6 sums to 100% even though the tally columns in Tables 14-3 and 14-4 tally different amounts.
5. Tables 14-5 and 14-6 enable one not only to do a predictive analysis but also to do a comparative analysis across different predictors. Screens also enable one to do a causal analysis by holding constant hypothesized causal factors to determine the effects of holding them constant.

APPLYING THRESHOLD ANALYSIS TO STATISTICAL INFERENCE

Evaluative and Explanatory Analysis

Threshold analysis can be useful in a variety of ways in a prescriptive or evaluative analysis, such as:

Table 14-5
How the Judicial Characteristics Relate to the Case Outcomes, Showing Percentages on the First Five Characteristics

	PART / WHOLE %				
	REPUBLICAN	DEMOCRAT	PROTESTANT	CATHOLIC	CONSERVATIVE
EMPLOYEE ORIENT	35.29	67.86	29.63	66.67	28.12
EMPLOYER ORIENT	64.71	32.14	70.37	33.33	71.87

Table 14-6
How the Judicial Characteristics Relate to the Case Outcomes, Showing Percentages on the Second Five Characteristics

	PART /WHOLE %				
	LIBERAL	REP.CONS.	DEM.CONS.	REP. LIB.	DEM.LIB.
EMPLOYEE ORIENT	73.33	25.00	37.50	60.00	80.00
EMPLOYER ORIENT	26.67	75.00	62.50	40.00	20.00

1. Determining how strong a hold a first-place alternative has on first place.
2. Determining what it would take to bring a first-place alternative down to second place.
3. Determining what it would take to bring a second-place alternative up to first place.
4. Determining which non-first-place alternative has the best chance of getting into first place.
5. Determining what weights or perceptions one should seek to change in order to make a nonwinner into a winner.

Threshold analysis can also be useful in a variety of ways in a predictive or explanatory analysis, such as:

1. Determining what it would take to move an inconsistent case that is below the cutoff level up to the cutoff level.
2. Determining what it would take to move an inconsistent case that is above the cutoff level down to the cutoff level.
3. Determining whether a case that is below or above the cutoff level really deserves to be there.
4. Obtaining insights into whether a predictive decision rule can be improved by a change in the weights of the predictive criteria, in the scoring of the cases or casetypes, or in other inputs.

Evaluation-prescription and explanation-prediction are two of the most important reasoning processes in social science. Another important process is statistical inference, in which one inductively reasons from a sample of data to a universal or a generalization. Threshold analysis can also be helpful here. The most common and important generalizations in social science are generalizations that relate one variable to another, such as the religion of decision-makers and their decisional propensities.

Testing a Single Relationship

Table 14-7 provides an illustrative example. It deals with the *relation between the religion of judges and whether they are defense-oriented or prosecution-oriented* in their decisions. The basic data show that Catholic judges are more likely to be defense-oriented than Protestant judges. The reason may be a tendency of minority group members to be more sympathetic to poorer people, including those who are accused of crimes. The key question here is not why this relation exists, but how much confidence we can have that the relation really does exist in light of what we know about how Catholics differ from Protestants on other related political issues.

Doing a threshold analysis in this context means asking what it would take

Table 14-7
Threshold Values in Cross-Tabulation Analysis

Predictive Criteria / Alternative Outcomes	THE BASIC DATA				FORMULAS FOR THE THRESHOLD VALUES		NUMERICAL THRESHOLD VALUES	
	Protestants	Jews	Catholics	Average	First Predictive Criterion	Second Predictive Criterion	First Predictive Criterion	Second Predictive Criterion
Defense Oriented	12 (31%) = <u>P1</u>	6 (75%)	10 (56%) = p1	28 (43%)	(p1)(<u>N1</u>)	(<u>P1</u>)(N2)	(.56)(39) = 22	(.31)(18) = 6
Prosecution Oriented	27 (69%) = <u>P2</u>	2 (25%)	8 (44%) = p2	37 (57%)	(p2)(<u>N1</u>)	(<u>P2</u>)(N2)	(.44)(39) = 17	(.69)(18) = 12
Totals	39 = <u>N1</u>	8	10 = N2	65	<u>N1</u>	N2	39	18

NOTES:

1. The basic data for the Protestant and Catholic judges come from S. Nagel, "Ethnic Affiliations and Judge Propensities," 24 <u>Journal of Politics</u> 92-110 (1962). The data for the Jewish judges is hypothetical since there were too few Jewish judges on the state supreme courts to analyze as of 1962.

2. The steps involved in doing a threshold analysis for a cross-tabulation are:
   (1) Select two predictive criteria for comparison purposes; for example, being a Protestant or a Catholic judge as predictors of being defense-oriented or prosecution-oriented.
   (2) Determine the numerical threshold value for the first predictive criterion and then for the second. That involves applying the part/whole percentage of the first predictive criterion to the column total of the second predictive criterion, and vice versa.
   (3) Ask whether those numerical threshold values seem realistic. That means asking whether it seems reasonable that only 6 of 18 Catholic judges would be defense-oriented and 12 would be prosecution-oriented.

3. If the answer to the threshold question is yes, then the relative predictive power of those two criteria is questionable. If the answer is no, then one could have more confidence in the predictive power of those two criteria relative to each other.

4. In doing a threshold analysis for a cross-tabulation one can compare:
   (1) All the possible pairs of predictive criteria.
   (2) The most interesting comparisons, as indicated by the substance of what is involved.
   (3) Each predictive criterion and a combination of the others.

to eliminate the gap of 25 percentage points between the percentage of Catholics who are defense-oriented (56%) and the percentage of Protestants who are defense-oriented (31%). The answer from the data shown in Table 14-7 is that the 12–27 division among Protestants on being defense-oriented would have to change to 22–17. Then 56% of the 39 Protestants would also be defense-oriented like the 18 Catholics. The alternative is that the 10–8 division among Catholics would have to change to 6–12. Then 31% of the 18 Catholics would also be defense-oriented like the 39 Protestants. If those changes seem unrealistic given the substance of what is involved, one can have substantive confidence that Catholic judges are more defense-oriented than Protestant judges.

This analysis can be used to supplement *traditional tests of statistical significance*, in which one determines the chance probability of obtaining a 25-percentage point difference with a sample size of 57. If the chance probability is less than .05 or .01, it is traditional to assume that there is a real difference, rather than a chance difference. This approach depends on the size of the sample, and it is rather mechanistic, ignoring the substance of what is involved. The threshold analysis does not depend on the size of the sample. It requires thinking on the part of the user and knowledge of the substance.

Testing Multiple Relationships

As an alternative to comparing Protestants and Catholics, one could compare Protestants and Jews, or Catholics and Jews. All *three comparisons* might make sense if the subject matter involves having confidence that there really is a difference between Protestant and Jewish judges and between Catholic and Jewish judges on being defense-oriented, as well as a difference between Protestant and Catholic judges. As another alternative, one might think it would make sense to compare Protestant, Jewish, and/or Catholic judges with *average judges*. None of these three comparisons, though, are especially meaningful because they all involve comparing each category partly with itself. This is especially so in comparing Protestant judges with average judges, since most of the average judges were Protestant judges. Even if one compares Jewish judges with average judges, one is comparing Jewish judges with judges who were 12% Jewish, since 8 out of 65 of the average or total judges were Jewish.

That observation may lead one to suggest comparing Protestants *with other judges*, Jews with other judges, and Catholics with other judges. The first comparison involves noting that 31% of the Protestant judges were defense-oriented, whereas 16 out of 26 of the other judges were defense-oriented, which means 61.5% of the other judges, for a gap of 30.5%. Such a comparison between Protestant judges and other judges is sometimes referred to as a *dummy variable comparison*. The concept implies that

Protestant versus other is somehow an artificial variable when in reality it may be a perfectly normal way of thinking about judges in religious terms.

The key point is that regardless of how one defines the two categories or subsamples of judges, one can apply a threshold analysis to help one *decide whether to have confidence* in the difference observed. In this situation of Protestants versus other judges, the threshold question becomes how realistic it is to believe that the 26 other judges might really divide into only 8 defense-oriented judges and 18 prosecution-oriented judges, instead of 16 and 10. It would take an 8 and 18 split to eliminate the 30.5% gap, or else the 39 Protestants would have to split 24 and 15 instead of 12 and 27.

One might object to this kind of threshold analysis as being applicable only to *cross-tabulation tables*. Any relation, however, can be analyzed as a cross-tabulation. If a variable is normally measured on a continuum, as age is, the variable can always be divided into two, three, four, or more categories. Likewise, any relation that involves three or more variables can be analyzed as a cross-tabulation with two or more variables on each axis, such as urban Protestants, rural Protestants, urban Jews, rural Jews, urban Catholics, and rural Catholics. The threshold analysis stimulates one to think more about which categories are the most meaningful for purposes of comparison or prediction in light of the subject matter, rather than in light of mechanistic rules about measures of chance probability.

This discussion is not meant to imply that threshold analysis should replace chance probability calculations or that threshold analysis is a better perspective. What it does imply is that when one is talking about the confidence one can have in a relation, it may be quite helpful to supplement traditional chance probability calculations with threshold analysis applied to statistical inference. The two approaches combine precision-objectivity with a kind of streetwise knowledge of the subject matter. *Doing both* should clearly be better than doing either alone.

15

SOS Causation

THINKING ABOUT THE CONCEPT OF SOS PREDICTION

A super-optimum solution (SOS) is a policy alternative in which both liberal and conservative come out ahead of their initial best expectations. It implies a normative analysis of what alternative should be adopted. In dealing with SOS prediction, we are talking about what alternative will be adopted or why an alternative was adopted rather than what alternative should be adopted.

They are closely related in the following senses:

1. In order to decide what should be adopted, we should show some awareness of what can be or will be under various circumstances. We should not recommend impossible alternatives.
2. If we want to explain why an alternative was adopted, it is best to do so in terms of what the participants or decision-makers think should be adopted, or what they thought should be adopted. This also means taking their goals into consideration in order to predict or explain.
3. Thus, prescription makes use of prediction in order to prescribe. Likewise, prediction makes use of prescription in order to predict.

An ordinary prediction differs from an SOS prediction in the following ways:

1. An SOS prediction may be concerned with predicting what SOS alternative will be adopted, and especially whether an SOS alternative will be adopted or whether the SOS alternative will be adopted.
2. It can also involve an attempt to explain why some situations lead to SOS alternatives and others do not.

CAUSAL ANALYSIS OF SOS ADOPTION

Merely arriving at a suggested policy that is capable of enabling conservatives, liberals, and holders of other major viewpoints all to come out ahead of their best expectations simultaneously does not guarantee that the policy will be adopted or that it will be successfully implemented even if it is adopted. Since SOS policies enable all sides to be better off than their best expectations, one would think that merely developing such policies would get them adopted. There are, however, at least four factors that can interfere with successful adoption. Their presence should be watched for, and one should plan accordingly in order to deal with them. The four factors are referred to as (1) upping the ante, (2) satisfying the representatives or mediator, (3) the revenge factor, and (4) suspicion that a trap is involved.

Upping the Ante

One phenomenon that tends to occur more with an SOS than with an ordinary solution is that after the solution has been suggested, each side feels the other side is getting such a good deal that each side ups the ante by increasing its demands. That is an aspect of the psychology of super-optimum solutions. Each side should really do just the opposite. Each side should say, "I am getting such a good deal that I should not be so demanding or the whole thing may fall through."

An example is a farm-labor dispute. The attorney for the farm workers was bothered by the fact that the growers were getting off lightly, regardless of how much the farm workers might be benefiting. As a result, he came up with new demands that had not been mentioned before.

This is the phenomenon that occurs in dispute resolution when people are oriented not toward maximizing their own goals but, are oriented toward keeping down the benefits of other people in the dispute. This is also the age-old phenomenon of cutting off one's nose to spite one's face, or suffering great costs in order to ensure that the other side will not get any benefits. It is a mind-set that tends to view dispute resolution as being a defeat if the other person comes out well.

Satisfying the Representatives

Not only the disputants, but also their representatives, must come out ahead of their best expectations. If the representatives do not come out well, they may present a serious roadblock to implementing the SOS. In the Sanyo case, one solution would have been to provide for cash side payments. The

Sanyo company was not willing to do that because it would defeat the SOS if they had to make payments to the plaintiff's lawyer, rather than giving low-cost computers or television sets to the plaintiff.

Another solution would have been to make it an explicit part of the agreement that the plaintiff (Traveler's Insurance Company) would gladly give a cash payment to its lawyer in view of the benefits that it was getting. In such a case, the plaintiff that is getting $1 million worth of computers and television sets should pay, not necessarily one third of $1 million in cash to the lawyer, but at least one third of half the $900,000 which was the plaintiff's original best expectation. The most the lawyers expected to get was probably $150,000, which would be one third of $450,000, or half the $900,000 demand. They could argue, however, that the $900,000 demand would be cut in half only if the defendant were offering zero. If the defendant were offering $300,000, then $1,200,000 would be cut in half; the settlement would be $600,000, and the plaintiff's lawyers would get $200,000, or one third of $600,000. The Traveler's Insurance Company would come out ahead even if it gave its lawyer one third of $900,000, or $300,000. It would still have $700,000 worth of computers, plus insurance claims worth, perhaps, more than the $300,000. The important point is that explicit attention has to be paid to how the plaintiff's lawyer is going to be compensated and not just to how the plaintiff is going to be compensated.

The Revenge Factor

A second key point is somehow to educate both sides to seek to maximize their own benefits minus costs, regardless of how well the other side does. That should not be so hard to do even if one side considers it a benefit to make the other side suffer or to deprive the other side of benefits. Surely even people with that point of view would value receiving direct benefits themselves over the indirect satisfaction of depriving the other side of benefits.

One can say that the labor lawyer in the farm-labor case may have caused more trouble than the workers. The lawyer may have been more emotionally involved in the case than the plaintiffs were. That is partly an ego thing. Lawyers sometimes tend to have big egos, and maybe even more so with lawyers who represent migrant labor. They may have a tendency to view themselves as the powerful saviors coming to rescue the helpless and have all kinds of complexes about their importance. The labor lawyer in that case did indicate that he was having revenge problems with regard to status matters and was especially bothered by the defendant's lawyer's talking longer.

Suspicion that a Trap Is Involved

The Camp David Accords almost fell apart as a result of suspicion that a trap was involved. The passage of time tends to cure such attitudes, although the agreement had to be reached before the passage of time could occur.

Removing versus Adding Goals

As SOS may sometimes be more readily found or implemented by the subtraction of a goal rather than the addition of one. That is true if one side is especially interested in Goal X, toward which the other side feels negative or indifferent. If Goal *X* is dividing the two sides, removing it as a goal may facilitate a solution. Normally, adding more goals provides one side with a package of things that it values, and removes from the other side a package of things that costs it little to give up. The package solution is a most meaningful SOS approach, and it involves multicriterion thinking.

If A rejects an SOS solution because B will also benefit, A is being spiteful. If A fails to think toward an SOS solution because a gain by B is perceived to mean a loss by A, A may be unduly narrow in its thinking. The result is missed opportunities of finding ways in which both A and B can benefit. An example is the opposition of the American Society for Public Administration to marketing the journals of its sections to libraries for fear that doing so would detract from its marketing of the *Public Administration Review*. However, it might have been quite possible to develop a marketing program that would benefit both the *Public Administration Review* and the section journals.

CAUSES OF SUCCESSFUL AND UNSUCCESSFUL SOS IMPLEMENTATION

Clarifying SOS Success

The concept of super-optimum solutions has not existed as a formal concept for very long. It is possible that even in prehistoric times, two people argued over something and resolved their dispute in such a way that they both came out better than their initial best expectations. However, the idea as a formal concept was probably not articulated until the 1950s, with the development of game theory in mathematics, operations research, and management science. The typical game or human interaction studied involved a relatively fixed pie in which the gains of one side were equal to the losses of the other side. These were referred to as *zero-sum games* because the combined results for both sides added to zero. Game theorists mentioned non-zero-sum games, in which both sides (or all sides) could come out ahead, rather than either winning or losing. However, they developed virtually no literature on the subject.

The idea of all sides' coming out ahead (or at least not taking a loss) was actually formalized as a concept in the early 1900s by Vilfredo Pareto, who formulated the Pareto optimum. For Pareto, this was a measurement concept, and he never discussed any ways of bringing the optimum about, nor did he explain why variance sometimes exists and sometimes does not in human interactions. His concept is also a very weak one in the sense that by using it, one could devise a policy for a billion inhabitants of China in which nobody gained or lost except one person, who gained one unit. That would be classified as a Pareto optimum. Common sense says that one can surely do better than that, and thus such a result does not deserve to be called an optimum except in an arbitrary definitional sense.

In the 1970s, alternative dispute resolution began to acquire popularity among lawyers, businesspeople, union leaders, and others. Basically it is resolving disputes by alternatives other than bringing a court case that one side wins and the other side loses. Part of the original motivation for going to an alternative arbitrator or mediator (rather than a judge) was avoiding delay. Later, more emphasis was put on the purpose of achieving win–win solutions in which everybody comes out ahead. Coming out ahead, however, tended to mean nothing more than coming out better than one's worst expectations.

Thus, in a damages suit, if the plaintiff demanded $100,000 and the defendant refused to offer more than $20,000, one might consider a $60,000 settlement a win–win settlement. The plaintiff might have received nothing as a result of losing, and the defendant might have paid $100,000, rather than $60,000. In more recent structured settlements, the plaintiff might receive $10,000 a year for every year over age 60, which would be worth more than $100,000 in the calculations of the plaintiff. The same arrangement might be worth less than $20,000 in the calculations of the defendant insurance company because of its actuarial calculations and its depositing a reserve that draws compound interest to establish an endowment or annuity until the payments must be made. That is more truly a super-optimum solution.

In the 1980s, super-optimizing took on a more meaningful form than the Pareto measurement concept, the non-zero-sum game, or the win–win dispute resolution. The new, more meaningful form in the field of public policy was the supply-side economics of the Reagan administration and economists like Arthur Laffer, along with the industrial policy of such opposition candidates as Gary Hart and economists like Robert Reich. The emphasis in both perspectives is on the idea of the expanded pie or gross national product (GNP), where all major viewpoints come out ahead of their best expectations largely through well-placed subsidies and tax breaks.

A good example relates to dealing with the national deficit. Traditional conservatives argue in favor of reducing domestic spending and increasing the taxes on consumers, like the value-added tax. Traditional liberals argue for reducing defense spending and increasing the taxes on the rich, like the progressive income tax. Both the SOS conservatives associated with supply-side economics and the SOS liberals associated with industrial policy tend to argue that the best way to reduce the deficit may be to increase spending, but spending that will stimulate increased productivity and thus increase the GNP, which is the tax base. One can then obtain more tax income to reduce the deficit even with a constant or lowered tax rate. Both sides also argue that the deficit might be better dealt with by reducing some kinds of taxes, where doing so is a tax break designed to stimulate increased productivity in a manner similar to a well-placed spending subsidy.

Some Experiences of the Reagan Administration

Thus going into the 1980s under the Reagan administration, the United States served as a partial laboratory for trying these new super-optimizing ideas of supply-side Reaganomics to see how well they would work in enabling all major segments of the population to come out ahead of their best expectations. Even those who have favorable attitudes toward the Reagan administration generally concede that Reaganomics did not do as well as expected. It certainly did not increase the GNP beyond inflation enough to reduce the deficit. In fact, the deficit during the eight years of the Reagan administration tripled, in the sense that the per capita deficit in 1988 was three times what it was in 1980. By 1984, President Reagan had also succeeded in incurring more of an accumulated national debt than all the previous presidents put together by causing the national debt to double even on a per capita basis.

What went wrong with the idea that well-placed subsidies and tax breaks could stimulate productivity and the GNP enough so that we could simultaneously have more spending, lower taxes, less deficit, and a higher standard of living? In hindsight, there seem to have been three key causal factors which can serve as a learning experience for improving future SOS policy-making and implementation. The first factor is that well-placed subsidies and tax breaks require that strings be attached in the sense of a quid pro quo for the subsidy or tax break that will be likely to result in increased national productivity. The 30% across-the-board tax cut was the opposite of that. It had no strings attached. The reasoning was that somehow the invisible hand of laissez-faire capitalism would guide the money saved from not having to pay taxes into improving the technology of U.S. steel-making, automobile-manufacturing, and other industries.

Instead, the money saved went disproportionately into three relatively unproductive uses. One was real estate, largely for speculative purposes. Buying real estate for the purpose of building a new modernized factory can add to national productivity. Buying real estate for the purpose of waiting for a highway to go through or for urban sprawl to expand does nothing for national productivity. The second unproductive use was luxury goods. It is interesting that in 1980, the only long-distance area codes in the United States were on land. After the 30% tax cut, the quantity of yachts with telephones became so great off the Atlantic coast and the Pacific coast that two new area codes had to be established just for all the cellular telephones. The third relatively unproductive purpose was high salaries for American corporate executives, which bore little relation to the extent to which they had improved the market share of their companies. For example, at General Motors the annual salary of the chief executive rose multiple times while the company's market share drastically decreased in favor of Toyota and other Japanese manufacturers, whose salaries were a fraction of the CEO's salary at General Motors.

Tax cuts that might have made a lot more sense include not a 30% tax cut to U.S. Steel, but a 60% tax cut or even a 100% tax cut, meaning no obligation to pay any corporate taxes for the time period covered. The key aspect is not the size of the tax cut, but the requirement that U.S. Steel, in return for the tax cut, introduce more oxygenated steel-making, which is more competitive than traditional blast furnaces. U.S. Steel has had a great deal of trouble getting needed capital for adopting new technologies ever since it was put into competition with Japanese, German, and Scandinavian steel and had to respond competitively.

The second big causal factor that interfered with the successful implementation of supply-side economics in the Reagan administration was that where strings were attached, the amount of money offered to get the strings accepted was too small. A good example was the enterprise zones idea. Its basic feature was offering inducements to private enterprise to locate or relocate in the inner city in order to provide productive employment opportunities for people who might otherwise be unemployed and a drain on the taxpayer and the deficit. The idea was partly borrowed from the British Labor Party and the Carter administration. The size of the subsidies, however, was too small to be much of an inducement. Insult was added to cheapness by the attempt to offer business firms partial exemptions from economic regulations governing minimum wages, maximum hours, child labor, equal employment, environmental protection, workplace safety, and whatever other regulations could be relaxed, but Congress would not go along with these exemptions. The amount of money involved in the 30% tax cut was huge, but no strings were attached. The enterprise zones idea had lots of strings attached, but the amount of money offered was too paltry.

The third causal factor in the failure of successful implementation was the lack of people who were knowledgeable about the technical aspects of a well-placed subsidy or tax break as opposed to useless expenditure. A good example is the grants made by the Department of Housing and Urban

Development (HUD) in the 1980s. Those grants involved very large amounts of money and had lots of strings attached. The grants could have been used for scattered-site housing and urban development that would have substantially improved the circumstances of poor and lower-middle-class people. However, the people who administered the grants frequently had no training in housing or urban development, although they did know how to distinguish a Republican campaign contributor from applicants who had not met that criterion. As a result, some of the HUD programs were filled with corruption that led to criminal prosecutions and missed opportunities.

Placing subsidies well requires people who have training not only in the substance of what they are administering, such as housing and urban development, but also in systematic public policy evaluation. Such training does not have to be part of a formal degree program. It could be offered within the Department of Housing and Urban Development or the Office of Personnel Management. It should, however, extend over more than a halfday or a weekend. It should probably involve at least the equivalent of a semester of solid reading, discussion, and lectures by practitioners and academics who have some recognized expertise in the substantive area and the general evaluative procedures.

The supply-side policies of the 1980s were clearly not as successful as they could have been. Maybe they were not successful at all if the goal was to reduce the deficit. Nevertheless, President Reagan deserves considerable credit for having been the first president (and he was not likely to be the last) to have a super-optimizing philosophy that emphasized expanding the GNP pie as a way of enabling both the rich and the poor to come out ahead rather than thinking in terms of trade-offs. That SOS orientation can also apply to blacks and whites, females and males, North and South, and other categories of people who are traditionally thought of as being in conflict over a relatively fixed pie. President Reagan did succeed in arriving at a super-optimum solution in foreign policy by bringing about arms control agreements that made both the United States and the Soviet Union better off than their best expectations, although the full benefits of the peace dividends have yet to be received. President Reagan seems to have been a more imaginative thinker on these SOS-related ideas than either the Republican or Democratic candidates who ran for the presidency to replace him.

Some Experiences from Great Society Legislation

In addition to having strings attached, big money, and competent personnel, other causal factors have already been observed in the short time that the American government has been experimenting with SOS-related policies. The above examples mainly involve Republicans. A good example involving Democrats as the key policy-makers is the air pollution legislation of

1972, which is closely associated with Senator Edmund Muskie. Like President Reagan, Senator Muskie deserves credit for innovative SOS thinking, but one should still recognize the errors that interfered with effective implementation, and more specifically, the provisions in the air pollution legislation designed to stimulate the development of the electric automobile.

If it were effective, the electric automobile would be a super-optimum solution to many problems simultaneously, including pollution, energy, and the sagging automobile industry. An electric automobile does not have an internal-combustion engine. It runs on a big battery, or on a small battery with big storage power. It therefore does not spew cancer-causing exhaust fumes. It does not run on gasoline, and thus it is not dependent on Arab countries or the oil companies. The price of an effective electric automobile would probably be substantially less than that of an internal-combustion automobile. That lower price would be good for consumers, and the volume of automobile sales would increase, possibly with an even better profit ratio.

The big problem with the present electric cars is that they either require a long extension cord like the electric cars in the Dodgem rides in amusement parks or require inconvenient recharging every few miles. The object is to develop a battery that will store enough electricity so that a car can go about 450 miles without recharging. That is the distance that internal-combustion cars can generally go without needing more gasoline, with 30 miles to the gallon and a 15-gallon tank. Batteries can now be created that will move a motor vehicle 450 miles without recharging, but one needs to attach a truck to the back of one's car to carry the huge battery, which is not a very efficient way to travel. It just so happens that although the electricity field has seen amazing developments over the last 150 years, such as electric lights, radio and TV, phonographs, movie projectors, refrigerators, telephones, and computers, there have been virtually no great breakthroughs in the storage battery since Count Volta invented the voltaic cell in the early 1800s. We now have dry batteries instead of his wet battery, but they do not store a lot more energy.

If we could get a real breakthrough in the storage of energy, we could not only solve the problem of air pollution due to automobiles but perhaps solve all our energy problems. For example, the biggest obstacle to using large-scale solar energy is our inability to store solar energy for rainy days. It has been proposed to build a large microwave in the sky above the cloud layer, and then never to have to worry about rainy or cloudy days. The microwave would tilt slightly every second toward a different place on earth and would send a laser beam of solar energy through the clouds to Dusseldorf, Tokyo, Chicago, and so on. Unfortunately, with current technology, the microwave platform would have to be about a mile square. We are having a great deal of trouble getting platforms in the sky that are 10 feet square, let alone 5,280 feet square. The cost is horrendous. We would not need any microwave in the sky if we had big storage batteries on earth. All we would need is a lot of saucer contraptions and solar-cell devices to pick up the sun when it is shining and to store its energy for the cloudy days.

In 1972, the air pollution legislation sought to stimulate the development of a powerful battery that would be small enough to fit into cars and inexpensive enough to be affordable by the average person. The traditional way to stimulate such a development has been to promise the inventor a monopolistic patent. The idea of monopolistic patents as incentives was one of the innovative contributions of the Founding Fathers of the United States; they incorporated the idea into Article I of the Constitution. For about 100 years, the monopolistic patent did serve the purpose of stimulating technological innovation. In the 20th century, though, there have probably been more cases in which innovative inventors have been discouraged by the patent system. What now often happens is that an imaginative thinker develops a truly new and useful idea, seeks to patent or market it, and is sued by a big corporation that has a related patent. The imaginative inventor cannot hold out for 10 years and a million dollars worth of litigation to establish his or her idea as being original and different.

Senator Muskie (as a precursor of the well-placed subsidy) specified in his 1972 air pollution legislation that the stimulant to inventing this highly useful storage battery would be a statutorily specified guarantee that the inventor would be able to count on the federal government's replacing its fleet of motor vehicles with the new battery-driven electric cars and trucks. That is a subsidy that may amount to billions of dollars with just the federal government as a customer, but much more than that since, with the federal prize, one could then service the world market for trillions of dollars.

This is a well-placed subsidy in the sense that (for one thing) it has strings attached. It specifies that the battery must enable a car to go about 450 miles, must be small, and must be inexpensive. It has big money as a reward. It is also being administered by the National Academy of Sciences. They are competent people when it comes to examining battery inventions, or at least they know where to find the right physicists and engineers. It even has super-optimum characteristics. Conservatives generally want to retain the patent system. Liberals want it abolished or greatly modified. The conservative approach may stimulate some inventiveness, even though the inventor may have a false notion of what is involved in creating and marketing a patentable product. The liberal approach may stimulate desirable competition among firms in an industry that might otherwise be controlled by a patent-holder. The well-placed subsidy can stimulate inventiveness and at the same time not create a stultifying monopoly.

In spite of the good characteristics of this kind of subsidy, no one has come forward to collect the prize. What is wrong? One could say that maybe the assignment is technologically too difficult. One could also say that maybe this is not such a well-placed subsidy after all. The defect here is that the subsidy is obtainable only after one has succeeded in developing the technological innovation. No provision was made for setting up a system of grants to enable physicists, engineers, and other would-be inventors to obtain funding to develop components and stages that would eventually lead to the final desired product. What is needed is a program somewhat like the National Science Foundation or the National Institutes of Health. They both provide grants for pure research and some applied research. Their grants are not big enough to develop an atomic bomb or to put a person on the moon, but they are big enough to move research incrementally in the right direction.

What may be lacking in delegating this kind of funding to the National Science Foundation (NSF) is a need to encourage unconventional thinking. A big problem with the NSF, which results in its subsidies' often not being so well placed, is that virtually all its subsidies must pass the test of peer review or review by other experts in one's field. That procedure is clearly an improvement on review by patronage personnel emphasizing partisan loyalty, but the people who participate in peer reviews may be overly sensitive to applicants who propose to do something that will make the conventional experts look wrong or unimaginative. In other words, what may be needed is a review of grant applications by technical experts in the Department of Energy who are not academics with sensitive egos, and who will be able to welcome unconventional but possibly promising grant applications.

Successful SOS Experiences

The above examples—the 30% tax cut, the enterprise zones, the HUD grants, and the subsidies for the invention of an electric car—were all defective in some important way. Perhaps no well-placed subsidy or tax break can be perfect. We need to learn from past experiences how to make future subsidies and tax breaks better. We also need to avoid the paralysis that comes from overemphasizing past mistakes. It may be better to try to achieve an imaginative, well-placed subsidy or tax break and only to get halfway to the goal than to resort to (1) conservative do-nothing approaches; (2) liberal overregulation approaches; or (3) half-hearted compromises.

We should also note that a number of liberal and conservative policies have been adopted within the last 20 years that could qualify as successful super-optimum solutions. One example is the rent-supplement policy for dealing with low-income housing. The traditional conservative approach is to leave low-income housing to the marketplace, where such housing is understandably nonexistent, since private enterprise cannot afford to provide decent housing to poor people without government help. The traditional liberal approach is government-owned public housing, which has concentrated poor people in junglelike dormitories, to the detriment of the tenants, HUD as a landlord, and the taxpayers. The super-optimum solution has been to provide a rent supplement to low-income people so they can rent decent housing in the private market. In such a system, the tenants have decent housing and an increased sense of self-worth, which may result in more productive ambition. The building owners have tenants who can afford to pay a reasonable rent. The taxpayer is better off because the government does not have to build or maintain the housing. The tenants may also be saving taxpayers money by being more productive wage earners, and thereby contributing multiplier and compounding effects to the gross national product. The system also results in integrated neighborhoods and better role models and peer groups for the children. This is partly a liberal SOS policy from the Great Society and the Carter administration, but it was carried on by the Reagan administration in recognition of its value and its emphasis on the private sector.

An example of a successful SOS policy from the Reagan administration (besides the arms control example already mentioned) is the marketable pollution right. It was implemented by the Environmental Protection Agency (EPA) under Reagan, although it had been discussed before then. It applies mainly to water or air pollution. In this system, each business firm on a river segment, for example, receives so many units of pollution rights. The quantity of the rights given depends on formulas which take into consideration the size of the firm, the nature of its products, and how well it is doing in keeping down pollution. A firm that is doing badly and is generating 500 pollution units may receive only 300 pollution rights. It then either has to reduce its pollution or has to buy further rights from other business firms that have a surplus. Those other business firms may demand high payment for rights in their surplus, especially if they are competing business firms. That system may cause the polluter to reduce its pollution more than it would under traditional government regulation, and more than it would if society relied on the generally irrelevant marketplace to reduce pollution. The system is super-optimum because it pleases conservatives because of its reliance on the private market in the buying and selling of pollution rights, and it pleases liberals because of its ease of adoption (unlike pollution taxes) and because it is reasonably effective in reducing pollution (unlike regulation, which is subject to easier evasions and delays).

From these examples, one might be able to conclude that successfully implemented super-optimum solutions tend to have the following characteristics:

1. Strings are attached if subsidies or tax breaks are involved, with monitoring that is capable of determining whether the strings or specifications are being properly met.
2. Sufficient money is appropriated to get the job done, regardless of whether we are talking about a subsidy, a tax break, or some other kind of government appropriation.

3. Competent and objective personnel administer the policy.
4. There is proper timing and sequencing of the stages involved in achieving the goals.
5. There is support from both conservatives and liberals.
6. The failure of previous do-nothing and overregulation policies is eliminated.
7. Imaginative thinking is used to develop the SOS solution in the first place and to get it adopted and implemented.
8. Other policy situations where SOS-type solutions were attempted or should have been attempted are studied so that information from past mistakes and successes can be used in future SOS policy implementation.[1]

NOTE

1. For further details on SOS causal explanation, see S. Nagel and M. Mills, "Arriving at Super-Optimum Solutions," in Marc Holzer (ed.), *Handbook of Public Productivity* (New York: Marcel Dekker, 1991), and "Causal Analysis in SOS Adoption and Implementation," in S. Nagel, *Policy Analysis Methods and Super-Optimum Solutions* (Ann Arbor: University of Michigan Press, 1992). Also see the books cited in note 1 of Chapter 9 dealing with SOS evaluation. Knowing how people evaluate is quite relevant to explaining why they decide the way they do.

Bibliography

Barzun, Jacques, and Henry Graff. *The Modern Researcher*. New York: Harcourt, Brace, 1957.

Borgatta, Edgar, and G. Bornstedt (eds.). *Sociological Methodology*. San Francisco: Jossey-Bass, 1970.

Break, George. *Intergovernmental Fiscal Relations in the United States*. Washington, D.C.: Brookings Institution, 1966.

Burns, John, and Jim Hodde. "Decision Analysis: Using Computers to Make Better Choices." 6 *Attorney's Computer Report* 1–4 (February 1988).

Carr, Robert. *The Supreme Court and Judicial Review*. New York: Rinehart, 1942.

Clark, R. *The Birth of the Bomb*. New York: Horizon, 1961.

Cohen, Jacob, and Patricia Cohen. *Applied Multiple Regression/Correlation Analysis for the Behavioral Sciences*. Hillsdale, N.J.: Erlbaum-Wiley, 1975.

Compton, Arthur. *Atomic Quest*. New York: Oxford University Press, 1956.

Conway, Richard, et al. *Theory of Scheduling*. Reading, Mass.: Addison-Wesley, 1967.

Cooper, George, et al. *Law and Poverty: Cases and Materials*. St. Paul: West, 1973.

Dixon, Robert. *Democratic Representation: Reapportionment in Law and Politics*. New York: Oxford, 1968.

Draper, N. R., and H. Smith. *Applied Regression Analysis*. New York: Wiley, 1966.

Edwards, Ward, and Robert Newman. *Multi-Attribute Evaluation*. Beverly Hills, Calif.: Sage, 1982.

Erikson, Warren, and Owen Hall. *Computer Models in Management Science*. Reading, Mass.: Addison-Wesley, 1986.

General Accounting Office. *Perspectives on Intergovernmental Policy and Fiscal Relations*. Washington, D.C.: Government Printing Office, 1979.

Gramlich, Edward. *Benefit-Cost Analysis of Government Programs*. Englewood Cliffs, N.J.: Prentice-Hall, 1981.

Haines, Charles G. *The Role of the Supreme Court in American Government and Politics, 1789–1835*. Berkeley: University of California Press, 1944.

Hale, George, and Marian Palley. *The Politics of Federal Grants*. Washington, D.C.: Congressional Quarterly Press, 1981.

Harris, Clifford. *The Break-Even Handbook*. Englewood Cliffs, N.J.: Prentice-Hall, 1978.

Hilton, Gordon. *Intermediate Politometrics*. New York: Columbia University Press, 1976.

Hirsch, Werner. *The Economics of State and Local Government*. New York: McGraw-Hill, 1970.

House Committee on Banking, Finance, and Urban Affairs. *Small Cities: How Can the Federal and State Governments Respond to Their Diverse Needs?* Washington, D.C.: Government Printing Office, 1978.

Humphreys, Patrick, and Ayleen Wisudha. *Methods and Tools for Structuring and Analyzing Decision Problems*. London: London School of Economics and Political Science, 1987.

Hwang, Ching-Lai, and Kwangsun Yoon. *Multiple Attribute Decision Making: Methods and Applications*. Berlin: Springer-Verlag, 1981.

Johnson, David, and Paul Mode. *Improving Law Firm Productivity by Encouraging Lawyers' Use of Personal Computers*. New York: Harcourt Brace Jovanovich, 1985.

Kotler, Philip. *Marketing Decision Making: A Model Building Approach*. New York: Holt, 1971.

LaFave, Wayne, and Austin Scott. *Handbook on Criminal Law*. St. Paul: West, 1972.

Lindsay, Peter, and Donald Norman. *Human Information Processing*. New York: Academic Press, 1972.

Lindzey, Gardner (ed.). *Handbook of Social Psychology: Theory and Method*. Reading, Mass.: Addison-Wesley, 1954.

McMillan, Claude. *Mathematical Programming: An Introduction to the Design and Application of Optimal Decision Machines*. New York: Wiley, 1970.

Mitra, Gautam (ed.). *Computer-Assisted Decision Making: Expert Systems, Decision Analysis, Mathematical Programming*. Amsterdam: North-Holland, 1986.

Nagel, S. "Alternative Prediction Methods and Criteria." *Policy Analysis: In Social Science Research*. Beverly Hills, Calif.: Sage, 1979.

______."Attorney Time Per Case: Finding an Optimum Level." 32 *University of Florida Law Review* 424–441 (1980).

______.*Policy Evaluation: Making Optimum Decisions*. New York: Praeger, 1982.

______."Dealing with Unknown Variables in Policy/Program Evaluation." 6 *Evaluation and Program Planning* 7–10 (1983).

______."Nonmonetary Variables in Benefit-Cost Evaluation." 7 *Evaluation Review* 37–64 (1983).

______."Applying Correlation Analysis to Case Prediction." 42 *Texas Law Review* 1006–1017 (1984).

______.*Public Policy: Goals, Means, and Methods*. New York: St. Martin's, 1984.

______."Economic Transformations of Nonmonetary Benefits in Program Evaluation." In James Catterall (ed.), *Economic Evaluation of Public Programs*. San Francisco: Jossey-Bass, 1985.

______."New Varieties of Sensitivity Analysis." 9 *Evaluation Review* 772–779 (1985).

______."Optimally Allocating Federal Money to Cities." 5 *Public Budgeting and Finance* 39–50 (1985).

______."P/G% Analysis: An Evaluation-Aiding Program." 9 *Evaluation Review* 209–224 (1985).

______."Using Microcomputers and P/G% to Predict Court Cases." 18 *Akron Law Review* 541–574 (1985).

______."Sequencing and Allocating Attorney Time to Cases." 13 *Pepperdine Law Review* 1021–1039 (1986).

______."Using Microcomputers for Assigning Judges to Case Types." 40 *University of Miami Law Review* 1317–1336 (1986).

______.*Using Personal Computers for Decision-Making in Law Practice*. Westport, Conn.: Greenwood-Quorum, 1986.

______."Comparing Multi-Criteria Decision Making and P/G% with Traditional Optimizing." In Yoshikazu Sawaragi (ed.), *Multiple-Criteria Decision Making*. Berlin: Springer-Verlag, 1987.

______."Computer-Aided Law Decisions." 21 *Akron Law Review* 73–96, (1987).

______.*Evaluation Analysis with Microcomputers*. Beverly Hills, Calif.: Sage, 1987.

______.*Microcomputers as Decision Aids in Law Practice*. Westport, Conn.: Greenwood-Quorum, 1987.

______."A Microcomputer Program for Dealing with Evaluation Problems." 9 *Evaluation and Program Planning* 159–168 (1987).

Nagel, S., Mark Beeman, and John Reed. "Optimum Sequencing of Court Cases to Reduce Delay." 37 *Alabama Law Review* 583–638 (1986).

Nagel, S., and M. Mills. "Systematic Allocation of Lawyers to Case Types." 15 *Capital University Law Review* 223–242 (1986).

Nagel, S., and M. Neef. *Legal Policy Analysis: Finding an Optimum Level or Mix*. Lexington, Mass.: Lexington-Heath, 1977.

Nathan, Richard, and Charles Adams. *Revenue Sharing: The Second Round*. Washington, D.C.: Brookings Institution, 1969.

Pelz, D., and F. M. Andrews. "Detecting Causal Priorities in Panel Study Data." 29 *American Sociological Review* 836–848 (1964).

Polsby, Nelson (ed.). *Reapportionment in the 1970s*. Berkeley: University of California Press, 1971.

Posner, Richard. *Economic Analysis of Law*. Boston: Little, Brown, 1977.

Quade, Edward. *Analysis for Public Decisions*. Amsterdam: North-Holland, 1982.

Radcliff, Benjamin. "Multi-Criteria Decision Making: A Survey of Software." 4 *Social Science Microcomputer Review* 38–55 (1986).

Reagan, Michael, and John Sanzone. *The New Federalism*. New York: Oxford University Press, 1981.

Richmond, Samuel. *Operations Research for Management Decisions*. New York: Ronald, 1968.

Saaty, Thomas. *The Analytic Hierarchy Process: Planning, Priority Setting, and Resource Allocation*. New York: McGraw-Hill, 1980.

Schockley, James. *The Brief Calculus: With Applications in the Social Sciences*. New York: Holt, 1971.

Schubert, Glendon. *Quantitative Analysis of Judicial Behavior*. New York: Free Press, 1959.

Smyth, H. *Atomic Energy for Military Purposes: The Official Report on the Devel-*

opment of the Atomic Bomb. Princeton, N.J.: Princeton University Press, 1947.

______. *Decision Analysis for Program Evaluation*. Cambridge, Mass.: Ballinger, 1982.

Tullock, Gordon. *The Logic of the Law*. New York: Basic Books, 1971.

Warren, Charles. *The Supreme Court in United States History*. Boston: Little, Brown, 1935.

Wright, Deil. *Federal Grants-in-Aid: Perspectives and Alternatives*. Washington, D.C.: American Enterprise Institute for Public Policy Research, 1968.

Zeleny, Milan. *Multiple Criteria Decision Making*. New York: McGraw-Hill, 1982.

Name Index

Subject Index

About the Author

STUART S. NAGEL is Professor of Political Science at the University of Illinois and a member of the Illinois bar. He has been an attorney to the United States Senate Judiciary Committee, the National Labor Relations Board, and the Legal Services Corporation.

www.ingramcontent.com/pod-product-compliance
Ingram Content Group UK Ltd.
Pitfield, Milton Keynes, MK11 3LW, UK
UKHW020810290926
15470UKWH00003B/1073